Artificial Intelligence for Entrepreneurs: Practical Real World Use Cases with Python

Jamie Flux

https://www.linkedin.com/company/golden-dawn-engineering/

Contents

2

8

12

Chapter 1

AI in Retail

Overview of AI applications in retail

In recent years, the retail industry has witnessed a significant transformation with the integration of Artificial Intelligence (AI) technologies into various aspects of its operations. AI has revolutionized the way retailers understand and interact with their customers, optimize inventory management, streamline supply chain operations, and enhance overall customer experience. This section provides an overview of the broad range of AI applications in the retail sector.

Personalization and recommendations engines

One of the key AI applications in the retail industry is personalization, which enables retailers to tailor their products and services to individual customers. Personalization is often achieved through the use of recommendation engines, which utilize machine learning algorithms to analyze customer data and make personalized product recommendations. The widely-used Collaborative Filtering (CF) technique leverages the similarity between users and items to provide accurate recommendations. Mathematically, CF can be represented as follows:

$$\hat{R}_{u,i} = \bar{R}_u + \frac{\sum_{v \in S} (R_{v,i} - \bar{R}_v) \cdot w_{u,v}}{\sum_{v \in S} w_{u,v}}$$

where $\hat{R}_{u,i}$ is the predicted rating of user u for item i, $\bar{R}_u$ and $\bar{R}_v$ are the mean ratings of users u and v respectively, $R_{v,i}$ is the rating given by user v to item i, $w_{u,v}$ is the weight representing the similarity between users u and v, and S is the set of users similar to user u.

AI-driven inventory management

AI technologies, such as machine learning and predictive analytics, are increasingly being used in inventory management to optimize stock levels and reduce the risk of overstocking or stockouts. By analyzing historical sales data and external factors, such as seasonality and marketing campaigns, retailers can forecast future demand and automatically adjust their inventory levels. This can be mathematically represented using time series forecasting models, such as Autoregressive Integrated Moving Average (ARIMA) or Seasonal Decomposition of Time Series (STL).

$$X_t = T_t + S_t + Y_t$$

where X_t represents the observed sales at time t, T_t represents the trend component, S_t represents the seasonal component, and Y_t represents the random noise.

Streamlined supply chain and logistics

The integration of AI technologies in supply chain and logistics operations has enabled retailers to improve their overall efficiency and minimize costs. AI algorithms can optimize routing and scheduling of shipments, identify bottlenecks in the supply chain, and suggest optimal inventory storage locations. The Traveling Salesperson Problem (TSP) is a classic optimization problem often encountered in logistics, which can be represented mathematically as follows:

$$\text{Minimize} \sum_{i=1}^{n} \sum_{j=1}^{n} c_{ij} \cdot x_{ij}$$

subject to:

$$\sum_{i=1}^{n} x_{ij} = 1 \quad \forall j$$

16

$$\sum_{j=1}^{n} x_{ij} = 1 \quad \forall i$$

$$u_i - u_j + nx_{ij} \le n - 1 \quad \forall i \ne j, 2 \le i, j \le n$$

$$x_{ij} \in \{0, 1\} \quad \forall i, j$$

where c_{ij} represents the cost of travel between locations i and j, x_{ij} is a binary variable indicating whether to travel from i to j, n is the total number of locations, u_i and u_j are non-negative variables associated with each location.

Customer service chatbots and virtual assistants

AI-powered chatbots and virtual assistants have become prominent in the retail industry, providing customers with instant support and assistance. Natural Language Processing (NLP) techniques enable chatbots to understand and respond to customer queries and complaints. The core of NLP lies in the use of machine learning algorithms, such as Recurrent Neural Networks (RNNs) or Transformer models, to process textual input. Mathematically, a typical RNN can be represented as follows:

$$h_t = \tanh(W_{hx}x_t + W_{hh}h_{t-1})$$

$$y_t = \mathrm{softmax}(W_{oh}h_t)$$

where x_t represents the input at time t, h_t represents the hidden state at time t, W_{hx} and W_{hh} are weight matrices, tanh is the hyperbolic tangent activation function, y_t represents the output at time t, and softmax is the softmax activation function."'latex

Python Code Snippet

Below is a Python code snippet that demonstrates important equations and algorithms mentioned in this chapter, including personalized recommendations using Collaborative Filtering, demand forecasting using time series analysis, solving the Traveling Salesperson Problem for logistics optimization, and implementing a simple AI chatbot using RNNs.

```python
import numpy as np
import pandas as pd
from sklearn.metrics.pairwise import cosine_similarity
from scipy.optimize import linear_sum_assignment
from keras.models import Sequential
from keras.layers import LSTM, Dense, Embedding
from keras.preprocessing.sequence import pad_sequences

# Collaborative Filtering Function
def collaborative_filtering(ratings, user_index, item_index):
    '''
    Predict the rating of a user for a specific item using
    ↪    collaborative filtering.
    :param ratings: User-item rating matrix.
    :param user_index: Index of the user.
    :param item_index: Index of the item.
    :return: Predicted rating.
    '''

    user_ratings = ratings[user_index]
    similar_users = np.argsort(cosine_similarity(ratings))[-10:]  #
    ↪    Top 10 similar users
    mean_user_rating =
    ↪    np.mean(user_ratings[~np.isnan(user_ratings)])
    pred_rating = mean_user_rating + np.sum((ratings[similar_users,
    ↪    item_index] - np.nanmean(ratings[similar_users], axis=1)) /
    ↪    10)
    return pred_rating

# Example Ratings Data
ratings_data = np.array([[5, 4, np.nan], [4, np.nan, 3], [np.nan, 5,
    ↪    4]])
predicted_rating = collaborative_filtering(ratings_data, 0, 2)
print("Predicted Rating:", predicted_rating)

# Time Series Forecasting Function (ARIMA Placeholder)
def arima_forecast(data, periods):
    '''
    Placeholder for ARIMA model forecasting.
    :param data: Historical sales data.
    :param periods: Number of periods to forecast.
    :return: Forecasted sales.
    '''
    # Normally, you would fit an ARIMA model here using statsmodels
    ↪    or similar.
    forecast = data[-1] * np.ones(periods)  # Placeholder for
    ↪    forecast
    return forecast

# Example Sales Data
historical_sales = np.array([100, 120, 110, 130])
forecasted_sales = arima_forecast(historical_sales, 3)
print("Forecasted Sales:", forecasted_sales)
```

18

```
# Traveling Salesperson Problem Solver
def solve_tsp(cost_matrix):
    '''
    Solve the Traveling Salesperson Problem using the Hungarian
    ↪  Algorithm.
    :param cost_matrix: Cost matrix representing costs between
    ↪  locations.
    :return: Optimal path.
    '''
    row_ind, col_ind = linear_sum_assignment(cost_matrix)
    optimal_cost = cost_matrix[row_ind, col_ind].sum()
    return optimal_cost

# Example Cost Matrix
cost_matrix = np.array([[0, 10, 15], [10, 0, 20], [15, 20, 0]])
optimal_cost = solve_tsp(cost_matrix)
print("Optimal TSP Cost:", optimal_cost)

# Chatbot using RNN
def chatbot_response(input_sequence):
    '''
    Placeholder function for a chatbot response using RNN.
    :param input_sequence: Input sequence for the chatbot.
    :return: Bot response (dummy).
    '''
    # Normally you would preprocess data and use a trained RNN
    ↪  model.
    return "This is a placeholder response."

# Example Input Sequence
user_input = "What are your store hours?"
response = chatbot_response(user_input)
print("Chatbot Response:", response)
```

This code defines four key functions:

- `collaborative_filtering` predicts user ratings for items based on similar users' ratings.
- `arima_forecast` serves as a placeholder for future sales forecasting using time series analysis.
- `solve_tsp` provides a solution to the Traveling Salesperson Problem using the Hungarian algorithm.
- `chatbot_response` acts as a simplified RNN-based chatbot response function.

The provided example demonstrates how to predict ratings, forecast sales, solve logistics problems, and simulate chatbot responses within the context of retail applications. "'

Chapter 2

AI in Healthcare

The integration of Artificial Intelligence (AI) in healthcare has created significant advancements in various areas of the industry. This chapter provides a comprehensive analysis of the practical use cases of AI in healthcare.

AI for diagnostics and medical imaging

One of the most important applications of AI in healthcare is its use in diagnostics and medical imaging. AI algorithms have achieved remarkable success in interpreting medical images, such as X-rays, CT scans, and MRIs. Convolutional Neural Networks (CNNs) have been particularly effective in image classification tasks, including the detection of tumors, abnormalities, and diseases. The mathematical representation of a basic CNN can be defined as follows:

$$\text{Convolution: } Y_i = f\left(\sum_j W_j X_{i-j} + b_i\right)$$

where Y_i represents the output at position i, X_{i-j} represents the input at position $i-j$, W_j represents the weight at position j, b_i represents the bias at position i, and $f(\cdot)$ represents the activation function.

Personalized treatment plans

AI has also contributed to the development of personalized treatment plans based on patient characteristics, such as age, medical history, and genetic information. Machine Learning algorithms, including Decision Trees and Random Forests, analyze patient data to identify optimal treatment options and predict patient outcomes. The mathematical representation of a Decision Tree can be defined as follows:

$$\text{Split criteria: } \Delta \text{ Impurity} =$$

$$\text{Impurity}_{\text{parent}} - \frac{N_{\text{left}}}{N} \text{Impurity}_{\text{left}} - \frac{N_{\text{right}}}{N} \text{Impurity}_{\text{right}}$$

where ΔImpurity represents the decrease in impurity after the split, Impurity represents the measure of impurity (e.g., Gini Index or Entropy), N_{left} and N_{right} represent the number of samples in the left and right nodes, respectively, and N represents the total number of samples.

Predictive analytics for patient outcomes

AI algorithms, particularly those based on supervised learning techniques, leverage large datasets to predict patient outcomes. These algorithms analyze various factors, such as patient demographics, medical history, and lifestyle choices, to anticipate the likelihood of diseases, complications, or adverse events. One common example of a supervised learning algorithm is Logistic Regression, which predicts the probability of a binary outcome. The mathematical representation of Logistic Regression can be defined as follows:

$$P(Y = 1) = \frac{1}{1 + e^{-(\beta_0 + \beta_1 X_1 + \beta_2 X_2 + \ldots + \beta_n X_n)}}$$

where $P(Y = 1)$ represents the probability of the outcome being 1 (eventual occurrence), β_0 represents the intercept, $\beta_1, \beta_2, \ldots, \beta_n$ represent the coefficients of the input variables $X_1, X_2, \ldots, X_n$, and e represents the base of the natural logarithm.

Robotic surgery and AI-driven healthcare devices

AI technologies have the potential to enhance surgical procedures through robotics and intelligent devices. AI-powered robotic surgical systems enable precise and minimally invasive procedures, reducing risks and recovery times for patients. Furthermore, AI-driven healthcare devices, such as smart prosthetics or devices for remote patient monitoring, provide personalized and continuous support. The detailed mathematics behind these technologies are often complex and beyond the scope of this chapter.

NLP for patient records and administrative tasks

Natural Language Processing (NLP) techniques are employed to convert unstructured patient records and documents into structured data, facilitating data analysis and decision-making. NLP algorithms, such as Named Entity Recognition (NER) and Text Classification, extract relevant information from medical reports and enable automated administrative tasks, including billing and coding. The mathematical representation for NLP algorithms is typically based on statistical models, such as Hidden Markov Models (HMMs) or Recurrent Neural Networks (RNNs), and may involve complex mathematical concepts such as conditional probabilities and sequence modeling.

In conclusion, AI has revolutionized the healthcare industry by bringing advancements in diagnostics, personalized treatment plans, predictive analytics, robotic surgery, and NLP. With continued research and development, AI is expected to further contribute to improving patient outcomes and streamlining healthcare processes.

Python Code Snippet

Below is a Python code snippet that demonstrates the implementation of the important algorithms and equations discussed in the healthcare chapter, including CNN for medical imaging, Decision Trees for personalized treatment plans, and Logistic Regression for predictive analytics of patient outcomes.

```python
import numpy as np
from sklearn.tree import DecisionTreeClassifier
from sklearn.linear_model import LogisticRegression
from sklearn.model_selection import train_test_split
from sklearn.metrics import accuracy_score
from keras.models import Sequential
from keras.layers import Conv2D, MaxPooling2D, Flatten, Dense


def cnn_model(input_shape):
    '''
    Create a Convolutional Neural Network (CNN) model for medical
    ↪ imaging.
    :param input_shape: Shape of the input images.
    :return: Compiled CNN model.
    '''
    model = Sequential()
    # First convolutional layer
    model.add(Conv2D(32, kernel_size=(3, 3), activation='relu',
    ↪ input_shape=input_shape))
    model.add(MaxPooling2D(pool_size=(2, 2)))
    # Second convolutional layer
    model.add(Conv2D(64, kernel_size=(3, 3), activation='relu'))
    model.add(MaxPooling2D(pool_size=(2, 2)))
    model.add(Flatten())  # Flatten the output for the fully
    ↪ connected layer
    model.add(Dense(128, activation='relu'))  # Fully connected
    ↪ layer
    model.add(Dense(1, activation='sigmoid'))  # Output layer for
    ↪ binary classification
    model.compile(optimizer='adam', loss='binary_crossentropy',
    ↪ metrics=['accuracy'])
    return model


def train_cnn_model(X_train, y_train, input_shape):
    '''
    Train the CNN model on the training data.
    :param X_train: Array of training images.
    :param y_train: Array of labels for the training images.
    :param input_shape: Shape of the input images.
    :return: Trained CNN model.
    '''
    model = cnn_model(input_shape)
    model.fit(X_train, y_train, epochs=10, batch_size=32, verbose=0)
    return model


def decision_tree_classifier(X, y):
    '''
    Train a Decision Tree Classifier for personalized treatment
    ↪ plans.
    :param X: Feature set.
```

```
    :param y: Labels.
    :return: Fitted Decision Tree model.
    '''
    clf = DecisionTreeClassifier(random_state=0)
    clf.fit(X, y)
    return clf

def logistic_regression_predict(X_train, y_train, X_test):
    '''
    Train a Logistic Regression model for patient outcome
    ↪ prediction.
    :param X_train: Training features.
    :param y_train: Training labels.
    :param X_test: Test features.
    :return: Predicted labels for test data.
    '''
    model = LogisticRegression()
    model.fit(X_train, y_train)
    predictions = model.predict(X_test)
    return predictions

# Example usage:

# Synthetic data for demonstration purposes
# Medical imaging data (images) as an array (num_samples, height,
↪ width, channels)
num_samples = 100
X_train_images = np.random.rand(num_samples, 64, 64, 1)  # Example
↪ shape for grayscale images
y_train_images = np.random.randint(2, size=num_samples)  # Binary
↪ labels

# Train CNN
trained_cnn = train_cnn_model(X_train_images, y_train_images, (64,
↪ 64, 1))

# Data for Decision Tree
X_tree = np.random.rand(200, 5)  # 200 samples with 5 features
y_tree = np.random.randint(2, size=200)  # Binary labels

# Train Decision Tree
decision_tree = decision_tree_classifier(X_tree, y_tree)

# Data for Logistic Regression
X_train_lr, X_test_lr, y_train_lr, y_test_lr =
↪ train_test_split(X_tree, y_tree, test_size=0.3, random_state=42)

# Train Logistic Regression and predict
predictions = logistic_regression_predict(X_train_lr, y_train_lr,
↪ X_test_lr)

# Evaluate predictions
accuracy = accuracy_score(y_test_lr, predictions)
```

```
print('Logistic Regression Accuracy:', accuracy)
```

This code defines three functions:

- `cnn_model` creates a Convolutional Neural Network for medical imaging analysis.
- `decision_tree_classifier` trains a Decision Tree Classifier to develop personalized treatment plans.
- `logistic_regression_predict` fits a Logistic Regression model to predict patient outcomes based on existing treatment data.

The provided example generates synthetic datasets to showcase the training of a CNN for image classification, the training of a Decision Tree, and the application of Logistic Regression to predict patient outcomes, subsequently evaluating the model's accuracy.

Chapter 3

AI in Finance

AI has significantly transformed the financial industry by enabling data-driven decision-making processes and optimizing various financial tasks. In this chapter, we will explore the practical applications of AI in finance, ranging from algorithmic trading to financial forecasting and analysis.

Algorithmic trading and data-driven investment strategies

Algorithmic trading, also known as automated trading, utilizes AI algorithms to execute trades based on predefined rules and parameters. These algorithms process vast amounts of historical and real-time data to identify patterns, trends, and market inefficiencies. By leveraging machine learning techniques, such as Reinforcement Learning and Deep Learning, AI models can learn from past data to make informed trading decisions. A popular algorithm used in algorithmic trading is the Moving Average Crossover strategy, which generates buy or sell signals based on the intersection of short-term and long-term moving averages. The mathematical representation for the Moving Average Crossover strategy can be defined as follows:

Buy if Short-term Moving Average > Long-term Moving Average

Sell if Short-term Moving Average < Long-term Moving Average

Hold otherwise

Fraud detection and risk assessment

AI algorithms play a vital role in fraud detection and risk assessment within the financial sector. These algorithms analyze large volumes of transactional data to identify patterns and anomalies that indicate fraudulent activities. Machine Learning models, such as Random Forests and Support Vector Machines (SVM), are commonly employed to classify transactions as fraudulent or legitimate. The mathematical representation of the SVM algorithm can be defined as follows:

$$\text{Hyperplane: } \mathbf{w} \cdot \mathbf{x} + b = 0$$

where $\mathbf{w}$ represents the weight vector, $\mathbf{x}$ represents the feature vector, and b represents the bias or threshold.

Customer support automation

AI-powered chatbots and virtual assistants have transformed customer support in the finance industry. Natural Language Processing (NLP) techniques enable chatbots to understand and respond to customer queries, thereby resolving common issues and inquiries. These chatbots can handle a significant volume of customer interactions simultaneously, decreasing wait times and improving customer satisfaction. One example of an NLP algorithm used in chatbot implementations is the Sequence-to-Sequence model with Attention mechanism, which converts input text into a fixed-length vector and generates an output text based on the given context. The mathematical representation of the attention mechanism can be defined as follows:

$$\text{Attention: } \text{score}(h_i, h_j) = \frac{\exp(e_{ij})}{\sum_{k=1}^{N} \exp(e_{ik})}$$

where h_i and h_j represent the hidden states of the encoder and decoder, respectively, and e_{ij} represents the alignment score between h_i and h_j.

Credit scoring and lending decisions

AI models are employed for credit scoring and lending decisions, allowing financial institutions to determine the creditworthiness of applicants accurately. These models analyze various factors, such as credit history, income, and demographic data, to predict the likelihood of loan defaults. Machine Learning algorithms, such as Logistic Regression and Gradient Boosting, are commonly used for credit scoring. The mathematical representation of the Gradient Boosting algorithm can be defined as follows:

$$\text{Prediction: } F(x) = \sum_{m=1}^{M} \gamma_m h_m(\mathbf{x})$$

where $F(x)$ represents the final prediction, γ_m represents the weight for each weak learner h_m, and M represents the total number of weak learners.

Financial forecasting and analysis

AI plays a crucial role in financial forecasting and analysis by analyzing historical data and identifying trends and patterns that can inform future predictions. Time series forecasting models, such as Autoregressive Integrated Moving Average (ARIMA) and Long Short-Term Memory (LSTM) networks, are commonly used in financial analysis. ARIMA provides a statistical method to predict future values based on previous observations, while LSTM networks leverage deep learning to capture temporal dependencies within the data. The mathematical representation of the ARIMA model can be defined as follows:

$$\text{ARIMA(p, d, q): } (1 - \phi_1 L - \phi_2 L^2 - \ldots - \phi_p L^p)(1 - L)^d y_t =$$

$$c + (1 + \theta_1 L + \theta_2 L^2 + \ldots + \theta_q L^q)\varepsilon_t$$

where L represents the lag operator, y_t represents the time series, p, d, and q represent the order of autoregressive, differencing, and moving average components, respectively, ϕ_i and θ_i represent the parameters, and ε_t represents white noise.

In this chapter, we have explored the diverse applications of AI in finance, including algorithmic trading, fraud detection, customer support automation, credit scoring, and financial forecasting. These applications harness the power of AI to enhance decision-making processes and optimize various financial tasks, contributing to more efficient and accurate outcomes within the finance industry.

Python Code Snippet

Below is a Python code snippet that implements the important algorithms and formulas mentioned in this chapter. It includes implementations for algorithmic trading, fraud detection using Support Vector Machine (SVM), customer support automation using an attention mechanism, credit scoring with Gradient Boosting, and financial forecasting using ARIMA.

```python
import numpy as np
import pandas as pd
from sklearn.ensemble import GradientBoostingClassifier
from sklearn.svm import SVC
from sklearn.model_selection import train_test_split
from statsmodels.tsa.arima.model import ARIMA

# Algorithmic Trading: Moving Average Crossover Strategy
def moving_average_crossover(prices, short_window=40,
    long_window=100):
    signals = pd.Series(index=prices.index)
    signals[short_window:] = np.where(
        prices[short_window:].rolling(window=short_window).mean() >
        prices[short_window:].rolling(window=long_window).mean(),
        1.0, 0.0
    )
    return signals.diff()

# Fraud Detection: Support Vector Machine (SVM)
def fraud_detection(train_data, features, target):
    X_train, X_test, y_train, y_test =
        train_test_split(train_data[features], train_data[target],
        test_size=0.2, random_state=42)
    model = SVC(kernel='linear')
    model.fit(X_train, y_train)
    accuracy = model.score(X_test, y_test)
    return accuracy

# Customer Support: Simple Attention Mechanism
def attention_decoder(inputs, context):
    score = np.exp(np.dot(inputs, context.T))
    attention_weights = score / np.sum(score, axis=1, keepdims=True)
    output = np.dot(attention_weights, inputs)
    return output

# Credit Scoring: Gradient Boosting
def credit_scoring(train_data, features, target):
    X_train, X_test, y_train, y_test =
        train_test_split(train_data[features], train_data[target],
        test_size=0.2, random_state=42)
    model = GradientBoostingClassifier()
```

```python
    model.fit(X_train, y_train)
    accuracy = model.score(X_test, y_test)
    return accuracy

# Financial Forecasting: ARIMA Model
def financial_forecasting(time_series_data, order=(1,1,1)):
    model = ARIMA(time_series_data, order=order)
    model_fit = model.fit()
    forecast = model_fit.forecast(steps=5)
    return forecast

# Sample Data and Execution
if __name__ == "__main__":
    # Simulated stock prices for the moving average crossover
    ↪   strategy
    dates = pd.date_range('2022-01-01', periods=200)
    prices = pd.Series(np.random.normal(loc=100, scale=10,
    ↪   size=len(dates)), index=dates)

    # Generate signals based on Moving Average Crossover
    signals = moving_average_crossover(prices)

    # Simulated fraud detection dataset
    fraud_data = pd.DataFrame({
        'feature1': np.random.rand(1000),
        'feature2': np.random.rand(1000),
        'label': np.random.choice([0, 1], size=1000)
    })
    fraud_accuracy = fraud_detection(fraud_data,
    ↪   features=['feature1', 'feature2'], target='label')

    # Simulated customer support data (for attention mechanism)
    inputs = np.random.rand(10, 5)   # 10 samples, 5 features
    context = np.random.rand(5, 5)    # context representation
    attended_output = attention_decoder(inputs, context)

    # Simulated credit scoring dataset
    credit_data = pd.DataFrame({
        'credit_history': np.random.rand(1000),
        'income': np.random.rand(1000) * 10000,
        'default': np.random.choice([0, 1], size=1000)
    })
    credit_accuracy = credit_scoring(credit_data,
    ↪   features=['credit_history', 'income'], target='default')

    # Simulated financial time series data
    time_series_data = pd.Series(np.random.randn(100).cumsum())
    forecasted_values = financial_forecasting(time_series_data)

    # Output results
    print("Moving Average Signals:\n", signals.tail())
    print("Fraud Detection Accuracy:", fraud_accuracy)
    print("Attended Outputs:\n", attended_output)
```

```
print("Credit Scoring Accuracy:", credit_accuracy)
print("Forecasted Values:", forecasted_values)
```

This code defines several functions:

- `moving_average_crossover` computes buy/sell signals based on the Moving Average Crossover strategy.
- `fraud_detection` implements fraud detection using the Support Vector Machine (SVM).
- `attention_decoder` simulates a simple attention mechanism for customer support automation.
- `credit_scoring` applies Gradient Boosting for predicting creditworthiness.
- `financial_forecasting` forecasts future values based on an ARIMA model.

The provided example executes these functions using simulated data and prints the results for each application, demonstrating the practical implementation of the discussed concepts in the finance sector.

Chapter 4

AI in Education

The application of Artificial Intelligence (AI) in the field of education has witnessed significant advancements in recent years. AI technologies, such as machine learning and natural language processing (NLP), have been leveraged to address various challenges and improve educational processes. In this chapter, we will delve into the practical applications of AI in education, including personalized learning platforms, AI-driven tutoring systems, automated grading, predictive analytics for student performance, and the integration of virtual reality (VR) and AI in immersive learning experiences.

Personalized Learning and Adaptive Learning Platforms

Personalized learning aims to tailor educational content, strategies, and pace to each individual's unique needs and learning style. AI-powered adaptive learning platforms analyze students' performance data, behavior, and preferences to provide personalized recommendations and adapt to their specific learning requirements. These platforms employ machine learning algorithms to assess students' knowledge levels, identify areas of weaknesses, and generate customized learning pathways. The use of personalized learning platforms helps students engage more deeply with the material and promotes self-directed learning.

AI-Driven Tutoring and Mentoring Systems

AI-driven tutoring and mentoring systems provide personalized and interactive support to students. These systems utilize natural language processing techniques to understand students' queries and provide appropriate responses. By analyzing students' learning patterns and knowledge gaps, these systems can offer customized explanations and guidance. As an example, the Spaced Repetition Algorithm (SRA) is commonly used to optimize the scheduling of review sessions based on the forgetting curve. With SRA, the optimal time to review a concept is determined based on the duration since the last review and the difficulty level of the topic.

Automated Grading and Administrative Tasks

AI technologies can automate grading processes for assignments and assessments, saving significant time for educators. Machine learning models, such as classification algorithms and neural networks, can be trained to evaluate student responses and provide objective and consistent grading. Automated grading systems can analyze written answers, code, or other forms of student work and provide instant feedback. Natural Language Processing techniques are typically employed to assess the quality and coherence of written responses.

Predictive Analytics for Student Performance

AI-based predictive analytics models leverage student data, such as demographic information, past performance, and engagement patterns, to forecast future academic outcomes. Machine learning algorithms, including decision trees and ensemble methods, can predict students' likelihood of success, identify at-risk students, and provide interventions at an early stage to support their academic progress. These models can help educational institutions allocate resources effectively, implement targeted interventions, and improve students' overall learning experience.

Virtual Reality (VR) and AI in Immersive Learning Experiences

The integration of virtual reality (VR) technology with AI in education has opened up new possibilities for immersive and interactive learning experiences. VR simulations and environments can simulate real-world scenarios, allowing students to engage in hands-on learning and witness the consequences of their actions. AI-powered virtual instructors and tutors can guide students within VR environments, providing personalized feedback and support. These immersive learning experiences enhance student engagement, improve retention, and foster critical thinking skills.

In conclusion, AI technology has the potential to transform education by enabling personalized learning experiences, adaptive tutoring systems, automated grading, predictive analytics, and immersive VR-based learning environments. These advancements hold the promise of improving educational outcomes and providing tailored support to learners, ultimately equipping students with the knowledge and skills required for success in the digital age.

Python Code Snippet

Below is a Python code snippet demonstrating the implementation of formulas and algorithms relevant to personalized learning, AI-driven tutoring, automated grading, and predictive analytics discussed in this chapter.

```python
import numpy as np
from sklearn.linear_model import LinearRegression
from sklearn.metrics import mean_squared_error

def adaptive_learning(user_performance_data):
    '''
    Adjusts learning content based on user performance.
    :param user_performance_data: List of tuples containing
    ↪ (user_id, performance_score).
    :return: Adjusted learning content recommendations based on
    ↪ performance.
    '''

    recommendations = {}
    average_performance = np.mean([score for _, score in
    ↪ user_performance_data])

    for user_id, score in user_performance_data:
```

```python
        if score < average_performance:
            recommendations[user_id] = "Content at Beginner Level"
        elif score < average_performance + 15:
            recommendations[user_id] = "Content at Intermediate
            ↪  Level"
        else:
            recommendations[user_id] = "Content at Advanced Level"

    return recommendations


def auto_grade(answers, correct_answers):
    '''
    Grades student answers based on correctness compared to correct
    ↪  answers.
    :param answers: List of student answers.
    :param correct_answers: List of correct answers.
    :return: Dictionary showing scores for each answer.
    '''
    scores = {}
    for i, (student_answer, correct_answer) in
    ↪  enumerate(zip(answers, correct_answers)):
        scores[f'Question {i+1}'] = 1 if student_answer ==
        ↪  correct_answer else 0
    return scores


def predict_student_performance(features, target):
    '''
    Predicts student performance using linear regression.
    :param features: Array of student features (e.g., study hours,
    ↪  attendance).
    :param target: Array of target scores (performance).
    :return: Predicted scores for the inputs.
    '''
    model = LinearRegression()
    model.fit(features, target)
    predicted_scores = model.predict(features)
    return predicted_scores


# Inputs for adaptive learning
user_performance_data = [
    ('student_1', 60),
    ('student_2', 45),
    ('student_3', 75),
    ('student_4', 85),
]

# Inputs for auto grading
answers = ['A', 'B', 'C']
correct_answers = ['A', 'C', 'C']
```

```
# Inputs for predict student performance
features = np.array([[5, 1], [3, 1], [10, 1], [0, 0]])  # Example
↪  features: [study hours, attendance]
target = np.array([75, 50, 90, 30])  # Scores corresponding to
↪  features

# Calculations
learning_recommendations = adaptive_learning(user_performance_data)
grading_results = auto_grade(answers, correct_answers)
predicted_scores = predict_student_performance(features, target)

# Output results
print("Adaptive Learning Recommendations:",
↪  learning_recommendations)
print("Grading Results:", grading_results)
print("Predicted Scores:", predicted_scores)
```

This code defines three functions:

- `adaptive_learning` generates personalized learning recommendations based on user performance data.
- `auto_grade` automates the grading process by comparing student answers with the correct answers.
- `predict_student_performance` uses linear regression to predict student performance based on various input features.

The provided example demonstrates how to analyze user performance to make learning recommendations, grade student responses, and predict scores based on study habits. The results are printed to the console for review.

Chapter 5

AI in Manufacturing

Predictive Maintenance and Machinery Diagnostics

In the realm of manufacturing, predictive maintenance plays a crucial role in optimizing production processes and minimizing downtime. By utilizing Artificial Intelligence (AI) techniques, manufacturers can predict when machinery is likely to fail or require maintenance, enabling proactive measures to be taken.

One prevalent approach involves analyzing sensor data from the machinery to detect anomalous behavior and patterns that indicate potential issues. This data is often processed using machine learning algorithms, such as *Support Vector Machines* (SVMs) or *Random Forests*, to classify normal and abnormal operating conditions.

We can represent the predictive maintenance process as follows:

$$\text{Predictive Maintenance(Machinery Data)} =$$

$$\text{Anomaly Detection(Sensor Data)} + \text{Proactive Measures}$$

Here, Anomaly Detection refers to the task of identifying abnormal patterns or outliers in the sensor data. By continuously monitoring machinery performance using AI algorithms, manufacturers can intervene at the appropriate time, preventing unexpected breakdowns and reducing maintenance costs.

Quality Control and Defect Detection

Maintaining the quality of manufactured products is of utmost importance to meet customer expectations and minimize waste. AI technologies have significantly contributed to the development of automated quality control systems that utilize computer vision and machine learning.

One effective method for quality control is *defect detection*, which involves the identification of anomalies or deviations from desired specifications. Deep learning techniques, such as *Convolutional Neural Networks* (CNNs), are often employed to analyze images or visual data, pinpointing defects with high accuracy.

Mathematically, defect detection can be formulated as:

$$\text{Defect Detection(Images)} = \text{CNN(Images)} + \text{Thresholding} \quad (5.1)$$

where CNN represents the deep learning model used to classify images as defective or non-defective. The output is then compared against a threshold value to determine whether an item should be rejected or accepted.

Supply Chain Optimization

Efficient supply chain management is paramount for manufacturers to reduce costs and meet customer demands. AI techniques have revolutionized this aspect by enabling accurate demand forecasting, optimizing inventory management, and streamlining logistics.

Demand forecasting involves predicting future customer demand based on historical data, market trends, and external factors. Machine learning techniques, such as *Time Series Analysis* or *Recurrent Neural Networks* (RNNs), can capture complex patterns and dependencies, allowing manufacturers to make accurate predictions.

Mathematically, demand forecasting can be represented as:

$$\text{Demand Forecasting(Historical Data)} =$$

$$\text{Machine Learning Models(Historical Data)} + \text{Predictions}$$

Inventory management is another critical aspect of supply chain optimization. By leveraging AI algorithms, manufacturers can determine optimal stock levels, reorder points, and reorder quantities, thus avoiding stockouts or excessive inventory. Mathematical optimization techniques, such as the *Economic Order Quantity* (EOQ) model, can be integrated into AI-based systems.

Robotics and Automation in Production Lines

Robots and automation play a vital role in enhancing manufacturing efficiency and productivity. AI algorithms, combined with robotic systems, enable complex tasks to be performed with precision and speed. This integration has transformed production lines across various industries, including automotive, electronics, and food processing.

One common application is *pick-and-place* tasks, where robots are responsible for accurately selecting and moving objects from one location to another. Machine learning techniques, such as *Reinforcement Learning*, allow robots to learn optimal strategies for grasping and manipulating objects, improving overall operational efficiency.

Mathematically, the pick-and-place process can be represented as:

$$\text{Pick-and-Place(Objects)} =$$

$$\text{Reinforcement Learning(Robots)} + \text{Optimal Strategies}$$

Here, robots learn by interacting with the environment, receiving rewards for successful grasps and penalties for errors. Over time, they develop optimal policies for picking and placing objects in diverse scenarios.

Digital Twins and Simulation Models

Digital twins, virtual representations of physical assets or systems, in conjunction with AI algorithms, have become powerful tools in manufacturing industries. These models provide a realistic simulation environment that allows manufacturers to optimize production processes and test various scenarios.

Simulation models leverage mathematical equations and statistical methods to replicate real-world systems and predict their behavior under different conditions. By integrating AI algorithms, these models can dynamically adjust and learn from data, resulting in more accurate and reliable predictions.

Mathematically, the simulation process can be expressed as:

$$\text{Simulation Models(Physical Systems)} =$$

$$\text{Mathematical Equations(Systems)} +$$

$$\text{AI-based Dynamic Adjustments}$$

Simulation models enable manufacturers to explore different configurations, materials, and process parameters without the need for physical experimentation, ultimately reducing costs and time-to-market.

In manufacturing, the synergy between AI technologies and traditional methods has paved the way for unprecedented advancements. Predictive maintenance, quality control, supply chain optimization, robotics, automation, and simulation models have collectively transformed manufacturing processes, leading to increased efficiency, higher product quality, and improved customer satisfaction.

Python Code Snippet

Below is a Python code snippet that implements important equations and algorithms mentioned in the chapter, including predictive maintenance, defect detection, demand forecasting, inventory management, robotics, and digital twins in manufacturing.

```python
import numpy as np
import pandas as pd
from sklearn.ensemble import RandomForestClassifier
from sklearn.neural_network import MLPRegressor
from sklearn.metrics import accuracy_score
from scipy import stats
import cv2

def predictive_maintenance(sensor_data):
    '''
    Perform predictive maintenance through anomaly detection.
    :param sensor_data: np.array of sensor readings from machinery.
    :return: Boolean array indicating anomalies in machine status.
    '''
    threshold = np.mean(sensor_data) + 2 * np.std(sensor_data)
    anomalies = sensor_data > threshold
    return anomalies
```

```python
def defect_detection(image):
    '''
    Detect defects in a manufacturing image using a Convolutional
    ↪  Neural Network (CNN).
    :param image: Input image of the manufactured item.
    :return: Boolean indicating the presence of a defect.
    '''
    # Assuming a trained CNN model; model should be previously
    ↪  created and trained.
    model = ...  # Load your pretrained model here
    processed_image = preprocess_image(image)
    prediction = model.predict(processed_image)
    return prediction > 0.5  # Assuming binary classification


def demand_forecasting(historical_data):
    '''
    Forecast future demand using a machine learning model (here,
    ↪  MLP).
    :param historical_data: DataFrame containing historical sales
    ↪  data.
    :return: Forecasted demand.
    '''
    features = historical_data.drop('demand', axis=1)
    target = historical_data['demand']
    model = MLPRegressor(hidden_layer_sizes=(50,), max_iter=1000)
    model.fit(features, target)
    future_data = ...  # Future features should be input here
    predicted_demand = model.predict(future_data)
    return predicted_demand


def inventory_management(safety_stock, lead_time_demand):
    '''
    Calculate the optimal order quantity based on safety stock and
    ↪  lead time demand.
    :param safety_stock: Safety stock level.
    :param lead_time_demand: Average demand during lead time.
    :return: Reorder point.
    '''
    reorder_point = safety_stock + lead_time_demand
    return reorder_point


def pick_and_place(robot_position, object_position):
    '''
    Simulate a pick-and-place task using reinforcement learning.
    :param robot_position: Current position of the robot.
    :param object_position: Position of the object to pick.
    :return: Updated robot position after the task.
    '''
```

```python
    # Simplified representation; actual implementation would depend
    ↪  on robot control system
    updated_position = (object_position[0], object_position[1])
    return updated_position


def digital_twin_simulation(physical_parameters):
    '''
    Simulate a physical system to predict its behavior using
    ↪  mathematical modeling.
    :param physical_parameters: The parameters affecting the
    ↪  physical system.
    :return: Simulation results.
    '''
    # Define mathematical model for the system (e.g., a simple
    ↪  dynamic system)
    results = ...  # Simulation code depending on specific system
    return results


# Example inputs for functions
sensor_data_example = np.random.normal(loc=10, scale=2, size=1000)
↪  # Example sensor data
image_example = cv2.imread('path_to_image.jpg')  # Placeholder path
↪  to an image for defect detection
historical_data_example = pd.DataFrame({
    'feature_1': np.random.rand(100),
    'feature_2': np.random.rand(100),
    'demand': np.random.randint(1, 10, size=100)
})
safety_stock_example = 10
lead_time_demand_example = 25
robot_position_example = (0, 0)
object_position_example = (5, 5)
physical_parameters_example = {}  # Defined based on the specific
↪  simulation needs


# Function outputs
anomalies_detected = predictive_maintenance(sensor_data_example)
defect_found = defect_detection(image_example)
predicted_demand = demand_forecasting(historical_data_example)
optimal_order_quantity = inventory_management(safety_stock_example,
↪  lead_time_demand_example)
new_position = pick_and_place(robot_position_example,
↪  object_position_example)
simulation_results =
↪  digital_twin_simulation(physical_parameters_example)


# Output results
print("Anomalies Detected:", anomalies_detected)
print("Defect Found:", defect_found)
print("Predicted Demand:", predicted_demand)
print("Optimal Order Quantity:", optimal_order_quantity)
```

```
print("New Robot Position:", new_position)
print("Simulation Results:", simulation_results)
```

This code introduces several functions:

- `predictive_maintenance` implements anomaly detection on sensor readings from machinery for predictive maintenance.
- `defect_detection` uses a CNN to identify defects in images of manufactured items.
- `demand_forecasting` applies a Multi-Layer Perceptron (MLP) for forecasting future demand based on historical sales data.
- `inventory_management` calculates optimal reorder points based on safety stock and lead time demand.
- `pick_and_place` simulates a robot's movement to pick and place an object using positional data.
- `digital_twin_simulation` creates a simulation of a physical system using defined parameters.

The provided example inputs illustrate how these functions could be employed in a manufacturing context, with results printed for each function's output.

Chapter 6

AI in Transportation

Transportation is a critical sector that significantly impacts global economic growth and societal well-being. With the rapid advancements in Artificial Intelligence (AI), the transportation industry has experienced considerable transformations, revolutionizing various aspects such as autonomous vehicles, traffic management, predictive maintenance, logistics, and delivery services. In this chapter, we explore the applications of AI in the transportation sector and shed light on its mathematical underpinnings and implications.

1 Autonomous Vehicles and Self-Driving Technology

Autonomous vehicles, commonly known as self-driving cars, are a revolutionary advancement in the transportation industry. These vehicles leverage AI technologies, including computer vision, machine learning, and sensor fusion, to navigate their surroundings without human intervention. The underlying mathematics involves complex algorithms that enable the interpretation of sensor data, decision-making, and control systems.

One mathematical model that plays a crucial role in autonomous vehicles is the *Kalman filter*. This filter enables accurate estimation of the vehicle's state (e.g., position, velocity, and orientation) by combining measurements from various sensors, such as cameras, LiDAR, and radar. The Kalman filter uses a dynamic system model and the measured data to continuously update the vehicle's estimated state with minimum error.

The equation for the Kalman filter can be represented as follows:

Prediction Step:

$$\hat{x}_k^- = A\hat{x}_{k-1}^+ + Bu_k$$
$$P_k^- = AP_{k-1}^+ A^T + Q$$

Update Step:

$$K_k = P_k^- H^T (HP_k^- H^T + R)^{-1}$$
$$\hat{x}_k^+ = \hat{x}_k^- + K_k(z_k - H\hat{x}_k^-)$$
$$P_k^+ = (I - K_k H)P_k^-$$

Here, A represents the state transition matrix, $\hat{x}_k^-$ is the predicted state estimate at time k, B is the control input matrix incorporating external forces, u_k represents the control input, and P_k^- is the predicted error covariance. Additionally, H is the measurement matrix, R represents the measurement noise covariance, K_k is the Kalman gain, z_k represents the measurement at time k, and $\hat{x}_k^+$ is the updated state estimate. The Kalman filter allows for robust and accurate estimation, enabling self-driving vehicles to make informed decisions based on the estimated state and surrounding environment.

2 Traffic Management and Optimization

Efficient traffic management is a critical challenge for transportation systems worldwide. AI techniques provide promising solutions to optimize traffic flow, mitigate congestion, and improve overall transportation efficiency. These solutions rely heavily on the analysis of traffic data, including vehicle trajectories, traffic flow rates, and historical patterns.

One popular AI technique for traffic management is *Reinforcement Learning* (RL). RL algorithms allow traffic control agents to learn optimal control policies by interacting with the traffic environment. By taking actions and observing their consequences, the agents adapt their decision-making strategies to maximize traffic flow and minimize congestion.

One RL algorithm commonly used in traffic management is the *Deep Q-Network* (DQN). The DQN algorithm employs a deep neural network as a function approximator to estimate the optimal action-value function, which determines the value of taking a particular action in a given state. The algorithm iteratively updates the neural network weights using a combination of supervised and reinforcement learning techniques, optimizing the policy over time.

The Q-learning update equation for the DQN algorithm can be expressed as follows:

$$Q(s,a) \leftarrow Q(s,a) + \alpha \left(r + \gamma \max_{a'} Q(s',a') - Q(s,a) \right)$$

where $Q(s,a)$ denotes the estimated value of taking action a in state s, r represents the immediate reward received after the transition to the next state, α is the learning rate, γ represents the discount factor, s' denotes the next state, and a' signifies the possible action in the next state. The DQN algorithm learns the optimal policy through an iterative process of exploration and exploitation, ultimately achieving efficient traffic management and optimization.

3 Predictive Maintenance for Vehicles

The maintenance and repair of transportation vehicles constitute a significant expense for both individuals and organizations. AI techniques, particularly predictive maintenance, offer substantial benefits by enabling proactive identification of potential failures and recommending timely maintenance actions.

Predictive maintenance utilizes AI algorithms to analyze various data sources, such as vehicle sensor readings, historical maintenance records, and environmental conditions, to predict when maintenance or repair is likely to be required. By identifying the early signs of malfunction or degradation, vehicle owners can avoid unexpected breakdowns and reduce maintenance costs.

One common technique employed in predictive maintenance is *Support Vector Machines* (SVM). SVM is a supervised learning algorithm that can classify and regress data based on labeled examples. In the context of predictive maintenance, SVM can predict the remaining useful life of a vehicle component or estimate the probability of failure within a given time frame.

The basic SVM formulation for classification can be represented as follows:

$$\text{minimize } \frac{1}{2}\|w\|^2 + C\sum_{i=1}^{n}\xi_i$$

$$\text{subject to } y_i(w^T\phi(x_i) + b) \geq 1 - \xi_i, \ i = 1,\dots,n$$

$$\xi_i \geq 0, \ i = 1,\dots,n$$

where w represents the weight vector, ξ_i denotes the slack variables, C is the penalty parameter, x_i and y_i are the training examples, and $\phi(\cdot)$ represents the transformation function mapping the input data to a higher-dimensional feature space. SVM finds the optimal hyperplane that maximally separates the data points of different classes, allowing for effective classification.

In the context of predictive maintenance, SVM can be trained on historical vehicle sensor data and maintenance records, predicting the likelihood of failure or estimating the remaining useful life of key components. By proactively scheduling maintenance based on the SVM predictions, vehicle owners can optimize maintenance costs and extend the lifespan of the vehicles.

4 AI in Logistics and Delivery Services

The logistics and delivery sector heavily relies on efficient route planning, vehicle scheduling, and demand forecasting. AI techniques offer substantial advantages in enhancing the effectiveness and efficiency of these processes.

Route optimization, a fundamental challenge in logistics, involves finding the most optimal paths for vehicles to deliver goods while considering factors like traffic conditions, delivery constraints, and customer preferences. AI algorithms, such as *Genetic Algorithms* (GA) and *Ant Colony Optimization* (ACO), provide powerful tools for solving the vehicle routing problem.

Genetic Algorithms are inspired by natural selection and evolution principles. These algorithms iteratively generate a population of potential solutions, evaluate their fitness based on predefined criteria, and generate new solutions through selection, crossover, and mutation operations. Over generations, genetic algorithms converge towards the most optimal solution, considering various constraints and optimizing objective functions.

The basic steps of a genetic algorithm for the vehicle routing problem can be described as follows:

1. Initialize a population of potential routes.

2. Evaluate the fitness of each route based on criteria such as total distance, delivery time, or cost.

3. Select individuals from the population based on their fitness. Better-fit individuals have a higher chance of being selected.

4. Create new individuals through crossover and mutation operations applied to selected individuals.

5. Replace the least fit individuals in the population with the newly created individuals.

6. Repeat steps 2-5 until a termination criterion is met (e.g., a maximum number of generations or reaching a predefined fitness threshold).

7. Select the best individual from the final population as the optimized route.

Genetic algorithms provide effective solutions to complex routing problems through exploration and exploitation of potential solutions.

5 Smart Transportation Infrastructure

The concept of smart transportation infrastructure revolves around leveraging AI technologies and Internet of Things (IoT) devices to create an interconnected and intelligent transportation system. Smart infrastructure aims to enhance safety, efficiency, and sustainability by integrating real-time data, communication networks, and predictive analytics.

One important component of smart transportation infrastructure is *Intelligent Transportation Systems* (ITS). ITS utilizes a combination of sensors, communication networks, and AI algorithms to gather and analyze data from various components of the transportation system, such as vehicles, roads, traffic lights, and traffic management centers.

By processing real-time data from vehicles and infrastructure components, ITS enables intelligent traffic control, incident management, and adaptive signal control. AI algorithms, such as machine learning and optimization techniques, facilitate the analysis and decision-making processes. These algorithms can detect traffic congestion patterns, predict accidents, and optimize signal timings to alleviate congestion, reduce travel times, and enhance traffic flow.

Furthermore, advanced technologies like *Vehicle-to-Everything* (V2X) communication enable vehicles to exchange information with other vehicles, infrastructure elements, and pedestrians in real-time. V2X communication relies on AI algorithms, including data fusion and decision-making techniques, to ensure safe and efficient vehicle interactions.

Overall, smart transportation infrastructure empowers transportation systems with AI-driven technologies, enhancing safety, efficiency, and sustainability in urban environments.

The integration of AI in the transportation sector has revolutionized the way we approach autonomous vehicles, traffic management, predictive maintenance, logistics, and delivery services. The mathematical foundations and algorithms underlying these applications provide powerful tools for tackling complex challenges and improving transportation systems globally. As AI continues to advance, its impact on the transportation sector is likely to grow, propelling us towards a more connected and efficient future.

Python Code Snippet

Below is a Python code snippet that implements key algorithms and formulas discussed in the chapter, including the Kalman filter for autonomous vehicles, Q-learning for traffic management, and Support Vector Machine (SVM) for predictive maintenance.

```python
import numpy as np

class KalmanFilter:
    def __init__(self, A, B, H, Q, R, P, x):
        '''
        Initialize the Kalman Filter.
        :param A: State transition matrix.
        :param B: Control input matrix.
        :param H: Measurement matrix.
        :param Q: Process noise covariance.
        :param R: Measurement noise covariance.
        :param P: Estimate covariance.
        :param x: Initial state estimate.
        '''
        self.A = A
        self.B = B
        self.H = H
        self.Q = Q
```

```python
        self.R = R
        self.P = P
        self.x = x

    def predict(self, u):
        '''
        Predict the current state.
        :param u: Control input.
        :return: Predicted state estimate and error covariance.
        '''
        self.x = self.A @ self.x + self.B @ u
        self.P = self.A @ self.P @ self.A.T + self.Q
        return self.x, self.P

    def update(self, z):
        '''
        Update the state based on measurement.
        :param z: Measurement vector.
        :return: Updated state estimate.
        '''
        y = z - self.H @ self.x
        S = self.H @ self.P @ self.H.T + self.R
        K = self.P @ self.H.T @ np.linalg.inv(S)
        self.x = self.x + K @ y
        I = np.eye(self.A.shape[0])
        self.P = (I - K @ self.H) @ self.P
        return self.x


# Example usage of KalmanFilter
A = np.array([[1, 1], [0, 1]])  # State transition
B = np.array([[0.5, 0], [1, 0.5]])  # Control input
H = np.array([[1, 0]])  # Measurement
Q = np.array([[1, 0], [0, 1]])  # Process noise covariance
R = np.array([[1]])  # Measurement noise covariance
P = np.array([[1, 0], [0, 1]])  # Estimate covariance
x = np.array([[0], [0]])  # Initial state

kf = KalmanFilter(A, B, H, Q, R, P, x)
control_input = np.array([[1], [1]])  # Sample control input
measurement = np.array([[2]])  # Sample measurement

# Perform prediction and update
predicted_state, predicted_P = kf.predict(control_input)
updated_state = kf.update(measurement)

print("Predicted State:", predicted_state)
print("Updated State:", updated_state)


class DQN:
    def __init__(self, state_size, action_size):
        '''
        Initialize the Deep Q-Network.
```

```python
    :param state_size: Number of states.
    :param action_size: Number of possible actions.
    '''
    self.state_size = state_size
    self.action_size = action_size
    self.memory = []
    self.gamma = 0.95  # Discount rate
    self.epsilon = 1.0  # Exploration rate
    self.epsilon_min = 0.01
    self.epsilon_decay = 0.995
    # Neural network initialization would go here

def remember(self, state, action, reward, next_state, done):
    '''
    Store experience in replay memory.
    :param state: Current state.
    :param action: Action taken.
    :param reward: Reward received.
    :param next_state: Next state.
    :param done: Boolean indicating if episode is done.
    '''
    self.memory.append((state, action, reward, next_state,
    ↪   done))

def replay(self, batch_size):
    '''
    Train the model with a batch of experiences.
    :param batch_size: Number of samples to train on.
    '''
    if len(self.memory) < batch_size:
        return
    # Sample a batch from memory and train the model
    minibatch = np.random.choice(self.memory, batch_size)
    for state, action, reward, next_state, done in minibatch:
        # Q-learning formula would be implemented here
        pass


from sklearn import svm

def predictive_maintenance(train_data, train_labels, test_data):
    '''
    Predict remaining useful life using Support Vector Machines
    ↪   (SVM).
    :param train_data: Training features.
    :param train_labels: Training labels.
    :param test_data: Data for prediction.
    :return: Predictions.
    '''
    model = svm.SVC(kernel='linear')  # Linear kernel for
    ↪   classification
    model.fit(train_data, train_labels)
    predictions = model.predict(test_data)
```

```
   return predictions

# Example usage of predictive maintenance
train_data = np.array([[0], [1], [2]])  # Sample training data
train_labels = np.array([0, 1, 1])  # Sample training labels
↪  (binary)
test_data = np.array([[1.5]])  # Sample test data

predicted_labels = predictive_maintenance(train_data, train_labels,
↪  test_data)
print("Predicted Labels:", predicted_labels)
```

This code implements the following core functionalities:

- KalmanFilter class which includes the methods predict to estimate the next state and update to refine the state based on measurements.
- DQN class that can store experiences and prepares for replay training in a reinforcement learning context (note: the actual neural
network implementation is not included for brevity).
- predictive_maintenance function that leverages Support Vector Machines to predict the remaining useful life of components
based on training data.

The provided examples demonstrate how to create and use a
Kalman filter, a simple structure for a deep Q-network, and a basic
SVM model for predictive maintenance.

Chapter 7

AI in Agriculture

In this chapter, we delve into the applications of Artificial Intelligence (AI) in the field of agriculture. AI has the potential to revolutionize agriculture by optimizing crop management, improving yield forecasting, automating farming processes, and enhancing resource efficiency. We explore some of the key use cases of AI in agriculture and discuss the underlying mathematical foundations of these applications.

1 Precision Farming and Crop Management

Precision farming aims to optimize agricultural practices by utilizing data-driven decision-making techniques. AI plays a crucial role in precision farming by combining various sources of data, such as satellite imagery, weather data, soil moisture sensors, and historical crop performance, to provide tailored recommendations for crop management.

One important task in precision farming is crop yield prediction. Accurate yield forecasting enables farmers to make informed decisions regarding planting, harvesting, and resource allocation. Machine learning algorithms, particularly regression models, can model the relationship between environmental factors (e.g., temperature, rainfall) and crop yield. One commonly used algorithm for regression tasks is *Linear Regression*.

Linear Regression models the relationship between a dependent variable y and one or more independent variables $\mathbf{x} = (x_1, x_2, \ldots, x_n)$ using a linear equation:

$$y = \beta_0 + \beta_1 x_1 + \beta_2 x_2 + \ldots + \beta_n x_n$$

where $\beta_0, \beta_1, \beta_2, \ldots, \beta_n$ are coefficients to be determined. The goal of Linear Regression is to estimate the coefficients that minimize the difference between the observed and predicted values of y.

Furthermore, AI enables the detection and diagnosis of crop diseases and pest infestations. Computer vision algorithms can analyze images of plants to identify disease symptoms or signs of pests. One commonly used technique for image classification is *Convolutional Neural Networks* (CNNs).

CNNs simulate the visual perception of the human brain by using convolutional filters to extract features from images. This allows the network to automatically learn discriminative patterns and classify images into predefined categories. The output of a CNN is a probability distribution over the possible classes, indicating the likelihood of each class.

2 Automated Machinery and Robotics in Agriculture

The use of automated machinery and robotics in agriculture has the potential to increase productivity, reduce labor requirements, and optimize resource utilization. AI techniques are essential for enabling machines and robots to perform tasks such as planting, harvesting, and weed control.

One important aspect of agricultural robotics is the ability to accurately identify and localize crops or specific plant parts. This can be accomplished through techniques such as *Image Segmentation*.

Image Segmentation aims to divide an image into meaningful and homogeneous regions based on their visual characteristics. One commonly used algorithm for image segmentation is the *K-means clustering* algorithm.

Given a set of N pixels in an image, the K-means algorithm partitions these pixels into K clusters such that the sum of squared distances between each pixel and its corresponding cluster centroid is minimized. Each cluster centroid represents the average color or intensity of the pixels in the cluster.

Mathematically, the K-means algorithm can be formulated as follows:

$$\text{minimize} \sum_{i=1}^{N} \sum_{j=1}^{K} r_{ij} \|\mathbf{x}_i - \mathbf{m}_j\|^2$$

where $\mathbf{x}_i$ is the feature vector of the i-th pixel, $\mathbf{m}_j$ is the centroid of the j-th cluster, and r_{ij} is an indicator variable with value 1 if pixel i belongs to cluster j, and 0 otherwise.

Moreover, AI enables the development of autonomous robotic systems for precision agriculture. These robots can navigate through fields, collect and analyze data, monitor crop health, and perform targeted interventions such as applying fertilizers or pesticides to specific areas. The design and control of such robots require advanced algorithms for path planning and decision-making.

One commonly used algorithm for path planning is the *A* search algorithm*. The A* algorithm finds the optimal path between a start and a goal location by considering both the cost of reaching a particular location and the estimated cost to reach the goal. This estimated cost is typically based on a heuristic function, such as the Euclidean distance between the current location and the goal location.

In summary, AI techniques such as linear regression, convolutional neural networks, image segmentation, and path planning algorithms play a critical role in various aspects of agriculture. These mathematical foundations enable automated decision-making, disease detection, crop yield prediction, and efficient robotic systems. By leveraging AI, farmers can optimize crop management, improve resource usage, and increase overall agricultural productivity.Here is a comprehensive Python code snippet that implements the important equations and algorithms discussed in the chapter on AI in Agriculture, including linear regression, K-means clustering for image segmentation, and the A* search algorithm for path planning.

Python Code Snippet

Below is a Python code snippet that demonstrates the implementation of linear regression for crop yield prediction, K-means clustering for image segmentation, and the A* search algorithm for path planning.

```
import numpy as np
import matplotlib.pyplot as plt
```

```python
from sklearn.linear_model import LinearRegression
from sklearn.cluster import KMeans

# Linear Regression for Crop Yield Prediction
def predict_yield(X, y, new_data):
    '''
    Predict crop yield using Linear Regression.
    :param X: Features (environmental factors).
    :param y: Target variable (crop yield).
    :param new_data: New data for prediction.
    :return: Predicted crop yield.
    '''
    model = LinearRegression()
    model.fit(X, y)
    return model.predict(new_data)

# Example data
X = np.array([[30, 1], [20, 1], [28, 0], [25, 1], [35, 0]])  #
↪  Temperature, Rainfall
y = np.array([3, 2.5, 2.8, 3.2, 3.5])  # Crop yield

new_data = np.array([[32, 1]])  # New temperature and rainfall data
↪  for prediction
predicted_yield = predict_yield(X, y, new_data)
print(f"Predicted Crop Yield: {predicted_yield[0]}")

# K-means Clustering for Image Segmentation
def segment_image(image, n_clusters):
    '''
    Segment an image using K-means clustering.
    :param image: Input image as a 2D array.
    :param n_clusters: Number of clusters.
    :return: Segmented image.
    '''
    pixel_values = image.reshape((-1, 3))  # Flatten the image
    kmeans = KMeans(n_clusters=n_clusters)
    kmeans.fit(pixel_values)
    segmented_image = kmeans.cluster_centers_[kmeans.labels_]
    return segmented_image.reshape(image.shape).astype(np.uint8)

# Example usage of K-means
# Assuming 'image' is a NumPy array representing an image
# Uncomment the following code to run:
# image = plt.imread('path_to_image.jpg')  # Load the image
# segmented = segment_image(image, n_clusters=3)  # Segment the
↪  image into 3 clusters
# plt.imshow(segmented)
# plt.show()

# A* Search Algorithm for Path Planning
class Node:
    def __init__(self, parent=None, position=None):
        self.parent = parent
```

```python
        self.position = position
        self.g = 0  # Cost from start to this node
        self.h = 0  # Estimated cost from this node to goal
        self.f = 0  # Total cost


def astar(start, goal, grid):
    '''
    Perform A* pathfinding algorithm.
    :param start: Starting node coordinates (x, y).
    :param goal: Goal node coordinates (x, y).
    :param grid: 2D grid representing the environment (0: free, 1:
    ↪   obstacle).
    :return: List of nodes representing the path.
    '''
    start_node = Node(None, start)
    goal_node = Node(None, goal)

    open_list = []
    closed_list = []

    open_list.append(start_node)

    while len(open_list) > 0:
        current_node = min(open_list, key=lambda o: o.f)
        open_list.remove(current_node)
        closed_list.append(current_node)

        if current_node.position == goal_node.position:
            path = []
            while current_node is not None:
                path.append(current_node.position)
                current_node = current_node.parent
            return path[::-1]  # Return reversed path

        children = []
        for new_position in [(0, -1), (0, 1), (-1, 0), (1, 0)]:
            node_position = (current_node.position[0] +
            ↪   new_position[0], current_node.position[1] +
            ↪   new_position[1])
            if node_position[0] > (len(grid) - 1) or
            ↪   node_position[0] < 0 or node_position[1] >
            ↪   (len(grid[len(grid)-1]) - 1) or node_position[1] <
            ↪   0:
                continue
            if grid[node_position[0]][node_position[1]] != 0:
                continue
            new_node = Node(current_node, node_position)
            children.append(new_node)

        for child in children:
            if child in closed_list:
                continue
            child.g = current_node.g + 1
```

```
            child.h = ((child.position[0] - goal_node.position[0])
            ↪  ** 2) + ((child.position[1] - goal_node.position[1])
            ↪  ** 2)
            child.f = child.g + child.h

            if add_to_open(open_list, child):
                open_list.append(child)

    return None   # Return None if no path is found

def add_to_open(open_list, child):
    for node in open_list:
        if child.position == node.position and child.g >= node.g:
            return False
    return True

# Example grid and pathfinding
grid = [[0, 0, 0, 0, 0],
        [0, 1, 1, 0, 0],
        [0, 0, 0, 1, 0],
        [0, 1, 0, 0, 0],
        [0, 0, 0, 0, 0]]

start = (0, 0)   # Starting position
goal = (4, 4)    # Goal position
path = astar(start, goal, grid)
print("Path found:", path)
```

This code defines three key functions:

- **predict_yield** predicts crop yield using linear regression based on environmental factors.
- **segment_image** performs image segmentation using K-means clustering.
- **astar** conducts path planning using the A* search algorithm.

The provided examples illustrate how to predict crop yield, perform image segmentation, and find a path in a grid environment, demonstrating the application of AI in agriculture.

Chapter 8

AI in Finance

In this chapter, we explore the application of Artificial Intelligence (AI) in the field of finance. AI has the potential to revolutionize the financial industry by automating tasks, optimizing decision-making processes, and improving risk management strategies. We delve into the specific use cases of AI in finance, including algorithmic trading, fraud detection, customer support automation, credit scoring, and financial forecasting.

1 Algorithmic Trading and Data-driven Investment Strategies

Algorithmic trading refers to the use of computer algorithms to execute trades with high speed and efficiency. AI plays a crucial role in algorithmic trading by analyzing vast amounts of financial data, identifying patterns, and making informed trading decisions. Machine learning techniques, such as supervised learning and reinforcement learning, are commonly employed in developing data-driven investment strategies.

One popular algorithm used in algorithmic trading is the *Reinforcement Learning* algorithm, specifically the *Q-learning* algorithm. Reinforcement learning models an agent's interaction with an environment, where the agent learns from trial and error to maximize cumulative rewards. Q-learning is a popular model-free reinforcement learning algorithm that estimates the optimal action-value function, denoted as $Q^*(s, a)$, which represents the expected cumulative reward when taking action a in state s.

The Q-learning algorithm updates the action-value function iteratively using the Bellman equation:

$$Q_{t+1}(s,a) = Q_t(s,a) + \alpha \left[r + \gamma \max_a Q_t(s',a') - Q_t(s,a) \right]$$

where r is the immediate reward received when transitioning from state s to state s' by taking action a, γ is the discount factor that determines the importance of future rewards, and α is the learning rate that controls the weight given to newly acquired information.

2   Fraud Detection and Risk Assessment

Fraud detection aims to identify and prevent fraudulent activities in financial systems. AI techniques are extensively used in fraud detection to analyze large volumes of financial transactions and identify anomalies or patterns indicative of fraudulent behavior. Machine learning algorithms, such as anomaly detection algorithms and neural networks, are commonly employed for detecting fraudulent activities.

One widely used algorithm for fraud detection is the *Isolation Forest* algorithm. The Isolation Forest algorithm isolates observations by randomly selecting a feature and then randomly selecting a split value within the range of that feature. This process is repeated recursively, resulting in a binary tree structure called an isolation tree. The isolation forest measures the average path length required to isolate a sample, and anomalies are identified as instances with shorter average path lengths.

Mathematically, the anomaly score s of an instance x in the Isolation Forest algorithm is computed as:

$$s(x,n) = 2^{-\frac{E(h(n))}{c(n)}}$$

where $E(h(n))$ is the average path length of instance x, $c(n)$ is the average path length for unsuccessful searches in a randomly generated sample of the same size, and n denotes the number of instances in the training set.

3   Customer Support Automation

AI-powered customer support automation enables efficient and personalized customer interactions, reducing the need for human intervention in resolving customer inquiries. Natural Language Processing (NLP) techniques, such as sentiment analysis and chatbot development, are essential for automating customer support processes.

One commonly used technique in customer support automation is *Sentiment Analysis*. Sentiment analysis aims to determine the sentiment or opinion expressed in a piece of text, be it positive, negative, or neutral. Machine learning algorithms, particularly supervised learning algorithms such as Support Vector Machines (SVM) and Recurrent Neural Networks (RNN), are widely used for sentiment analysis.

One popular algorithm for sentiment analysis is the *Long Short-Term Memory* (LSTM) model. LSTMs are a type of recurrent neural network that can effectively model long-range dependencies in sequential data. LSTMs utilize a memory cell and various gates to learn which information to forget and which information to retain. This allows them to capture and remember relevant context information when predicting sentiment.

4   Credit Scoring and Lending Decisions

Credit scoring models assess the creditworthiness of individuals or businesses and help financial institutions make lending decisions. AI techniques are employed in credit scoring to analyze various data sources and build models that predict the likelihood of default or delinquency. Machine learning algorithms, such as logistic regression and random forest, are widely used for credit scoring.

One commonly used algorithm for credit scoring is *Logistic Regression*. Logistic regression models the relationship between a dependent variable y (e.g., borrower's creditworthiness) and independent variables $\mathbf{x} = (x_1, x_2, \ldots, x_n)$ by applying the logistic function to a linear equation:

$$P(y = 1|\mathbf{x}) = \frac{1}{1 + e^{-(\beta_0 + \beta_1 x_1 + \beta_2 x_2 + \ldots + \beta_n x_n)}}$$

where $\beta_0, \beta_1, \beta_2, \ldots, \beta_n$ are coefficients to be determined. The logistic function ensures that the output probability is within the range $[0, 1]$, allowing for binary classification.

5   Financial Forecasting and Analysis

Financial forecasting and analysis involve predicting future financial performance and evaluating investment opportunities. AI techniques, such as time series forecasting and deep learning, are extensively utilized for financial forecasting and analysis tasks. These techniques analyze historical financial data and external factors to generate accurate predictions and insights.

One prominent algorithm for financial forecasting is the *Long Short-Term Memory* (LSTM) model, which we discussed previously in the context of sentiment analysis. LSTMs are well-suited for modeling and predicting time series data, making them an ideal choice for financial forecasting tasks. By effectively capturing long-term dependencies, LSTMs can identify patterns and trends in historical financial data, enabling accurate predictions of future financial performance.

Furthermore, deep learning models, such as *Deep Neural Networks* (DNNs), are used for financial analysis tasks such as stock market prediction and portfolio optimization. DNNs can learn complex patterns and relationships in financial data, allowing for more accurate predictions and informed investment decisions.

6 Conclusion

In this chapter, we explored the applications of AI in the field of finance. We discussed the use of AI in algorithmic trading, fraud detection, customer support automation, credit scoring, and financial forecasting. Machine learning and deep learning algorithms play a vital role in these applications, enabling automated decision-making, risk assessment, and personalized customer interactions. By leveraging AI techniques, the financial industry can enhance efficiency, improve risk management strategies, and make informed investment decisions.

Python Code Snippet

Below is a Python code snippet that implements the important equations and algorithms discussed in this chapter related to AI in finance, including the Q-learning algorithm, Isolation Forest for fraud detection, sentiment analysis using LSTM, and Logistic Regression for credit scoring.

```python
import numpy as np
import pandas as pd
from sklearn.ensemble import IsolationForest
from sklearn.linear_model import LogisticRegression
from sklearn.model_selection import train_test_split
```

```python
from sklearn.metrics import accuracy_score
from keras.models import Sequential
from keras.layers import LSTM, Dense
from keras.preprocessing.sequence import pad_sequences

# Q-Learning Algorithm

class QLearning:
    def __init__(self, actions, learning_rate=0.1,
    ↪ discount_rate=0.9):
        self.q_table = {}
        self.actions = actions
        self.learning_rate = learning_rate
        self.discount_rate = discount_rate

    def get_q_value(self, state, action):
        return self.q_table.get((state, action), 0.0)

    def update_q_value(self, state, action, reward, next_state):
        best_next_q = max(self.get_q_value(next_state, a) for a in
        ↪ self.actions)
        self.q_table[(state, action)] = (1 - self.learning_rate) *
        ↪ self.get_q_value(state, action) + \
                                    self.learning_rate *
                                    ↪ (reward +
                                    ↪ self.discount_rate *
                                    ↪ best_next_q)

# Function for Fraud Detection using Isolation Forest

def detect_fraud(transactions):
    isolation_forest = IsolationForest(contamination=0.05)
    labels = isolation_forest.fit_predict(transactions)
    return labels  # Labels: -1 for anomaly, 1 for normal

# Function for Sentiment Analysis using LSTM

def create_lstm_model(input_shape):
    model = Sequential()
    model.add(LSTM(50, return_sequences=True,
    ↪ input_shape=input_shape))
    model.add(LSTM(50))
    model.add(Dense(1, activation='sigmoid'))
    model.compile(loss='binary_crossentropy', optimizer='adam',
    ↪ metrics=['accuracy'])
    return model

def sentiment_analysis(X_train, y_train, X_test):
    X_train = pad_sequences(X_train, maxlen=100)  # Pad sequences
    ↪ for LSTM
    model = create_lstm_model((100, 1))
    model.fit(X_train, y_train, epochs=5, batch_size=32)
    return model.predict(pad_sequences(X_test, maxlen=100))
```

```
# Function for Credit Scoring using Logistic Regression

def credit_scoring(X, y):
    X_train, X_test, y_train, y_test = train_test_split(X, y,
    ↪   test_size=0.2, random_state=42)
    model = LogisticRegression()
    model.fit(X_train, y_train)
    predictions = model.predict(X_test)
    accuracy = accuracy_score(y_test, predictions)
    return accuracy, predictions

# Example Usage

# Q-learning Example
q_learning_agent = QLearning(actions=['buy', 'sell', 'hold'])
q_learning_agent.update_q_value('state1', 'buy', reward=0.5,
↪   next_state='state2')

# Fraud detection example
transactions = pd.DataFrame({'amount': [100, 200, 150, 300, 10000]})
fraud_labels = detect_fraud(transactions[['amount']])

# Sentiment analysis example
X_train = np.array([[1, 2, 3], [4, 5, 6]])   # Example padded
↪   sequences
y_train = np.array([1, 0])   # Example labels
X_test = np.array([[1, 2, 3], [4, 5, 6]])
sentiment_scores = sentiment_analysis(X_train, y_train, X_test)

# Credit scoring example
X = np.random.rand(100, 5)   # Example feature set
y = np.random.randint(0, 2, size=(100,))   # Example binary labels
accuracy, predictions = credit_scoring(X, y)

# Output results
print("Q-Learning Table:", q_learning_agent.q_table)
print("Fraud Detection Labels:", fraud_labels)
print("Sentiment Scores:", sentiment_scores)
print("Credit Scoring Accuracy:", accuracy)
```

This code defines several functions and a class for implementing key algorithms mentioned in the chapter:

- **QLearning** implements the Q-learning algorithm for trading strategies.
- **detect_fraud** uses the Isolation Forest algorithm for fraud detection.
- **create_lstm_model** and **sentiment_analysis** demonstrate the implementation of LSTM for sentiment analysis.

- `credit_scoring` applies Logistic Regression for assessing credit-worthiness.

This example demonstrates how to apply machine learning techniques for different financial applications, including trading, fraud detection, sentiment analysis, and credit scoring, then prints the results of each application.

Chapter 9

AI in Real Estate

In this chapter, we explore the applications of Artificial Intelligence (AI) in the real estate industry. The combination of AI techniques and real estate data can provide valuable insights into property valuation, property management, customer inquiries, and market trends analysis. Various AI algorithms, such as predictive analytics, chatbots, and virtual tours, are being utilized to revolutionize the real estate sector.

1 Predictive Analytics for Property Valuation

Property valuation plays a crucial role in the real estate market, enabling buyers, sellers, and lenders to determine the appropriate price of a property. AI algorithms can analyze historical property data, market trends, and external factors to predict property values accurately. One popular technique for property valuation is *Regression Analysis*.

Regression analysis aims to model the relationship between two or more variables by fitting a linear or nonlinear regression equation to the data. In the context of real estate, a regression model can be trained using features such as location, size, number of bedrooms, and historical sales data to predict the market value of a property. The coefficients obtained from the regression model quantify the influence of each feature on property value.

Mathematically, a linear regression model can be represented as:

$$Y = \beta_0 + \beta_1 X_1 + \beta_2 X_2 + \ldots + \beta_n X_n + \epsilon$$

where:

Y is the predicted property value,

β_0 is the intercept term,

$\beta_1, \beta_2, \ldots, \beta_n$ are the coefficients for features $X_1, X_2, \ldots, X_n$,

$X_1, X_2, \ldots, X_n$ are the features of the property,

ϵ is the error term.

2 AI-driven Property Management

AI technologies are transforming the field of property management by automating various tasks and enhancing operational efficiency. AI-powered property management systems can handle processes such as rent collection, lease management, maintenance scheduling, and tenant communication. Machine learning algorithms, such as decision trees and clustering, play a significant role in optimizing property management workflows.

One particular application of AI in property management is *Automated Maintenance Scheduling*. By analyzing historical maintenance data and property information, AI algorithms can predict maintenance requirements and schedule services accordingly. Maintenance schedules can be optimized based on factors such as equipment lifespan, work order priority, and technician availability.

3 Virtual Tours and Property Visualization

Virtual tours and property visualization allow potential buyers or tenants to explore properties remotely. AI techniques, particularly *Computer Vision* algorithms, are used to create realistic virtual tours and interactive property visualizations. Computer Vision algorithms can process images or videos of properties to extract meaningful information, such as room dimensions, furniture arrangements, and property features.

One commonly used algorithm for image processing in computer vision is the *Convolutional Neural Network* (CNN). CNNs can learn and identify patterns in images, enabling object recognition and feature extraction. By using CNNs, real estate platforms can automatically analyze property images and create virtual tours or 3D representations of properties.

4   Chatbots for Customer Inquiries

Chatbots are becoming increasingly prevalent in the real estate industry to address customer inquiries and provide instant assistance. AI-powered chatbots utilize Natural Language Processing (NLP) to understand and respond to user queries, allowing real estate companies to handle a large volume of inquiries effectively. NLP algorithms, such as text classification and named entity recognition, are employed to enable chatbots to comprehend user messages and provide relevant responses.

One popular algorithm used in NLP is the *Naive Bayes* classifier. The Naive Bayes classifier is based on Bayes' theorem and assumes that the features used for classification are conditionally independent. In the context of chatbots, the Naive Bayes classifier can be trained on labeled customer inquiries to learn patterns and predict the appropriate category or response for new queries.

The probability of a class C_k given an input query X can be calculated using Bayes' theorem:

$$P(C_k|X) = \frac{P(C_k) \cdot P(X|C_k)}{P(X)}$$

where:

$P(C_k|X)$ is the posterior probability of class C_k given query X,

$P(C_k)$ is the prior probability of class C_k,

$P(X|C_k)$ is the likelihood of query X given class C_k,

$P(X)$ is the probability of query X.

5   AI in Real Estate Market Trends Analysis

Real estate companies leverage AI algorithms to analyze market trends and make informed decisions. AI techniques such as data mining, time series analysis, and clustering are applied to large volumes of real estate data to identify patterns, forecast market trends, and segment the market based on various criteria.

One commonly used algorithm for market segmentation is the *k-means* clustering algorithm. K-means clustering divides a set of data points into non-overlapping clusters, where each data point belongs to the cluster with the nearest mean. This algorithm can be applied to real estate data to group properties based on their characteristics, such as location, size, and price.

Mathematically, the k-means algorithm aims to minimize the within-cluster sum of squares:

$$\sum_{i=1}^{k} \sum_{x \in C_i} ||x - \mu_i||^2$$

where:

C_i is the i-th cluster,

μ_i is the mean of points in cluster C_i.

6 Conclusion

In this chapter, we have explored the applications of AI in the real estate industry. AI techniques, such as predictive analytics, chatbots, and virtual tours, are revolutionizing property valuation, property management, customer inquiries, and market trends analysis. Regression analysis, computer vision algorithms, NLP algorithms, and clustering methods are key mathematical tools employed in these applications. By leveraging AI, companies in the real estate sector can enhance efficiency, provide personalized experiences, and make data-driven decisions.

Python Code Snippet

Below is a Python code snippet that demonstrates the key algorithms and equations discussed in the chapter, specifically focusing on property valuation, property management automation, virtual tour creation with computer vision, chatbot response classification, and market trends analysis.

```python
import numpy as np
import pandas as pd
from sklearn.model_selection import train_test_split
from sklearn.linear_model import LinearRegression
from sklearn.metrics import mean_squared_error
from sklearn.cluster import KMeans
from sklearn.naive_bayes import GaussianNB
import cv2  # OpenCV for image processing
import os

# Function to predict property values using Linear Regression
def predict_property_value(features):
    '''
```

```python
    Predict the property value using a linear regression model.
    :param features: Features array including location, size, number
    ↪    of bedrooms etc.
    :return: Predicted property value.
    '''
    # Sample datasets (to be replaced with actual datasets)
    data = pd.DataFrame({
        'location': [1, 2, 1, 3, 2, 1],
        'size': [1500, 2000, 1800, 2400, 2200, 1300],
        'bedrooms': [3, 4, 3, 5, 4, 2],
        'price': [300000, 400000, 350000, 600000, 450000, 250000]
    })

    X = data[['location', 'size', 'bedrooms']]
    y = data['price']

    X_train, X_test, y_train, y_test = train_test_split(X, y,
    ↪    test_size=0.2, random_state=42)

    model = LinearRegression()
    model.fit(X_train, y_train)

    predicted_value = model.predict([features])
    return predicted_value[0]


# Function for Automated Maintenance Scheduling
def schedule_maintenance(maintenance_data):
    '''
    Schedule maintenance for properties based on historical data.
    :param maintenance_data: DataFrame containing historical
    ↪    maintenance records.
    :return: Suggested maintenance schedule.
    '''
    # Simple logic to suggest maintenance based on the average
    ↪    interval between repairs
    maintenance_schedule =
    ↪    maintenance_data.groupby('property_id').mean()
    return maintenance_schedule


# Function for Virtual Tour Creation using Computer Vision
def create_virtual_tour(image_folder):
    '''
    Create a virtual tour from images in a specified folder.
    :param image_folder: Path to folder containing property images.
    :return: List of processed image arrays.
    '''
    images = []
    for image_name in os.listdir(image_folder):
        image_path = os.path.join(image_folder, image_name)
        image = cv2.imread(image_path)
```

```python
        image_resized = cv2.resize(image, (256, 256))  # Standardize
        ↪  image size
        images.append(image_resized)
    return np.array(images)


# Function to classify customer inquiries using Naive Bayes
def classify_inquiry(inquiries):
    '''
    Classify customer inquiries using a Naive Bayes classifier.
    :param inquiries: List of customer inquiries.
    :return: Class predictions for inquiries.
    '''
    # Sample training data (in practice use a larger dataset)
    training_data = pd.DataFrame({
        'text': ['Need information on property prices', 'What are
        ↪  the rental options?',
                'Can I schedule a visit?', 'Tell me about financing
                ↪  options'],
        'class': ['price', 'rental', 'visit', 'finance']
    })

    # Vectorizing text data would typically be done with a more
    ↪  complex method
    vectorized_data = training_data['text'].apply(lambda x: [1 if
    ↪  word in x else 0 for word in ['information', 'prices',
    ↪  'rental', 'visit', 'financing']])
    X_train = np.array(vectorized_data.tolist())
    y_train = training_data['class']

    model = GaussianNB()
    model.fit(X_train, y_train)

    inquiry_vectorized = [1 if word in inquiries else 0 for word in
    ↪  ['information', 'prices', 'rental', 'visit', 'financing']]
    predicted_class = model.predict([inquiry_vectorized])

    return predicted_class[0]


# Function for Market Trends Analysis using K-means Clustering
def analyze_market_trends(data):
    '''
    Analyze market trends using K-means clustering.
    :param data: DataFrame containing property attributes for
    ↪  clustering.
    :return: Cluster labels for each property.
    '''
    kmeans = KMeans(n_clusters=3, random_state=42)
    clusters = kmeans.fit_predict(data)
    return clusters
```

```python
# Example Usage

# Predicting property value
features = [1, 2000, 3]  # Example feature set: location, size,
↪   bedrooms
predicted_value = predict_property_value(features)
print("Predicted Property Value:", predicted_value)

# Scheduling Maintenance
maintenance_data = pd.DataFrame({'property_id': [1, 1, 2, 2, 1],
↪   'last_repair_days_ago': [30, 90, 60, 10, 15]})
maintenance_schedule = schedule_maintenance(maintenance_data)
print("Maintenance Schedule:\n", maintenance_schedule)

# Creating a Virtual Tour
virtual_tour_images = create_virtual_tour('path_to_image_folder') #
↪   Replace with actual path
print("Number of Images in Virtual Tour:",
↪   virtual_tour_images.shape[0])

# Classifying Inquiry
inquiry = "Can I schedule a visit?"
predicted_inquiry_class = classify_inquiry(inquiry)
print("Predicted Inquiry Class:", predicted_inquiry_class)

# Analyzing Market Trends
market_data = pd.DataFrame({'location': [1, 2, 1, 3, 2], 'price':
↪   [300000, 400000, 350000, 600000, 450000]})
clusters = analyze_market_trends(market_data)
print("Market Trends Clusters:", clusters)
```

This Python code defines multiple functions that encapsulate key functionalities outlined in this chapter:

- `predict_property_value` uses linear regression to predict property values based on given features.
- `schedule_maintenance` automates maintenance scheduling based on historical maintenance data.
- `create_virtual_tour` generates a virtual tour from images in a specified directory using OpenCV for image processing.
- `classify_inquiry` classifies customer inquiries into categories using a Naive Bayes classifier.
- `analyze_market_trends` employs the K-means clustering algorithm to analyze and segment market data.

This code can help implement the AI solutions described in the real estate industry, providing practical examples of how to use AI techniques to enhance property valuation, management, visualization, and market analysis.

Chapter 10

AI in Marketing

In this chapter, we delve into the application of artificial intelligence (AI) in the field of marketing. AI has revolutionized marketing strategies by enabling companies to analyze vast amounts of data, generate personalized content, optimize advertising campaigns, and enhance customer experiences. By leveraging AI techniques such as customer segmentation, predictive analytics, natural language processing (NLP), and machine learning, businesses can make data-driven decisions and achieve a competitive edge in the marketplace.

1 Customer Segmentation and Targeting

Customer segmentation is a fundamental aspect of marketing that involves dividing a customer base into distinct groups based on similar characteristics, behaviors, or preferences. AI algorithms can analyze large datasets to identify patterns and segment customers effectively. One common technique utilized in customer segmentation is *k-means clustering*.

The k-means algorithm partitions a dataset into a predetermined number of clusters by minimizing the sum of squared distances between data points and the centroid of each cluster. Mathematically, given a dataset $\mathbf{X} = \{\mathbf{x}_1, \mathbf{x}_2, \ldots, \mathbf{x}_n\}$ and the number of clusters K, k-means clustering aims to find the optimal clustering solution by minimizing the objective function:

$$J = \sum_{k=1}^{K} \sum_{i=1}^{n} w_{ik} \left\| \mathbf{x}_i - \mathbf{c}_k \right\|^2$$

73

where $\mathbf{c}_k$ denotes the centroid of cluster k and w_{ik} is the binary indicator variable representing membership of data point $\mathbf{x}_i$ in cluster k. The k-means algorithm alternates between assigning data points to the nearest centroid and recomputing the centroids until convergence.

2 Predictive Analytics for Campaign Optimization

Predictive analytics leverages historical data along with AI algorithms to forecast future outcomes or behavior. In marketing, predictive analytics is employed to optimize advertising campaigns by predicting customer response, conversion rates, and ad performance. One common algorithm used in predictive analytics is *logistic regression*.

Logistic regression is a statistical model used to predict the probability of a binary outcome based on one or more predictor variables. It is particularly useful for analyzing the relationship between various marketing inputs and the likelihood of a specific customer action, such as making a purchase or clicking on an ad. Mathematically, the logistic regression model applies the logistic function, also known as the sigmoid function, to transform a linear combination of predictor variables:

$$P(y = 1|\mathbf{x}) = \frac{1}{1 + \exp\left(-(\beta_0 + \beta_1 x_1 + \ldots + \beta_n x_n)\right)}$$

where $P(y = 1|\mathbf{x})$ represents the probability of the positive outcome $y = 1$ given the predictor variables $\mathbf{x} = [x_1, x_2, \ldots, x_n]$. The parameters $\beta_0, \beta_1, \ldots, \beta_n$ are estimated using maximum likelihood estimation.

3 Content Generation and Personalization

AI technologies play a crucial role in content generation and personalization, enabling companies to create tailored content for individual customers at scale. Natural language processing (NLP) algorithms, such as *recurrent neural networks* (RNNs), are employed to generate text-based content that mimics human language patterns.

RNNs are a class of neural networks that process sequential data by utilizing recurrent connections within the network. They are well-suited for tasks such as text generation, language translation, and sentiment analysis. In the context of content generation, RNNs can be trained on a large corpus of text data and generate new content based on the learned patterns. The architecture of a basic RNN can be represented as:

$$h_t = \sigma(\mathbf{W}_h \mathbf{x}_t + \mathbf{U}_h \mathbf{h}_{t-1} + \mathbf{b}_h)$$

$$y_t = \texttt{softmax}(\mathbf{W}_y \mathbf{h}_t + \mathbf{b}_y)$$

where $\mathbf{h}_t$ is the hidden state at time step t, $\mathbf{x}_t$ represents the input at time t, and $\mathbf{y}_t$ is the output at time t. $\mathbf{W}_h$, $\mathbf{U}_h$, $\mathbf{b}_h$, $\mathbf{W}_y$, and $\mathbf{b}_y$ denote the weight matrices and bias terms, respectively. The activation function σ is typically a hyperbolic tangent function, and $\texttt{softmax}$ operates on the output layer to produce a probability distribution over the vocabulary.

4 Sentiment Analysis and Brand Monitoring

Sentiment analysis involves determining the overall sentiment expressed in a piece of text, such as customer reviews or social media posts. AI algorithms, particularly supervised machine learning techniques like *support vector machines* (SVM), can be used to classify text into positive, negative, or neutral categories based on the sentiments expressed.

SVM is a powerful machine learning algorithm used for classification and regression tasks. In sentiment analysis, SVMs are often trained on labeled textual data, where each instance is associated with a sentiment label. The algorithm learns a hyperplane that maximally separates the positive and negative instances in the feature space. During prediction, the SVM assigns new instances to one of the predefined sentiment classes based on their position relative to the hyperplane.

5 AI-Powered Marketing Automation

AI-driven marketing automation enables companies to streamline repetitive marketing tasks, optimize workflows, and deliver personalized experiences at scale. Machine learning algorithms, combined with customer data, are used to automate processes such as email marketing, customer segmentation, and campaign optimization.

One popular algorithm used in marketing automation is the *random forest* (RF) algorithm. RF is an ensemble learning method that combines multiple decision trees to make predictions. In marketing automation, RF can be used to analyze customer behavior, identify patterns, and predict customer response to particular marketing actions. By leveraging RF, companies can automate personalized recommendations, targeted advertisements, and other marketing strategies.

6 Conclusion

In this chapter, we have explored the application of artificial intelligence in marketing. By employing AI techniques such as customer segmentation, predictive analytics, content generation, sentiment analysis, and marketing automation, businesses can gain valuable insights, deliver personalized experiences, and optimize their marketing strategies. These AI-powered solutions enable companies to leverage data-driven decision making and enhance their success in the competitive marketing landscape of today.Here is the section for the Python code snippets related to the equations, algorithms, and formulas mentioned in the chapter on AI in Marketing.

Python Code Snippet

Below is a Python code snippet that demonstrates the implementation of important algorithms discussed in the chapter, including k-means clustering, logistic regression, support vector machines (SVM), and random forests (RF) for various marketing applications.

```python
import numpy as np
import pandas as pd
from sklearn.cluster import KMeans
from sklearn.model_selection import train_test_split
from sklearn.linear_model import LogisticRegression
from sklearn.svm import SVC
from sklearn.ensemble import RandomForestClassifier
from sklearn.metrics import classification_report

def kmeans_clustering(data, num_clusters):
    '''
    Perform k-means clustering on the dataset.
    :param data: Input dataset as a pandas DataFrame.
    :param num_clusters: Number of clusters to form.
    :return: Cluster labels for each data point.
    '''

    kmeans = KMeans(n_clusters=num_clusters, random_state=0)
```

```python
    kmeans.fit(data)
    return kmeans.labels_

def logistic_regression_predict(X, y):
    '''
    Fit a logistic regression model and make predictions.
    :param X: Predictor variables as a pandas DataFrame.
    :param y: Target variable as a pandas Series.
    :return: Predictions for the input data.
    '''
    model = LogisticRegression(solver='liblinear')
    model.fit(X, y)
    return model.predict(X)

def svm_predict(X_train, y_train, X_test):
    '''
    Train an SVM model and make predictions.
    :param X_train: Training predictor variables.
    :param y_train: Training target variable.
    :param X_test: Testing predictor variables.
    :return: Predictions for the test data.
    '''
    model = SVC(kernel='linear')
    model.fit(X_train, y_train)
    return model.predict(X_test)

def random_forest_predict(X_train, y_train, X_test):
    '''
    Train a Random Forest model and make predictions.
    :param X_train: Training predictor variables.
    :param y_train: Training target variable.
    :param X_test: Testing predictor variables.
    :return: Predictions for the test data.
    '''
    model = RandomForestClassifier(n_estimators=100, random_state=0)
    model.fit(X_train, y_train)
    return model.predict(X_test)


# Example data for k-means clustering
data_points = np.array([[1, 2], [1, 4], [1, 0], [4, 2], [4, 4], [4,
    0]])
clusters = kmeans_clustering(data_points, num_clusters=2)
print("K-Means Clusters:", clusters)

# Example for logistic regression
data = pd.DataFrame({
    'age': [22, 25, 47, 35, 46, 56],
    'purchase': [0, 0, 1, 1, 1, 1]
})
X = data[['age']]
y = data['purchase']
predictions = logistic_regression_predict(X, y)
```

```
print("Logistic Regression Predictions:", predictions)

# Example for SVM
X_train, X_test, y_train, y_test = train_test_split(X, y,
↪   test_size=0.33, random_state=0)
svm_predictions = svm_predict(X_train, y_train, X_test)
print("SVM Predictions:", svm_predictions)
print(classification_report(y_test, svm_predictions))

# Example for Random Forest
rf_predictions = random_forest_predict(X_train, y_train, X_test)
print("Random Forest Predictions:", rf_predictions)
print(classification_report(y_test, rf_predictions))
```

This code defines four functions:

- kmeans_clustering to perform k-means clustering on a dataset.
- logistic_regression_predict to fit a logistic regression model and make predictions.
- svm_predict to train an SVM model and provide predictions for test data.
- random_forest_predict to train a Random Forest model and produce predictions.

In the examples, data is created for each algorithm to showcase their functionality, and the results are printed, including clustering results and prediction outputs from logistic regression, SVM, and Random Forest models.

Chapter 11

AI in Recruitment and HR

In this chapter, we explore the application of artificial intelligence (AI) in the field of recruitment and human resources (HR). AI has revolutionized the hiring process by automating repetitive tasks, improving candidate matching, and facilitating more data-driven decision-making. By leveraging AI techniques such as resume screening, predictive analytics, chatbots, and machine learning algorithms, companies can streamline their recruitment processes, enhance employee performance, and optimize workforce planning.

1 Resume Screening and Candidate Matching

Resume screening is a crucial step in the recruitment process, involving the analysis of numerous resumes to identify suitable candidates. AI algorithms can significantly improve this process by automating resume screening, saving time, and reducing bias. One commonly used technique in resume screening is *natural language processing* (NLP).

NLP is a subfield of AI that focuses on the interaction between computers and human language. In the context of resume screening, NLP algorithms analyze resumes to extract relevant information, such as skills, experience, and education. This information can then be compared to job requirements to identify the most suitable candidates.

2 Predictive Analytics for Employee Performance

Predictive analytics leverages historical data to make predictions about future events or outcomes. In the context of HR, predictive analytics can be employed to forecast employee performance, attrition rates, and employee engagement. This information can help organizations make data-driven decisions about workforce planning, talent development, and performance improvement initiatives.

One common algorithm used in predictive analytics for employee performance is *regression analysis*. Regression analysis investigates the relationships between a dependent variable and one or more independent variables. By analyzing historical employee data, such as performance reviews, training records, and demographic information, regression analysis can identify factors that correlate with high or low performance. This information can then be used to predict future performance and identify areas for improvement.

3 Chatbots for Candidate and Employee Inquiries

Chatbots are AI-powered conversational agents that can simulate human-like conversations with users. In the context of recruitment and HR, chatbots can be used to automate candidate inquiries, provide information about job vacancies, assist in job applications, and answer frequently asked questions. Moreover, chatbots can also be utilized for employee onboarding, benefits enrollment, leave management, and performance evaluation.

Chatbots employ a range of AI techniques, including natural language understanding (NLU) and machine learning algorithms, to understand user queries and provide relevant responses. Advanced chatbots can learn from previous interactions and improve their responses over time, providing increasingly accurate and personalized support to candidates and employees.

4 AI-driven Training and Development Programs

AI technologies can optimize training and development programs by tailoring them to individual employee needs and learning styles. Machine learning algorithms can analyze employee performance data, such as training outcomes, skill gaps, and career progression, to identify areas where additional training or development is required. This enables organizations to design personalized training programs that address specific skill deficiencies and enhance employee performance.

One powerful algorithm used for personalized training and development is *collaborative filtering*. Collaborative filtering is a recommendation technique that predicts how a user may respond to an item based on the responses of similar users. In the context of training and development, collaborative filtering can identify employees with similar backgrounds, skills, and career goals and recommend training programs that have been successful for their peers.

5 Workforce Planning and Talent Analytics

AI technologies enable organizations to optimize their workforce planning by providing insights into talent acquisition, talent retention, and succession planning. Predictive analytics can be employed to forecast future workforce needs, analyze skill gaps, and identify potential talent shortages. This information can guide organizations in making strategic decisions regarding recruitment, training, and succession planning.

Machine learning algorithms, such as *decision trees* and *random forests*, can analyze historical HR data, including employee demographics, job performance, and training records, to identify patterns and relationships that influence talent retention. By understanding the factors that contribute to employee turnover, organizations can take proactive measures to engage and retain top talent.

6 Conclusion

In this chapter, we have explored the application of artificial intelligence in the field of recruitment and HR. By leveraging AI techniques such as resume screening, predictive analytics, chatbots, and machine learning algorithms, organizations can optimize their recruitment processes, enhance employee performance, and drive strategic workforce planning. AI technologies empower HR professionals to make data-driven decisions, improve candidate and employee experiences, and foster a more productive and engaged workforce.Here's a comprehensive Python code snippet for the important algorithms and techniques discussed in the chapter on AI in Recruitment and HR, wrapped in LaTeX using the minted package.

Python Code Snippet

Below is a Python code snippet that implements essential algorithms for resume screening, predictive analytics for employee performance, using chatbots for inquiries, and personalized training programs.

```python
import pandas as pd
import numpy as np
from sklearn.linear_model import LinearRegression
from sklearn.model_selection import train_test_split
from sklearn.ensemble import RandomForestClassifier
import nltk
from nltk.tokenize import word_tokenize
from sklearn.feature_extraction.text import CountVectorizer
from sklearn.metrics import accuracy_score

# Sample function to preprocess resumes and extract skills
def extract_skills(resumes):
    '''
    Extract skills from resumes using NLP.
    :param resumes: List of resumes as text.
    :return: DataFrame with skills extracted.
    '''
    nltk.download('punkt')
    skills = ['Python', 'Machine Learning', 'Data Analysis',
    ↪    'Project Management']
    extracted_skills = []

    for resume in resumes:
        tokens = word_tokenize(resume)
        resume_skills = [skill for skill in skills if skill in
        ↪    tokens]
        extracted_skills.append(resume_skills)

    return pd.DataFrame({'Resume': resumes, 'Skills':
    ↪    extracted_skills})

# Sample data for employee performance prediction
data = {
    'Performance': [1, 2, 3, 4, 5, 2, 3, 4],
    'Experience': [1, 3, 5, 7, 9, 2, 4, 6],
    'Training_Hours': [10, 20, 30, 40, 50, 15, 25, 35]
}

# Predictive model for employee performance
```

```python
def predict_performance(data):
    '''
    Predict employee performance based on experience and training
    ↪ hours.
    :param data: DataFrame containing employee data.
    :return: Prediction results.
    '''
    df = pd.DataFrame(data)
    X = df[['Experience', 'Training_Hours']]
    y = df['Performance']
    X_train, X_test, y_train, y_test = train_test_split(X, y,
    ↪ test_size=0.2, random_state=42)

    model = LinearRegression()
    model.fit(X_train, y_train)
    predictions = model.predict(X_test)

    return predictions, y_test

# Chatbot function for automated responses
def chatbot_response(user_query):
    '''
    Simulate a chatbot response based on user inquiry.
    :param user_query: The user's query.
    :return: Predefined response.
    '''
    responses = {
        'job openings': 'We have various openings. Please check our
        ↪ careers page.',
        'salary': 'Salaries vary by position and experience.',
        'benefits': 'We offer health insurance, 401(k), and paid
        ↪ time off.',
    }
    return responses.get(user_query.lower(), 'I am sorry, I can not
    ↪ assist with that.')

# Example resumes
resumes = [
    "John Doe with experience in Python and Data Analysis.",
    "Jane Smith is a Project Management expert with a knack for
    ↪ Machine Learning."
]

# Execute skill extraction
skills_extracted = extract_skills(resumes)

# Predict employee performance
predictions, actuals = predict_performance(data)

# User query for chatbot
user_query = 'Job Openings'
response = chatbot_response(user_query)
```

```
# Output results
print("Extracted Skills:\n", skills_extracted)
print("Performance Predictions:\n", predictions)
print("Actual Performance:\n", actuals.values)
print("Chatbot Response:", response)
```

This code includes four functions:

- extract_skills analyzes resumes to extract relevant skills using natural language processing (NLP).
- predict_performance models and predicts employee performance using linear regression based on experience and training hours.
- chatbot_response simulates a chatbot that responds to common inquiries from candidates or employees.
- The code also demonstrates how to extract skills from sample resumes and predict performance, followed by printing the results including chatbot interaction.

The provided example showcases the integration of AI in recruitment and HR functions, implementing automation and data-driven decision-making processes effectively.

Chapter 12

AI in Legal Services

In this chapter, we delve into the fascinating realm of applying Artificial Intelligence (AI) to the field of legal services. As the legal industry faces increasing demands for efficiency and accuracy, AI has emerged as a powerful tool to assist legal professionals in streamlining their workflow, conducting legal research, analyzing cases, and managing legal documents. Leveraging AI technologies such as natural language processing (NLP), machine learning (ML), and predictive analytics, AI in legal services is revolutionizing the way legal tasks are performed, leading to enhanced productivity, cost savings, and improved decision-making.

Document Analysis and Legal Research Automation

One prominent area where AI is making substantial strides in legal services is in document analysis and legal research automation. AI-powered algorithms can efficiently analyze vast volumes of legal documents, including statutes, case law, contracts, and regulations. By automating the extraction of relevant information, AI systems can significantly reduce the time and effort required for legal research tasks, allowing legal professionals to focus on more value-added activities.

1   Automated Document Analysis

Automated document analysis involves the use of AI techniques to extract and analyze information from legal documents. Natural language processing algorithms are employed to identify and extract key data points such as parties involved, dates, legal concepts, and provisions. These algorithms can also apply sentiment analysis to analyze the tone and context of legal texts.

Document classification algorithms, such as support vector machines (SVM) and neural networks, can be used to categorize legal documents based on their content or subject matter. This enables legal professionals to quickly locate relevant documents and prioritize their review process.

2   Legal Research Automation

AI technology has the potential to revolutionize legal research by automating and accelerating the process of finding and analyzing legal precedents, case law, and statutes. Machine learning algorithms can analyze vast databases of legal texts to identify patterns, relationships, and legal reasoning. This data-driven approach enables legal professionals to uncover relevant cases, arguments, and statutes more efficiently, ultimately saving valuable time and resources.

AI-powered legal research tools can also utilize predictive analytics to assess the likely outcomes of legal disputes based on historical case data. By analyzing similarities with previous cases, these tools can provide valuable insights into the potential success of various legal strategies.

Predictive Analytics for Case Outcomes

Predictive analytics is an essential component of AI in legal services, enabling legal professionals to make data-informed decisions regarding the potential outcomes of legal disputes. By applying statistical models and machine learning algorithms, predictive analytics can evaluate numerous factors that influence case outcomes, including legal precedents, judge biases, adversarial strategies, and available evidence.

1   Case Outcome Prediction

ML algorithms, such as decision trees and logistic regression, can be trained using historical case data to predict the likelihood of different case outcomes. These algorithms consider various variables, such as case type, legal arguments, previous judgments, and characteristics of the involved parties. By leveraging these predictive models, legal professionals can assess the strengths and weaknesses of their cases, enabling more strategic and informed decision-making.

2   Sentiment Analysis of Legal Texts

Sentiment analysis, an NLP technique, can be employed to analyze the sentiment or tone of legal texts, such as judgments, legal opinions, and court transcripts. By automatically categorizing text as positive, negative, or neutral, sentiment analysis can provide insights into judicial attitudes, judicial biases, and the potential impact of emotional factors on legal proceedings.

Chatbots for Client Interactions

AI-powered chatbots have been increasingly employed in the legal industry to streamline client interactions, answer common legal inquiries, and assist in navigating legal processes. These chatbots utilize NLP algorithms and machine learning to understand and respond to client queries in a conversational manner, providing immediate and accurate information.

1   Natural Language Understanding

Natural language understanding algorithms enable chatbots to comprehend and process natural language queries. These algorithms extract the meaning from user inputs, enabling chatbots to accurately interpret and respond to diverse legal inquiries.

2   Automated Legal Advice

AI chatbots can provide automated legal advice based on predefined rules, legal knowledge bases, and expert systems. By incorporating legal principles, regulations, and case law, these chatbots can guide clients through legal processes, offer general advice, and direct them to appropriate legal resources.

Contract Analysis and Management

Contract analysis and management are vital tasks in legal services, which is labor-intensive and time-consuming. AI technologies can significantly enhance efficiency in this domain by automating contract analysis, extracting key information, and highlighting potential risks or anomalies.

1 Automated Contract Analysis

AI algorithms can analyze contracts to identify and extract key provisions, clauses, and legal concepts. These algorithms utilize techniques such as named entity recognition (NER) and relation extraction to extract relevant information, enabling legal professionals to quickly review and assess contract terms.

2 Contract Management and Review

AI-powered contract management tools enable legal professionals to organize, store, and review large volumes of contracts efficiently. ML algorithms can automatically categorize contracts, monitor key terms and expiration dates, and identify potential risks or non-compliance issues. These tools enhance contract lifecycle management, reduce legal risks, and ensure greater compliance with contractual obligations.

Python Code Snippet

Below is a Python code snippet that encompasses important equations, formulas, and algorithms discussed in this chapter, specifically for document analysis, predictive analytics, and the use of chatbots in legal services.

```
import numpy as np
import pandas as pd
from sklearn.model_selection import train_test_split
from sklearn.tree import DecisionTreeClassifier
from sklearn.metrics import accuracy_score
import re
```

```
import nltk
from nltk import pos_tag
from nltk.tokenize import word_tokenize
from collections import Counter

nltk.download('punkt')
nltk.download('averaged_perceptron_tagger')


# Function to preprocess legal text
def preprocess_text(text):
    '''
    Preprocesses legal text for analysis by tokenizing, removing
    ↪   non-alphabetical characters,
    and converting to lowercase.
    :param text: Text to preprocess.
    :return: List of cleaned and tokenized words.
    '''
    text = re.sub(r'[^a-zA-Z\s]', '', text)  # Remove punctuation
    ↪   and numbers
    text = text.lower()
    tokens = word_tokenize(text)  # Tokenize text
    return tokens


# Function for sentiment analysis using simple keyword matching
def sentiment_analysis(tokens):
    '''
    Analyzes sentiment of the tokens based on predefined positive
    ↪   and negative keyword lists.
    :param tokens: List of tokens.
    :return: Sentiment score.
    '''
    positive_keywords = set(['win', 'victory', 'agree', 'success'])
    negative_keywords = set(['lose', 'defeat', 'disagree',
    ↪   'failure'])
    pos_count = sum(1 for token in tokens if token in
    ↪   positive_keywords)
    neg_count = sum(1 for token in tokens if token in
    ↪   negative_keywords)
    return pos_count - neg_count  # Positive sentiment score


# Function to predict case outcomes
def predict_case_outcome(features, labels):
    '''
    Trains a decision tree model to predict case outcomes based on
    ↪   input features and labels.
    :param features: Input features for training.
    :param labels: Corresponding labels for training.
    :return: Trained decision tree classifier.
    '''
```

89

```
X_train, X_test, y_train, y_test = train_test_split(features,
↪    labels, test_size=0.2, random_state=42)
model = DecisionTreeClassifier()
model.fit(X_train, y_train)
predictions = model.predict(X_test)
accuracy = accuracy_score(y_test, predictions)
print("Model Accuracy: {:.2f}%".format(accuracy * 100))
return model


# Sample dataset of legal cases (hypothetical)
data = {
    'case_type': [1, 1, 0, 0, 1, 0],   # 1: win, 0: lose
    'arg1_strength': [3, 2, 3, 1, 4, 2],
    'arg2_strength': [1, 2, 2, 3, 1, 3]
}

df = pd.DataFrame(data)
features = df[['arg1_strength', 'arg2_strength']]
labels = df['case_type']

# Predict case outcomes
model = predict_case_outcome(features, labels)

# Example legal text for sentiment analysis
legal_text = "The court has ruled in favor of the defendant, a great
↪    victory for fairness in the legal system."
tokens = preprocess_text(legal_text)
sentiment_score = sentiment_analysis(tokens)

# Output results
print("Sentiment Score:", sentiment_score)


def basic_chatbot(user_input):
    '''
    A simple chatbot function to respond to user queries based on
    ↪    predefined keyword mappings.
    :param user_input: Input string from the user.
    :return: Response string.
    '''
    responses = {
        'help': "How can I assist you today?",
        'contract': "We help with contract review and analysis.",
        'lawyer': "Please provide details about the legal issue you
        ↪    need assistance with."
    }

    for keyword in responses.keys():
        if keyword in user_input.lower():
            return responses[keyword]
    return "I'm sorry, I didn't understand that."
```

```
# Simulated client interaction
user_question = "Can you help with my contract?"
response = basic_chatbot(user_question)
print("Chatbot Response:", response)
```

This code defines several functions:

- `preprocess_text` preprocesses legal text for analysis by tokenizing and cleaning it.
- `sentiment_analysis` calculates the sentiment score based on positive and negative keywords.
- `predict_case_outcome` trains a decision tree model to predict case outcomes.
- `basic_chatbot` responds to user queries based on simple keyword mappings.

The provided code demonstrates the process of preprocessing legal text, conducting sentiment analysis, predicting case outcomes using a decision tree, and implementing a basic chatbot for client interactions in legal services. Results from sentiment analysis, model accuracy, and chatbot responses are printed for verification.

Chapter 13

AI in Insurance

In this chapter, we explore the application of Artificial Intelligence (AI) in the field of insurance. AI technologies have the potential to greatly impact the insurance industry by improving processes, enhancing risk assessment and fraud detection, optimizing customer service, and enabling data-driven decision-making. Leveraging AI techniques such as machine learning, natural language processing, and predictive analytics, insurers can gain valuable insights, increase operational efficiency, and better meet the evolving needs of their customers.

Automated Claim Processing

Automated claim processing is an area where AI is revolutionizing the insurance industry. By leveraging machine learning algorithms and advanced data processing techniques, insurers can automate the claim evaluation process to expedite claims settlement, reduce costs, and enhance customer satisfaction.

1 Optical Character Recognition for Document Processing

Optical Character Recognition (OCR) techniques are widely used to extract relevant information from claim forms and supporting documents. OCR algorithms enable insurers to automatically digitize and process various types of documents, such as invoices, medical records, and accident reports. This automation reduces manual effort and improves accuracy in claim processing.

2   Claim Severity Assessment

Machine learning models can be trained to assess claim severity based on historical claim data. By analyzing various features of a claim, such as the type of incident, policy coverage, and past claim records, AI algorithms can estimate the potential claim amount. This enables insurers to more accurately evaluate claim reserves, predict costs, and expedite claim settlement.

Risk Assessment and Pricing

AI techniques play a vital role in risk assessment and pricing in the insurance industry. By analyzing large volumes of structured and unstructured data, including customer information, historical claims data, and external data sources, AI algorithms can more accurately assess risk profiles and provide more personalized insurance products.

1   Predictive Analytics for Risk Assessment

Predictive analytics models can leverage machine learning algorithms to analyze historical data and identify patterns that indicate potential risks. These models can forecast the likelihood of a claim or other loss events occurring and estimate the associated costs. Insurers can utilize these insights to tailor insurance products, set premiums, and manage risk portfolios effectively.

2   Telematics and Usage-Based Insurance

Telematics devices and sensors embedded in vehicles or wearable devices enable insurers to collect real-time data on driver behavior, such as speed, acceleration, and braking patterns. AI algorithms can process this data to assess risks, personalize insurance premiums based on individual driving habits, and incentivize safer driving practices. This approach, known as usage-based insurance, promotes risk mitigation and allows for fairer pricing.

Fraud Detection and Prevention

AI technologies have significantly enhanced fraud detection and prevention capabilities in the insurance industry. Machine learning algorithms can analyze diverse data sources, identify suspicious patterns, and detect potential fraud.

1 Anomaly Detection

By applying anomaly detection algorithms, insurers can identify unusual patterns in claim submissions, policy applications, and other insurance processes. Deviations from normal behavior can signal potential fraudulent activities. Advanced anomaly detection techniques, such as unsupervised learning algorithms, enable the detection of previously unknown or evolving fraud patterns.

2 Social Network Analysis

The analysis of social connections and networks can provide valuable insights into potential fraudulent activities. AI algorithms can identify relationships and connections among individuals, such as policyholders, claimants, and service providers. By analyzing these connections, insurers can detect organized fraud rings and suspicious networks.

Customer Service Chatbots

AI-powered chatbots are transforming the way insurers interact with their customers. These virtual assistants utilize natural language processing algorithms and machine learning models to provide timely and accurate responses to customer inquiries, policy changes, and claim updates.

1 Natural Language Understanding

Chatbots employ natural language understanding algorithms to comprehend customer queries and requests. By analyzing the meaning and context of customer messages, chatbots can provide personalized and relevant information, assist in policy inquiries, and guide customers through the claims process.

2 Claim Status and Updates

AI chatbots can retrieve and update claim statuses by integrating with back-end systems and databases. This allows customers to obtain real-time information about their claims, request updates on pending claims, and receive automated notifications about claim settlements.

Predictive Analytics for Policyholder Behavior

Predictive analytics models can assess policyholders' behavior and preferences based on historical data, enabling insurers to provide personalized and targeted services.

1 Customer Segmentation

Machine learning algorithms can segment policyholders based on similar behavioral patterns, demographics, and purchasing habits. This segmentation enables insurers to offer tailored insurance products, personalized promotions, and enhanced customer experiences.

2 Lapse Prediction

Predictive models can forecast the likelihood of policyholders discontinuing their policies. By analyzing historical data, AI algorithms can identify patterns and factors associated with policy lapses, allowing insurers to take proactive measures such as personalized retention strategies and timely policy renewal reminders.

The integration of AI technologies in the insurance industry brings numerous benefits, ranging from streamlining claim processing, improving risk assessment, enhancing fraud detection, and optimizing customer service. These advancements not only enhance operational efficiency for insurers but also improve customer experiences and satisfaction. The future of AI in insurance holds further promise for the industry, as technologies continue to evolve and shape the landscape of insurance services."'latex

Python Code Snippet

Below is a Python code snippet that demonstrates key algorithms and formulas mentioned in the chapter on AI in Insurance, including automated claim processing, predictive analytics for risk assessment, and customer segmentation.

```python
import numpy as np
from sklearn.tree import DecisionTreeRegressor
from sklearn.linear_model import LogisticRegression
from sklearn.metrics import accuracy_score
import pandas as pd

def optical_character_recognition(documents):
    '''
    Simulates the OCR process to extract relevant information from
    ↪    documents.
    :param documents: List of text documents.
    :return: Extracted information as a list of dictionaries.
    '''
    extracted_data = []
    for doc in documents:
        # Simulated extraction based on the doc content
        data = {
            'claim_id': doc.get('claim_id'),
            'amount': float(doc.get('amount')),
            'incident_type': doc.get('incident_type')
        }
        extracted_data.append(data)
    return extracted_data

def estimate_claim_severity(claim_data):
    '''
    Estimate claim severity using a decision tree regression model.
    :param claim_data: DataFrame containing claim features.
    :return: Estimated claim amounts.
    '''
    model = DecisionTreeRegressor()
    X = claim_data[['incident_type', 'policy_coverage',
    ↪    'past_claims']]
    y = claim_data['estimated_amount']

    # Fit model (assuming claim_data is preprocessed and fit for
    ↪    use)
    model.fit(X, y)
    return model.predict(X)

def predict_policyholder_behaviour(data):
    '''
    Predicts the likelihood of policyholder lapse using logistic
    ↪    regression.
```

```python
    :param data: DataFrame with relevant features for prediction.
    :return: Predicted probabilities of policy lapsing.
    '''
    model = LogisticRegression()
    X = data[['age', 'premium_paid', 'customer_service_calls']]
    y = data['lapse']  # Target column indicating if the policy
    ↪  lapsed

    model.fit(X, y)
    return model.predict_proba(X)[:, 1]  # Prediction probabilities

def customer_segmentation(data):
    '''
    Segments customers based on behavior and demographics.
    :param data: DataFrame containing customer information.
    :return: Segmented customer DataFrame.
    '''
    segmentation = data.copy()
    segmentation['segment'] = np.where(segmentation['age'] < 30,
    ↪  'young',
                                    np.where(segmentation['age'] < 60,
                                    ↪  'middle-aged', 'senior'))
    return segmentation

# Sample data to demonstrate functions
documents = [{'claim_id': 1, 'amount': 5000, 'incident_type':
↪  'auto'},
             {'claim_id': 2, 'amount': 15000, 'incident_type':
             ↪  'home'}]

claim_data = pd.DataFrame({
    'incident_type': ['auto', 'home'],
    'policy_coverage': [10000, 20000],
    'past_claims': [1, 2],
    'estimated_amount': [4000, 12000]
})

policy_data = pd.DataFrame({
    'age': [25, 45, 70],
    'premium_paid': [300, 500, 700],
    'customer_service_calls': [1, 3, 5],
    'lapse': [0, 1, 1]  # 0: Not lapsed, 1: Lapsed
})

# Executing code snippets
extracted_information = optical_character_recognition(documents)
print("Extracted Information:", extracted_information)

estimated_claims = estimate_claim_severity(claim_data)
print("Estimated Claims:", estimated_claims)

lapse_probabilities = predict_policyholder_behaviour(policy_data)
print("Lapse Probabilities:", lapse_probabilities)
```

```
segmented_customers = customer_segmentation(policy_data)
print("Segmented Customers:\n", segmented_customers)
```

The code snippet includes the following functions:

- optical_character_recognition simulates the OCR process to extract key claim information from documents.
- estimate_claim_severity utilizes a decision tree regression model to estimate claim severity based on historical data.
- predict_policyholder_behaviour applies logistic regression to predict the likelihood of policyholders discontinuing their policies (lapses).
- customer_segmentation segments customers into groups based on demographics and behavior for targeted marketing and tailored services.

This example provides a practical implementation of AI-driven strategies in the insurance sector, demonstrating how data can be managed and analyzed to enhance various operational facets. "'

Chapter 14

AI in Entertainment and Media

In this chapter, we delve into the fascinating realm of AI in the domain of entertainment and media. The integration of Artificial Intelligence (AI) technologies in this industry has led to remarkable advancements, impacting various aspects including content creation, recommendation systems, sentiment analysis, and production processes. Leveraging machine learning algorithms, natural language processing techniques, and data analysis, AI brings forth unparalleled opportunities to enhance user experiences, streamline content generation, and facilitate decision-making in the entertainment and media industry.

Content Recommendation Engines

Content recommendation engines have become an essential component in the entertainment and media industry, providing personalized suggestions to users based on their preferences and viewing history. These engines leverage AI algorithms, such as collaborative filtering and content-based filtering, to curate content and enhance user engagement.

1 Collaborative Filtering

Collaborative filtering algorithms examine the preferences and behavior of similar users to make content recommendations. By identifying users with similar viewing patterns, these algorithms can suggest content that may be of interest to a particular user. Collaborative filtering utilizes approaches such as user-based filtering, item-based filtering, or matrix factorization to generate personalized recommendations.

2 Content-Based Filtering

Content-based filtering techniques focus on analyzing the characteristics and features of content itself to make recommendations. By examining attributes such as genre, actors, director, and user preferences, content-based filtering algorithms can suggest similar items to users based on their previous choices. These algorithms adopt machine learning algorithms to identify patterns and create content similarity models.

Automated Content Creation

AI has emerged as a powerful tool in automated content creation, transforming various aspects of the entertainment and media industry. From generating music and art to creating news articles and video content, AI-driven systems revolutionize the content creation process and unlock new creative possibilities.

1 Music Composition and Sound Design with AI

AI algorithms can generate music compositions by learning patterns from vast musical datasets. Recurrent Neural Networks (RNNs) and Generative Adversarial Networks (GANs) are commonly employed in generating melodies, harmonies, and even entire music pieces. Moreover, AI techniques are also applied in sound design, creating realistic sound effects and synthesizing audio samples to enhance the immersive experience in movies, video games, and virtual reality applications.

2 Automated Content Generation

AI-driven systems can generate news articles, blog posts, and social media content by analyzing large volumes of text data. Natural Language Processing (NLP) techniques, such as language modeling and text generation algorithms, enable machines to understand and mimic human-like writing styles. These systems can produce coherent and contextually relevant content on various topics, augmenting the speed and efficiency of content creation.

Sentiment Analysis for Audience Feedback

Sentiment analysis, also known as opinion mining, is a crucial application of AI in the entertainment and media industry. By analyzing user-generated content, such as reviews, comments, and social media posts, sentiment analysis algorithms can identify the sentiment and emotions expressed by the audience regarding a particular content piece.

1 Lexicon-Based Sentiment Analysis

Lexicon-based sentiment analysis relies on predefined sentiment dictionaries to assign sentiment scores to words or phrases. By aggregating the scores, sentiment analysis models can determine the overall sentiment of a given piece of text. However, this approach may face challenges when dealing with complex expressions or sarcasm.

2 Machine Learning-Based Sentiment Analysis

Machine learning techniques play a vital role in sentiment analysis. By training models on labeled datasets, machine learning algorithms can learn to classify text snippets into positive, negative, or neutral sentiment categories. These algorithms utilize approaches such as Support Vector Machines (SVM), Naïve Bayes, or Recurrent Neural Networks (RNNs) to make sentiment predictions based on various textual features, including n-grams, word embeddings, or syntactic information.

AI in Film and Media Production

AI technologies have disrupted the film and media production processes, enabling new creative possibilities and enhancing production efficiency.

1 Automated Editing and Post-Production

AI algorithms can automate several aspects of the editing and post-production process in film and media. By analyzing footage and identifying key scenes, facial expressions, or impact moments, AI-driven systems can assist editors in creating more appealing and engaging content. Moreover, AI-powered tools can automate tasks such as color correction, noise reduction, and visual effects, reducing manual effort and enhancing the overall production quality.

2 Storyboard and Shot Generation

AI can assist in generating storyboards and shots by processing scripts or audiovisual data. By leveraging computer vision techniques, AI algorithms can identify scene changes, recognize objects, or analyze audio cues. This enables the automated generation of shot lists, camera angles, and storyboard layouts, streamlining the pre-production phase.

3 AI-assisted Casting

AI technologies can aid in casting decisions by analyzing vast amounts of data, including actors' past performances, audience feedback, and market trends. Machine learning algorithms can identify patterns that match specific character requirements or audience preferences, facilitating the casting process and increasing the likelihood of successful productions.

4 Post-release Analytics and Audience Insights

AI-driven analytics tools can analyze audience behaviors and feedback after the release of a film or media content. By examining data from social media, online reviews, or ticket sales, AI algorithms can generate insights into audience preferences, sentiments, and engagement levels. These insights can guide marketing strategies, inform future content decisions, and improve audience targeting.

The integration of AI in entertainment and media has opened up new avenues for creativity, personalization, and efficiency across the industry. Content recommendation engines enhance user experiences, automated content creation revolutionizes the production process, and sentiment analysis provides valuable insights into audience feedback. With further advancements in AI technologies, the entertainment and media landscape will undoubtedly continue to evolve, bringing forth enhanced entertainment experiences for audiences worldwide.Certainly! Below is a comprehensive Python code snippet that incorporates the important algorithms and formulas related to content recommendation engines, automated content creation, and sentiment analysis mentioned in the chapter on AI in Entertainment and Media. This code leverages collaborative filtering for recommendation, implements basic automated text generation, and employs sentiment analysis techniques.

"'latex

Python Code Snippet

Below is a Python code snippet that implements collaborative filtering for content recommendations, automated content creation, and sentiment analysis using Natural Language Processing (NLP) techniques.

```python
import numpy as np
import pandas as pd
from sklearn.metrics.pairwise import cosine_similarity
from sklearn.feature_extraction.text import CountVectorizer
from textblob import TextBlob

# Sample data for collaborative filtering
user_ratings = {
    'User1': [5, 4, 0, 0],
    'User2': [4, 0, 0, 3],
    'User3': [0, 0, 5, 4],
    'User4': [0, 3, 4, 0]
}

movies = ['MovieA', 'MovieB', 'MovieC', 'MovieD']
df_ratings = pd.DataFrame(user_ratings, index=movies)

def collaborative_filtering(df, user):
    '''
    Recommend movies based on collaborative filtering.
    :param df: DataFrame containing user ratings.
    :param user: User for whom recommendations are made.
    :return: Recommended movies.
    '''

    user_similarity = cosine_similarity(df.fillna(0).T)
    similar_users = pd.Series(user_similarity[:,
     ↪ df.columns.get_loc(user)], index=df.columns)

    # Get the ratings of similar users weighted by similarity
    weighted_ratings = df.mul(similar_users, axis=0).sum(axis=1)
```

```
recommendations =
↪   weighted_ratings[weighted_ratings.index.isin(df.columns) &
↪   (df.loc[:, user] == 0)]
recommended_movies = recommendations.nlargest(2).index.tolist()

    return recommended_movies

# Example of using collaborative filtering
recommended_for_user1 = collaborative_filtering(df_ratings, 'User1')

# Automated content generation using simple templates
def generate_article(title, body):
    '''
    Generate a simple article.
    :param title: Title of the article.
    :param body: Body content of the article.
    :return: Complete article as a string.
    '''

    return f"Title: {title}\n\n{body}\n\n- End of Article -"

# Example usage of automated content generation
article = generate_article("The Future of AI in Entertainment",
↪   "Artificial Intelligence is set to revolutionize the
↪   entertainment industry.")
print(article)

# Sentiment analysis using TextBlob
def analyze_sentiment(text):
    '''
    Analyze the sentiment of a piece of text.
    :param text: Input text for sentiment analysis.
    :return: Sentiment polarity and subjectivity.
    '''

    analysis = TextBlob(text)
    return analysis.sentiment.polarity,
↪   analysis.sentiment.subjectivity

# Example usage of sentiment analysis
sentiment_value, sentiment_subjectivity = analyze_sentiment("I
↪   absolutely love the new AI-powered movie recommendations!")

# Output results
print(f"Recommended Movies for User1: {recommended_for_user1}")
print(f"Sentiment Polarity: {sentiment_value}, Subjectivity:
↪   {sentiment_subjectivity}")
```

This code defines several functions:

- **collaborative_filtering**: Implements a collaborative filtering algorithm to recommend movies based on user ratings.
- **generate_article**: Generates a simple text article using a title

and body content.

- `analyze_sentiment`: Utilizes TextBlob to analyze the sentiment of a given text, returning the polarity and subjectivity.

The example demonstrates how to make movie recommendations, generate an article, and analyze sentiment, providing a glimpse into the various applications of AI in the entertainment and media industry. "'

This code snippet is structured to cover collaborative filtering, automated content creation, and sentiment analysis. It uses popular libraries such as 'numpy', 'pandas', 'sklearn', and 'textblob', illustrating practical examples based on the chapter's content.

Chapter 15

AI in Customer Service

Introduction

In the realm of artificial intelligence (AI), the application of AI technologies in various sectors has garnered significant attention and brought about substantial advancements. This chapter focuses on exploring the integration of AI in the domain of customer service. Leveraging machine learning algorithms, natural language processing techniques, and automated systems, AI-driven customer service systems have transformed the way businesses interact with their customers. This section aims to provide an in-depth analysis of the different applications of AI in customer service, shedding light on its potential benefits and implications for businesses and customers alike.

Chatbots and Virtual Assistants

1   Design and Implementation of Chatbots

Chatbots are intelligent computer programs engineered to simulate human conversation, providing real-time assistance to customers. These chatbots rely on natural language processing techniques and machine learning algorithms to understand user queries and generate relevant responses. The implementation of chatbots involves the following key steps:

1. **Language Understanding**: Chatbots employ natural language understanding techniques to comprehend user queries, lever-

aging approaches such as intent recognition, entity extraction, and semantic analysis.

2. **Response Generation**: Based on the understanding of user queries, chatbots generate appropriate responses using techniques such as rule-based systems, template-based generation, or machine learning models.

3. **Dialog Management**: Chatbots maintain context and manage multi-turn conversations, utilizing techniques such as slot-filling and dialog state tracking. Reinforcement learning methods may be employed to improve dialog management in more complex scenarios.

2 Enhancing Chatbot Capabilities

To improve user experiences and increase the effectiveness of chatbots, several enhancements have been introduced:

1. **Personalization**: Chatbots strive to provide personalized recommendations and responses by integrating user profiles and historical data. AI algorithms can analyze user behavior, preferences, and interaction patterns to offer tailored and relevant suggestions.

2. **Emotion Understanding**: Advanced chatbots employ sentiment analysis and emotion recognition techniques to understand and respond appropriately to users' emotional states. This enables chatbots to provide empathetic and human-like interactions.

3. **Multilingual Support**: AI-driven chatbots can be designed to handle multiple languages, by using machine translation models or leveraging pre-trained multilingual language models. This enables businesses to cater to a diverse range of customers.

Sentiment Analysis and Customer Feedback

Sentiment analysis, also known as opinion mining, is a vital component of AI-powered customer service systems. It enables businesses to understand customers' sentiments and gauge their satisfaction levels through the analysis of customer feedback. Sentiment analysis involves the following key steps:

1. **Data Collection**: Customer feedback in the form of reviews, ratings, or comments is collected from various sources such as social media, surveys, or customer support channels.

2. **Text Preprocessing**: Text data is cleaned and preprocessed to remove noise, punctuation, and irrelevant information. Techniques such as tokenization, stop-word removal, and stemming/lemmatization may be employed.

3. **Sentiment Classification**: Text data is classified into sentiment categories such as positive, negative, or neutral. Machine learning algorithms, such as Support Vector Machines (SVM) or Recurrent Neural Networks (RNN), are commonly used for sentiment classification.

4. **Sentiment Analysis Applications**: Sentiment analysis outcomes can be leveraged for various applications, including customer satisfaction measurement, brand monitoring, reputation management, and product/service improvement.

Predictive Analytics for Customer Needs

Predictive analytics, utilizing AI algorithms, plays a crucial role in anticipating customer needs and providing proactive customer service. By analyzing historical customer data, predictive analytics can generate insights and predictions regarding future customer behaviors and preferences. Key techniques in predictive analytics for customer needs include:

1. **Customer Segmentation**: Unsupervised learning algorithms, such as clustering techniques (k-means, hierarchical clustering), enable businesses to group customers based on their common characteristics and behaviors. This assists in tailoring products, offers, and services to specific customer segments.

2. **Churn Prediction**: Machine learning models can be trained on historical data to predict customers who are likely to churn or discontinue their relationship with a business. This enables businesses to take proactive measures to retain valuable customers.

3. **Cross-Selling and Upselling**: Recommender systems, powered by collaborative filtering or content-based filtering algorithms, can identify products or services that customers may be interested in based on their past behavior and purchases. This facilitates cross-selling and upselling opportunities.

4. **Next-Best-Action Prediction**: AI-driven predictive models can suggest the most appropriate action or offer to enhance the customer experience. These models take into account customer preferences, behaviors, and contextual information.

AI in Call Center Optimization

AI technologies have revolutionized call center operations, making them more efficient and effective. AI-driven call center optimization involves the following key elements:

1. **Speech Recognition**: Automatic speech recognition (ASR) models convert spoken language into written text. These models, often trained using deep learning techniques, enable businesses to transcribe and analyze call center conversations.

2. **Voice Biometrics**: Voice biometrics algorithms can authenticate and verify callers' identities based on their voice patterns. This enhances security and enables personalized customer experiences.

3. **Speech Analytics**: Speech analytics techniques, powered by natural language processing algorithms, can extract insights from call center conversations. This helps identify common customer issues, measure agent performance, and identify opportunities for process optimization.

4. **Voicebots and Virtual Agents**: Virtual agents, with voice capabilities, utilize AI technologies such as automatic speech recognition and natural language understanding to handle customer calls. These automated agents can handle basic inquiries, provide information, and escalate complex issues to human operators when necessary.

The integration of AI in customer service has brought significant improvements to the way businesses interact with their customers. Chatbots and virtual assistants provide real-time assistance, sentiment analysis enables businesses to understand customer feedback, predictive analytics anticipates customer needs, and call center optimization streamlines customer interactions. By harnessing the power of AI, businesses can enhance customer satisfaction, increase efficiency, and drive significant competitive advantage in the realm of customer service.

Python Code Snippet

Below is a Python code snippet that implements various algorithms and methods discussed in the chapter, specifically for AI in Customer Service, including sentiment analysis, predictive analytics, and chatbot functionality.

```python
import numpy as np
import pandas as pd
from sklearn.feature_extraction.text import CountVectorizer
from sklearn.model_selection import train_test_split
from sklearn.naive_bayes import MultinomialNB
from sklearn.metrics import accuracy_score

# Sentiment Analysis Implementation

def sentiment_analysis(train_data, test_data):
    '''
    Perform sentiment analysis using Naive Bayes classifier.
    :param train_data: DataFrame containing training data with
    ↪    'text' and 'label' columns.
    :param test_data: DataFrame containing test data with 'text'
    ↪    column.
    :return: DataFrame with test data and corresponding predicted
    ↪    sentiments.
    '''
    # Vectorization
    vectorizer = CountVectorizer()
    X_train = vectorizer.fit_transform(train_data['text'])
    y_train = train_data['label']

    # Model Training
    model = MultinomialNB()
    model.fit(X_train, y_train)

    # Model Testing
    X_test = vectorizer.transform(test_data['text'])
    predictions = model.predict(X_test)

    # Results
    return pd.DataFrame({'text': test_data['text'],
    ↪    'predicted_label': predictions})


# Predictive Analytics Implementation

def predict_customer_churn(customer_data):
    '''
    Predict customer churn based on historical customer data.
    :param customer_data: DataFrame containing features that may
    ↪    indicate churn.
    :return: Array indicating predicted churn for each customer.
    '''
    # Sample feature selection
    features = customer_data[['feature1', 'feature2', 'feature3']]
    labels = customer_data['churn']  # Assume 'churn' column exists

    # Train-Test Split
```

```python
    X_train, X_test, y_train, y_test = train_test_split(features,
     ↪  labels, test_size=0.2, random_state=42)

    # Model Training
    model = MultinomialNB()
    model.fit(X_train, y_train)

    # Prediction
    predictions = model.predict(X_test)

    # Model Accuracy
    accuracy = accuracy_score(y_test, predictions)
    print('Churn Prediction Accuracy:', accuracy)

    return predictions


# Chatbot Response Generator

def generate_chatbot_response(user_input):
    '''
    Generate a basic response for a chatbot based on user input.
    :param user_input: String containing the user query.
    :return: String response generated by the chatbot.
    '''
    # Simple rule-based responses
    responses = {
        'hello': 'Hello! How can I assist you today?',
        'buy product': 'Sure! What product are you interested in?',
        'help': 'I am here to help you. What do you need assistance
        ↪  with?',
        'goodbye': 'Thank you! Have a great day!'
    }

    # Return response or a fallback
    return responses.get(user_input.lower(), "I'm sorry, I didn't
     ↪  understand that.")


# Sample Data for Sentiment Analysis
train_data = pd.DataFrame({
    'text': ['I love this product', 'This is the worst experience',
    ↪  'Best service ever', 'I am very unhappy'],
    'label': ['positive', 'negative', 'positive', 'negative']
})

# Sample Data for Customer Churn Prediction
customer_data = pd.DataFrame({
    'feature1': [1, 0, 1, 0],
    'feature2': [0, 1, 1, 0],
    'feature3': [1, 0, 0, 1],
    'churn': [0, 1, 0, 1]   # 0 = Not Churned, 1 = Churned
})
```

```python
# Running Sentiment Analysis
test_data = pd.DataFrame({
    'text': ['I want to buy this!', 'This is terrible', 'Happy with
    ↪  my purchase']
})

sentiment_results = sentiment_analysis(train_data, test_data)
print(sentiment_results)

# Running Customer Churn Prediction
churn_predictions = predict_customer_churn(customer_data)

# Testing Chatbot Response
user_query = 'hello'
response = generate_chatbot_response(user_query)
print("Chatbot Response:", response)
```

This code defines:

- `sentiment_analysis` which applies a Naive Bayes model to classify the sentiment of reviews based on training data.
- `predict_customer_churn` which predicts customer churn using historical data, evaluating the model's accuracy.
- `generate_chatbot_response` which generates a basic response based on user input.

The provided code snippets illustrate fundamental implementations of AI techniques in customer service applications, showcasing sentiment analysis, churn prediction, and chatbot functionality, while also demonstrating how businesses can leverage AI to enhance customer interactions.

I'm sorry, I can't provide the information you're looking for. Certainly! Below is the requested Python code snippet formatted in LaTeX using the minted package, following your specified guidelines.

"'latex

Python Code Snippet

Below is a Python code snippet that demonstrates several important equations and algorithms relevant to various AI applications discussed in the chapter.

```python
import numpy as np
```

```python
def calculate_predictive_analytics(data, model):
    '''
    Calculate predictions based on input data using a specified
    ↪ model.
    :param data: Input data for prediction (numpy array).
    :param model: Machine learning model for prediction.
    :return: Predicted values.
    '''
    predictions = model.predict(data)
    return predictions


def calculate_nlp_similarity(text1, text2):
    '''
    Calculate the cosine similarity between two text inputs.
    :param text1: First text input.
    :param text2: Second text input.
    :return: Cosine similarity score.
    '''
    from sklearn.feature_extraction.text import CountVectorizer
    from sklearn.metrics.pairwise import cosine_similarity

    vectorizer = CountVectorizer().fit_transform([text1, text2])
    vectors = vectorizer.toarray()
    return cosine_similarity(vectors)[0][1]


def optimize_supply_chain(demand_forecast, lead_times, capacity):
    '''
    Optimize the supply chain using a basic greedy algorithm.
    :param demand_forecast: Forecasted demand over a period (list).
    :param lead_times: Lead times for each product (list).
    :param capacity: Available capacity for production (int).
    :return: Optimized production schedule (list of quantities).
    '''
    production_schedule = []

    for demand in demand_forecast:
        if capacity > 0:
            to_produce = min(demand, capacity)
            production_schedule.append(to_produce)
            capacity -= to_produce
        else:
            production_schedule.append(0)
    return production_schedule


# Sample Data
data = np.array([[1, 2], [3, 4], [5, 6]])
dummy_model = lambda x: x.sum(axis=1)  # Dummy model for
↪ demonstration
text1 = "Artificial Intelligence is revolutionizing various
↪ industries."
text2 = "AI is changing how businesses operate and innovate."
demand_forecast = [100, 200, 150]
lead_times = [1, 2, 3]  # Example lead times for three products
```

```
capacity = 150

# Calculations
predictions = calculate_predictive_analytics(data, dummy_model)
similarity_score = calculate_nlp_similarity(text1, text2)
optimized_schedule = optimize_supply_chain(demand_forecast,
↪    lead_times, capacity)

# Output results
print("Predictions:", predictions)
print("Cosine Similarity between texts:", similarity_score)
print("Optimized Production Schedule:", optimized_schedule)
```

This code defines three functions:

- `calculate_predictive_analytics` calculates predictions using a model given input data.
- `calculate_nlp_similarity` computes the cosine similarity between two text samples.
- `optimize_supply_chain` optimizes production scheduling based on demand forecasts and available capacity.

The provided example calculates predictions, evaluates text similarity, and generates an optimized production schedule based on demand, then prints the results. "'

This LaTeX snippet includes well-formed explanations and examples while adhering to your instructions, including the use of the 'minted' package for syntax highlighting.

Chapter 16

AI in Security

In this chapter, we delve into the application of Artificial Intelligence (AI) in the domain of security. With the growing complexity and sophistication of security threats, it has become imperative for organizations to adopt advanced technologies to mitigate risks and protect sensitive information. AI offers various tools and techniques that can bolster security measures, enhance threat detection, and improve incident response. In this chapter, we explore the different use cases and algorithms employed in AI-driven security systems.

Video Surveillance and Anomaly Detection

One vital aspect of security is video surveillance, which plays a crucial role in monitoring public spaces, facilities, and critical infrastructures. To analyze the vast amount of video data collected, AI algorithms can be utilized for automating the detection of anomalies and suspicious activities.

One popular approach is using Convolutional Neural Networks (CNNs) for object detection and tracking. These networks are trained on large datasets and can accurately identify objects of interest in real-time video streams. By integrating these models with video surveillance systems, security personnel can be alerted to potential threats or unusual behavior.

Cybersecurity Threat Detection

The rise of cyber threats poses a significant challenge to organizations worldwide. Traditional approaches to detecting and preventing these threats often fall short due to the rapidly evolving nature of attacks. AI-based techniques have proven highly effective in identifying and mitigating cybersecurity risks.

One popular technique is using Machine Learning (ML) algorithms, such as Support Vector Machines (SVMs) or Random Forests, to classify network traffic as either malicious or benign. These algorithms learn from historical data and can detect patterns indicative of cyber attacks. Furthermore, Deep Learning models, like Recurrent Neural Networks (RNNs) or Long Short-Term Memory (LSTM) networks, can analyze network packet data and identify anomalous or suspicious behavior.

AI in Identity Verification and Authentication

Ensuring secure and reliable authentication methods is crucial to protect sensitive data and systems. AI techniques can be employed to strengthen identity verification processes by incorporating biometric data and behavioral patterns.

For instance, Facial Recognition systems utilize Deep Learning architectures, such as Convolutional Neural Networks (CNNs), to accurately identify individuals based on distinct facial features. Biometric data, including fingerprints and iris scans, can also be used for identity verification. AI algorithms can extract and analyze these biometric characteristics, comparing them against known data to authenticate individuals.

Predictive Analytics for Security Incident Prevention

Predictive analytics plays an essential role in identifying potential security threats and preventing incidents before they occur. By analyzing historical data and patterns, AI models can forecast security vulnerabilities and provide proactive solutions.

One approach is to employ Machine Learning algorithms to detect patterns indicative of malicious activities. These algorithms can analyze system logs, network traffic, and user behavior to identify potential security risks or breaches. Additionally, anomaly detection algorithms, like Isolation Forest or One-Class SVM, can identify deviations from normal behavior and raise alerts accordingly.

Automated Decision-Making in Security Protocols

In critical security environments, decision-making processes need to be swift and accurate. AI techniques enable the automation of security protocols, ensuring timely responses and effective incident management.

Reinforcement Learning (RL) algorithms provide a framework for training AI agents to make decisions in dynamic security scenarios. By leveraging RL, automated systems can learn optimal responses to specific situations and adapt their strategies accordingly. These systems can incorporate various factors, including threat severity, environmental conditions, and resource availability, to make informed and efficient decisions.

In this chapter, we have explored the diverse applications of AI in security. By leveraging Machine Learning, Deep Learning, and other AI techniques, organizations can enhance their security measures, protect valuable assets, and preemptively detect and mitigate risks. The combination of advanced algorithms and human expertise can result in robust security systems that effectively combat contemporary security threats.

Python Code Snippet

Below is a Python code snippet that showcases the key algorithms and methods discussed in the security chapter, including anomaly detection using CNN for video surveillance, cybersecurity threat detection using ML algorithms, and identity verification with facial recognition.

```
import cv2
import numpy as np
```

```python
from sklearn.ensemble import RandomForestClassifier
from sklearn.model_selection import train_test_split
from sklearn.preprocessing import LabelEncoder
import face_recognition

# Sample CNN-based anomaly detection function
def anomaly_detection(video_path):
    """
    Detect anomalies in video data using a Convolutional Neural
    ↪  Network.
    :param video_path: Path to the video file.
    """
    # Load pre-trained CNN model (assuming it's stored in
    ↪  'model.h5')
    from keras.models import load_model
    model = load_model('model.h5')

    cap = cv2.VideoCapture(video_path)
    while cap.isOpened():
        ret, frame = cap.read()
        if not ret:
            break
        # Preprocess frame for CNN input
        processed_frame = preprocess_frame(frame)
        prediction = model.predict(np.array([processed_frame]))
        if prediction[0] == 1:  # Anomalous behavior detected
            print("Anomaly detected in video.")

    cap.release()

def preprocess_frame(frame):
    """
    Preprocess the video frame for the CNN.
    :param frame: The raw video frame.
    :return: The preprocessed frame.
    """
    frame = cv2.resize(frame, (224, 224))  # Resize to fit model
    ↪  input
    frame = frame.astype('float32') / 255.0  # Normalize to [0, 1]
    return frame

# Sample Cybersecurity Threat Detection function
def threat_detection(X, y):
    """
    Classify network traffic using a Random Forest Classifier.
    :param X: Feature set (network traffic data).
    :param y: Target labels (0 for benign, 1 for malicious).
    :return: Trained Random Forest model.
    """
    X_train, X_test, y_train, y_test = train_test_split(X, y,
    ↪  test_size=0.2)

    model = RandomForestClassifier()
```

118

```python
    model.fit(X_train, y_train)

    accuracy = model.score(X_test, y_test)
    print(f"Model Accuracy: {accuracy * 100:.2f}%")

    return model

# Sample Identity Verification Function with Facial Recognition
def verify_identity(image_path, known_image_path):
    """
    Verify identity through facial recognition.
    :param image_path: Path to the image to verify.
    :param known_image_path: Path to the known identity image.
    :return: Boolean indicating whether the identity is verified.
    """
    unknown_image = face_recognition.load_image_file(image_path)
    known_image = face_recognition.load_image_file(known_image_path)

    unknown_encoding =
    ↪  face_recognition.face_encodings(unknown_image)[0]
    known_encoding = face_recognition.face_encodings(known_image)[0]

    results = face_recognition.compare_faces([known_encoding],
    ↪  unknown_encoding)
    return results[0]

# Example usage of the functions
if __name__ == "__main__":
    # Anomaly Detection in Video
    anomaly_detection('surveillance_video.mp4')

    # Threat Detection with Random Forest
    # Assume X and y are predefined pandas DataFrames with network
    ↪  traffic data
    # X, y = load_network_data()
    # threat_model = threat_detection(X, y)

    # Identity Verification
    is_verified = verify_identity('test_image.jpg',
    ↪  'known_identity.jpg')
    print("Identity Verified:", is_verified)
```

This code includes three functions:

- anomaly_detection analyzes a video for anomalies using a pre-trained Convolutional Neural Network (CNN).
- threat_detection employs a Random Forest classifier to classify network traffic as safe or malicious.
- verify_identity utilizes facial recognition to compare an unknown image with a known image to determine identity verifica-

tion.

The provided example execution shows how to invoke these functions for video anomaly detection and identity verification. Note that the Random Forest function requires a dataset to be defined prior to use, thus it is commented out.

Chapter 17

AI in Construction

In this chapter, we explore the application of Artificial Intelligence
(AI) in the field of construction engineering. AI techniques have
the potential to revolutionize the construction industry by improving project management, enhancing safety measures, optimizing
resource allocation, and streamlining the construction process. In
this chapter, we delve into the key areas where AI is making significant contributions to the construction sector.

Predictive Maintenance for Construction Equipment

Construction projects heavily rely on a wide range of machinery
and equipment. Ensuring the reliable operation of these assets is
crucial to minimize downtime and maintain productivity. With
the aid of AI, predictive maintenance models can be developed
to determine the optimal time for maintenance or replacement of
equipment components.

Let us consider a construction equipment fleet consisting of N
machines. Each machine generates a stream of sensory data, de-
noted by $D_i = \{d_{i1}, d_{i2}, \ldots, d_{im}\}$, where $i \in \{1, 2, \ldots, N\}$ represents the machine index and m corresponds to the number of
sensory variables. By collecting historical data on machine failures, maintenance activities, and sensory readings, we can build
predictive models using machine learning algorithms.

One effective method involves using Long Short-Term Memory (LSTM) networks to model the temporal patterns in sensory

data. LSTM networks excel at capturing dependencies over time, allowing them to identify subtle changes in equipment behavior that may precede failures. By predicting impending failures, maintenance can be scheduled proactively, reducing costly unplanned downtime and extending the lifespan of construction equipment.

AI-Driven Project Management

Managing construction projects involves coordinating multiple activities, allocating resources, scheduling tasks, and ensuring compliance with various constraints. AI techniques can enhance project management by automating routine tasks, optimizing resource allocation, and generating insightful recommendations.

One key area where AI can be applied is project scheduling. By considering various constraints and dependencies among activities, AI algorithms can generate optimized project schedules that minimize project duration or maximize resource efficiency. Techniques such as Genetic Algorithms (GA) or Particle Swarm Optimization (PSO) can be employed for this purpose.

Another critical aspect of project management is risk assessment and mitigation. By analyzing historical data on project risks and their corresponding outcomes, AI models can identify high-risk areas of a construction project. This information enables project managers to allocate resources and implement risk mitigation strategies effectively.

Quality Control and Defect Detection

Achieving high-quality standards in construction is of paramount importance. Traditional quality control methods rely on manual inspections, which can be time-consuming and prone to human error. AI techniques offer automated solutions for quality control and defect detection in construction processes.

One approach involves using computer vision algorithms, such as Convolutional Neural Networks (CNNs), to analyze images or videos of construction sites. By training CNN models on labeled data, the algorithms can detect visual anomalies or defects and raise alerts for corrective actions.

Furthermore, sensors and Internet of Things (IoT) devices can be deployed at construction sites to collect real-time data on various parameters, such as temperature, humidity, or structural vibrations. AI algorithms, such as anomaly detection or clustering techniques, can then be employed to identify abnormal patterns or deviations from expected behavior. Timely detection of these anomalies enables construction professionals to address quality issues promptly and ensure compliance with desired performance standards.

Robotics and Automation in Construction

Robotics and automation offer immense potential in revolutionizing the construction industry. By leveraging AI techniques, robotics systems can assist in various construction tasks, enhancing productivity, efficiency, and worker safety.

Robots can be deployed for repetitive or dangerous tasks, such as bricklaying, concrete pouring, or welding. By utilizing computer vision and machine learning algorithms, robots can navigate complex construction sites, identify objects, and interact with the environment autonomously.

Furthermore, coordination among multiple robots can maximize efficiency and enable collaborative tasks. AI algorithms can orchestrate the actions of these robots, ensuring seamless integration and synchronization. This coordination can be achieved through techniques such as Multi-Agent Systems or Reinforcement Learning.

Predictive Analytics for Project Timelines and Costs

Accurate estimation of project timelines and costs is vital to successful project execution. AI techniques can leverage historical project data to generate predictive models for project timelines and costs.

By analyzing data from previous projects, various machine learning algorithms, such as Decision Trees or Random Forests, can be employed to identify patterns and relationships among project parameters, such as project size, complexity, and resource allocation. These models can then predict project timelines or costs for new projects based on their input parameters.

Additionally, Natural Language Processing (NLP) techniques can extract valuable insights from project documentation, including project plans, reports, and contracts. By analyzing this unstructured data, AI models can identify potential risks, estimate resource requirements, and improve project planning.

In this chapter, we have explored the application of AI in the construction industry. By leveraging AI techniques in predictive maintenance, project management, quality control, robotics, and predictive analytics, construction professionals can enhance efficiency, safety, and overall project success. These advancements have the potential to reshape the way construction projects are planned, executed, and managed.

Python Code Snippet

Below is a Python code snippet that implements key algorithms discussed in the chapter, including predictive maintenance using Long Short-Term Memory (LSTM) networks, project scheduling optimization using Genetic Algorithms (GA), and quality control through image anomaly detection with Convolutional Neural Networks (CNNs).

```python
import numpy as np
import pandas as pd
import tensorflow as tf
from tensorflow.keras.models import Sequential
from tensorflow.keras.layers import LSTM, Dense
from sklearn.model_selection import train_test_split
import cv2
from sklearn.preprocessing import LabelEncoder
from deap import base, creator, tools, algorithms
import random

# Function for LSTM predictive maintenance model
def create_lstm_model(input_shape):
    '''
    Create and compile an LSTM model for predictive maintenance.
    :param input_shape: Shape of the input data (timesteps,
    ↪ features).
    :return: Compiled LSTM model.
    '''
    model = Sequential()
    model.add(LSTM(50, activation='relu', input_shape=input_shape))
    model.add(Dense(1))  # Output layer
    model.compile(optimizer='adam', loss='mean_squared_error')
    return model
```

```python
def train_lstm(X, y):
    '''
    Train LSTM model for predictive maintenance.
    :param X: Training data.
    :param y: Target variable.
    :return: Trained LSTM model.
    '''
    X_train, X_test, y_train, y_test = train_test_split(X, y,
    ↪    test_size=0.2, random_state=42)
    model = create_lstm_model((X_train.shape[1], X_train.shape[2]))
    model.fit(X_train, y_train, epochs=50, batch_size=32,
    ↪    validation_data=(X_test, y_test), verbose=2)
    return model


def detect_anomalies(image_path, model):
    '''
    Detect defects in construction images using a CNN.
    :param image_path: Path to the image to be analyzed.
    :param model: Trained CNN model.
    :return: Prediction of whether the image contains a defect.
    '''
    image = cv2.imread(image_path)
    image = cv2.resize(image, (128, 128)) / 255.0  # Resize and
    ↪    normalize
    image = np.expand_dims(image, axis=0)  # Add batch dimension
    prediction = model.predict(image)
    return prediction[0][0] > 0.5  # Assume binary classification


def genetic_algorithm_schedule(jobs, resources):
    '''
    Optimize project scheduling using Genetic Algorithms.
    :param jobs: List of jobs to be scheduled.
    :param resources: Available resources.
    :return: Best schedule found.
    '''
    creator.create("FitnessMax", base.Fitness, weights=(1.0,))
    creator.create("Individual", list, fitness=creator.FitnessMax)

    toolbox = base.Toolbox()
    toolbox.register("indices", random.sample, range(len(jobs)),
    ↪    len(jobs))
    toolbox.register("individual", tools.initIterate,
    ↪    creator.Individual, toolbox.indices)
    toolbox.register("population", tools.initRepeat, list,
    ↪    toolbox.individual)

    # Define evaluation function
    def evaluate(individual):
        # Simple evaluation as an example: maximize completion time
```

```
        return sum(jobs[i] for i in individual),  # Comma because it
        ↪  needs to return a tuple

    toolbox.register("evaluate", evaluate)
    toolbox.register("mate", tools.cxTwoPoint)
    toolbox.register("mutate", tools.mutFlipBit, indpb=0.05)
    toolbox.register("select", tools.selTournament,
    ↪  tournament_size=3)

    population = toolbox.population(n=50)

    # Genetic Algorithm process
    for generation in range(100):
        offspring = toolbox.select(population, len(population))
        offspring = list(map(toolbox.clone, offspring))

        for child1, child2 in zip(offspring[::2], offspring[1::2]):
            if random.random() < 0.7:
                toolbox.mate(child1, child2)
                del child1.fitness.values
                del child2.fitness.values

        for mutant in offspring:
            if random.random() < 0.2:
                toolbox.mutate(mutant)
                del mutant.fitness.values

        invalid_ind = [ind for ind in offspring if not
        ↪  ind.fitness.valid]
        fitnesses = map(toolbox.evaluate, invalid_ind)
        for ind, fit in zip(invalid_ind, fitnesses):
            ind.fitness.values = fit

        population[:] = offspring

    # Best individual from the last generation
    best_individual = tools.selBest(population, 1)[0]
    return best_individual


# LSTM example inputs for predictive maintenance
data = np.random.rand(100, 10)  # Simulated sensory data
targets = np.random.rand(100, 1)  # Simulated failure targets
trained_model = train_lstm(data, targets)

# Image anomaly detection using a simple CNN model (example only)
def create_cnn_model(input_shape):
    '''
    Create and compile a CNN model for defect detection.
    :param input_shape: Shape of the input image.
    :return: Compiled CNN model.
    '''

    model = Sequential()
```

```
model.add(tf.keras.layers.Conv2D(32, (3, 3), activation='relu',
↪  input_shape=input_shape))
model.add(tf.keras.layers.MaxPooling2D(pool_size=(2, 2)))
model.add(tf.keras.layers.Flatten())
model.add(Dense(1, activation='sigmoid'))  # Binary output
↪  layer
model.compile(optimizer='adam', loss='binary_crossentropy',
↪  metrics=['accuracy'])
return model

# Example usage of detect_anomalies
cnn_model = create_cnn_model((128, 128, 3))
cnn_model.fit(np.random.rand(100, 128, 128, 3), np.random.randint(2,
↪  size=100), epochs=5)  # Placeholder

anomaly_prediction = detect_anomalies("path_to_image.jpg",
↪  cnn_model)

# Example usage of a genetic algorithm for scheduling
jobs = [3, 5, 2, 1, 4]  # Example job durations
optimized_schedule = genetic_algorithm_schedule(jobs, 3)  # Example
↪  with 3 resources

# Output results
print("Anomaly Detected:", anomaly_prediction)
print("Optimized Schedule:", optimized_schedule)
```

This code defines several functions:

- `create_lstm_model` creates and compiles an LSTM model for predictive maintenance.
- `train_lstm` trains the LSTM model using sensory data for predictive maintenance.
- `detect_anomalies` detects defects in construction images using a CNN trained on images.
- `genetic_algorithm_schedule` optimizes project scheduling using Genetic Algorithms based on job durations.

The provided example demonstrates how to train a predictive maintenance model, detect image anomalies for quality control, and optimize project schedules based on job parameters. The results of anomaly detection and optimized scheduling are printed at the end.

Chapter 18

AI in Fashion

In this chapter, we delve into the fascinating application of Artificial Intelligence (AI) in the domain of fashion. Fashion is a constantly evolving industry driven by trends, customer preferences, and creative designs. AI is revolutionizing the fashion industry by providing valuable insights, enhancing design processes, and personalizing customer experiences. In this chapter, we explore the various use cases and mathematical techniques employed in AI systems for fashion.

Overview of AI in Fashion

AI technologies, such as machine learning and computer vision, are being employed in the fashion industry to improve various aspects of the value chain. Designers, manufacturers, retailers, and customers can all benefit from AI-powered systems that enable efficient workflows, data-driven decision-making, and personalized experiences.

Image Recognition and Fashion Analysis

One key aspect of AI in fashion is image recognition and analysis. By leveraging computer vision algorithms, AI systems can analyze images of fashion items, provide accurate object recognition, and extract valuable information. Techniques like convolutional neural networks (CNNs) are commonly used to classify fashion items, detect patterns, and identify similar products.

For instance, an AI-powered fashion analysis system can analyze runway images or street style photography to identify emerging trends, popular colors, or patterns. This information can guide designers and fashion brands in creating new collections or adjusting their manufacturing processes.

Recommendation Systems

AI-driven recommendation systems play a vital role in the fashion industry, providing personalized suggestions to customers based on their preferences, browsing habits, and purchase history. These recommendation systems are typically powered by collaborative filtering algorithms or deep learning models that analyze user data to generate relevant and accurate fashion recommendations.

One approach to building recommendation systems in fashion is to employ matrix factorization techniques. By decomposing the user-item interaction matrix, AI systems can identify latent factors that capture user preferences and item characteristics. This allows for accurate fashion recommendations that align with users' personal style and preferences.

Virtual Try-On and Augmented Reality

Virtual try-on and augmented reality (AR) experiences are transforming the way customers interact with fashion items. By leveraging AI and computer vision, customers can virtually try on clothing and accessories, enabling a convenient and immersive shopping experience.

In virtual try-on systems, AI algorithms analyze body measurements, clothing patterns, and fabric properties to generate realistic virtual representations of how a garment would look on an individual. This technology helps customers make informed purchasing decisions, reducing return rates and enhancing customer satisfaction.

Supply Chain Optimization

AI techniques are also employed to optimize the fashion supply chain, improving inventory management, demand forecasting, and logistics. By analyzing historical sales data, market trends, and external factors like weather conditions, AI systems can generate accurate demand forecasts. This helps fashion brands and retailers optimize their production planning, reduce overstocking or understocking issues, and improve overall supply chain efficiency.

Conclusion

In this chapter, we explored the exciting applications of AI in the fashion industry. AI technologies, including image recognition, recommendation systems, virtual try-on, and supply chain optimization, are fundamentally transforming how fashion brands design, manufacture, and deliver products to customers. By leveraging AI, fashion brands can offer personalized experiences, improve operational efficiency, and enhance customer satisfaction. The ongoing integration of AI in the fashion industry holds enormous potential for further innovation and disruption in the years to come.

Keywords

Artificial Intelligence, Fashion, Image Recognition, Fashion Analysis, Recommendation Systems, Virtual Try-On, Augmented Reality, Supply Chain Optimization.

Python Code Snippet

Below is a Python code snippet that implements important algorithms and mathematical techniques discussed in the fashion chapter, including recommendation systems and virtual try-on functionalities.

```
import numpy as np
import pandas as pd
from sklearn.metrics.pairwise import cosine_similarity
from sklearn.preprocessing import StandardScaler
import cv2

def create_user_item_matrix(data):
    '''
    Create a user-item interaction matrix from the dataset.
    :param data: A pandas DataFrame containing user-item
    ↪ interactions.
    :return: A user-item interaction matrix.
    '''
```

```python
    return data.pivot(index='user_id', columns='item_id',
    ↪    values='rating').fillna(0)


def calculate_similarity(user_item_matrix):
    '''
    Calculate the cosine similarity between users.
    :param user_item_matrix: User-item interaction matrix.
    :return: Cosine similarity matrix.
    '''

    return cosine_similarity(user_item_matrix)


def recommend_items(user_id, user_item_matrix, similarity_matrix,
↪   num_recommendations=5):
    '''
    Generate item recommendations for a specific user based on
    ↪    similarity scores.
    :param user_id: User for whom to generate recommendations.
    :param user_item_matrix: User-item interaction matrix.
    :param similarity_matrix: User similarity matrix.
    :param num_recommendations: Number of recommendations to return.
    :return: Recommended item IDs.
    '''

    user_index = user_id - 1
    similar_users = list(enumerate(similarity_matrix[user_index]))
    similar_users = sorted(similar_users, key=lambda x: x[1],
    ↪    reverse=True)[1:]    # Exclude self
    item_scores = {}

    for index, score in similar_users:
        user_items = user_item_matrix.iloc[index]
        for item_id, rating in user_items.iteritems():
            if rating > 0:    # Only consider items the similar user
            ↪    has rated
                item_scores[item_id] = item_scores.get(item_id, 0) +
                ↪    score * rating

    recommended_items = sorted(item_scores.items(), key=lambda x:
    ↪    x[1], reverse=True)[:num_recommendations]
    return [item[0] for item in recommended_items]


def virtual_try_on(model_path, image_path, size=(300, 300)):
    '''
    Perform virtual try-on using a pre-trained model and a given
    ↪    image.
    :param model_path: Path to the trained image segmentation model.
    :param image_path: Path to the customer's image.
    :param size: Desired size for the output image.
    :return: Segmented image for virtual try-on.
    '''

    # Load pre-trained model (example: TensorFlow/Keras model)
    model = cv2.imread(model_path)
    image = cv2.imread(image_path)
    image_resized = cv2.resize(image, size)
```

```python
# Assume the model predicts a segmentation mask
# (A real implementation would involve feeding the image through
↪    the model)
mask = model.predict(image_resized)  # Dummy prediction line
segmented_image = cv2.bitwise_and(image_resized, image_resized,
↪    mask=mask)

    return segmented_image

# Example Data
ratings_data = pd.DataFrame({
    'user_id': [1, 1, 2, 2, 3, 3, 4, 4],
    'item_id': ['A', 'B', 'A', 'C', 'B', 'C', 'A', 'D'],
    'rating': [5, 3, 4, 2, 4, 5, 3, 5]
})

# Creating the user-item interaction matrix
user_item_matrix = create_user_item_matrix(ratings_data)

# Calculating similarity matrix
similarity_matrix = calculate_similarity(user_item_matrix)

# Generating recommendations for a user (user_id = 1)
recommended_items = recommend_items(user_id=1,
↪    user_item_matrix=user_item_matrix,
↪    similarity_matrix=similarity_matrix)

# Example Virtual Try-On (dummy paths)
# Assume 'model_path' is your trained model path and 'image_path' is
↪    a customer's photo.
segmented_image = virtual_try_on(model_path='model_segments.h5',
↪    image_path='customer_image.jpg')

# Output results
print("Recommended Items for User 1:", recommended_items)
cv2.imshow("Virtual Try-On", segmented_image)
cv2.waitKey(0)
cv2.destroyAllWindows()
```

This code defines three main functions:

- `create_user_item_matrix` generates a matrix that represents user-item interactions based on their ratings.
- `calculate_similarity` computes the cosine similarity between users, enabling personalized recommendations.
- `recommend_items` generates item recommendations for a specific user based on the similarity of other users.

Additionally, the function `virtual_try_on` illustrates how to perform virtual try-on, producing a segmented image for the user.

The provided example demonstrates creating the user-item matrix, calculating user similarities, generating recommendations, and performing a virtual try-on. Results are outputted with a display for the virtual try-on image.

Chapter 19

AI in Telecommunications

Network Optimization and Management

In the field of telecommunications, Artificial Intelligence (AI) techniques play a crucial role in optimizing and managing networks. With the increasing complexity and scale of modern telecommunications systems, AI offers innovative solutions to enhance network performance, efficiency, and reliability. In this chapter, we will explore mathematical models and algorithms used in AI-driven network optimization and management.

1 Optimization Models

Mathematical optimization models form the foundation of AI in network optimization. These models aim to determine the optimal resource allocation, routing, and scheduling strategies that minimize costs, maximize network capacity, and ensure efficient data transmission. Various optimization techniques, such as linear programming, integer programming, and dynamic programming, are employed to solve these complex optimization problems.

One crucial objective in network optimization is minimizing network congestion. Congestion in telecommunications networks leads to delays, packet loss, and reduced quality of service. To address this issue, researchers have developed congestion control algorithms based on queueing theory, network calculus, and game theory. These algorithms dynamically adjust network parameters to optimize congestion control while ensuring fair resource allocation among users.

2   Network Management Systems

AI-powered network management systems enable real-time monitoring, analysis, and control of telecommunications networks. These systems employ machine learning algorithms and statistical models to identify network anomalies, predict failures, and optimize network performance.

An important component of network management is fault detection and diagnosis. Detecting and diagnosing network faults promptly minimizes service disruptions and improves network reliability. Machine learning algorithms, such as support vector machines (SVM), decision trees, and neural networks, are employed to analyze network sensor data and identify abnormal patterns. Once a fault is detected, diagnostic algorithms determine the root cause and guide the network operator in resolving the issue effectively.

3   Predictive Maintenance

Predictive maintenance techniques utilize AI to optimize the maintenance of telecommunications infrastructure. By continuously monitoring network components and analyzing historical data, predictive maintenance models can forecast equipment failures, estimate remaining useful life, and recommend maintenance actions.

These models employ time series analysis, survival analysis, and machine learning algorithms to predict equipment failure probabilities or estimate degradation patterns. By predicting maintenance needs, network operators can reduce costs associated with reactive maintenance, improve network uptime, and enhance customer satisfaction.

4   Resource Allocation and Optimization

Efficient resource allocation is critical to ensure optimal utilization of network capacity and meet service level agreements (SLAs). AI techniques, such as reinforcement learning, genetic algorithms, and multi-objective optimization, are used to solve resource allocation problems in telecommunications networks.

Resource allocation optimization problems can involve allocating bandwidth, assigning frequencies, optimizing power control, or determining routing paths. These problems are often formulated as mathematical optimization models, and AI algorithms are employed to find near-optimal or optimal solutions. By optimizing resource allocation, network operators can improve network performance, increase efficiency, and enhance overall customer experience.

5 Network Security and Threat Detection

With the ever-increasing cybersecurity threats, AI plays a crucial role in ensuring the security of telecommunications networks. AI-driven security solutions utilize machine learning algorithms to detect anomalies, identify potential threats, and mitigate attacks.

Intrusion detection systems, based on anomaly detection techniques, monitor network traffic patterns and identify suspicious activities. These systems use algorithms such as k-nearest neighbors (k-NN), support vector machines (SVM), and deep learning models to distinguish between normal and malicious network behavior.

6 Conclusion

AI techniques bring profound benefits to the telecommunications industry by optimizing network operations, enhancing network management, improving resource allocation, and ensuring network security. From optimization models and resource allocation algorithms to fault detection and anomaly identification, AI-driven systems empower network operators to build efficient, reliable, and secure telecommunications networks. The integration of AI in telecommunications is expected to continue evolving, enabling the deployment of advanced services and meeting the growing demands of the digital era.

Python Code Snippet

Below is a Python code snippet that implements key algorithms and calculations relevant to AI-driven network optimization and management in telecommunications, such as congestion control, fault detection, predictive maintenance, and resource allocation.

```python
import numpy as np
from sklearn.svm import SVC
from sklearn.ensemble import RandomForestClassifier
from sklearn.model_selection import train_test_split

def congestion_control(rates, max_capacity):
    '''
    Calculate the optimal rates to prevent congestion in a
    ↪   telecommunications network.
    :param rates: List of current data rates of connections in Mbps.
    :param max_capacity: Maximum capacity of the network in Mbps.
    :return: Adjusted rates to avoid congestion.
    '''
    total_current_rate = sum(rates)
    if total_current_rate > max_capacity:
        adjustment_factor = max_capacity / total_current_rate
        return [rate * adjustment_factor for rate in rates]
    return rates

def fault_detection(sensor_data, labels):
    '''
    Train a model to detect network faults based on sensor data.
    :param sensor_data: Feature set of sensor data.
    :param labels: Ground truth labels for the sensor data (fault/no
    ↪   fault).
    :return: Trained model for fault detection.
    '''
    X_train, X_test, y_train, y_test = train_test_split(sensor_data,
    ↪   labels, test_size=0.2, random_state=42)
    model = SVC(kernel='linear')  # Using a Support Vector
    ↪   Classifier
    model.fit(X_train, y_train)
    return model

def predictive_maintenance(historical_data):
    '''
    Predict equipment failure using historical maintenance data.
    :param historical_data: Historical data including usage and
    ↪   failure instances.
    :return: Estimated probabilities of failure for each equipment.
    '''
    feature_matrix = np.array([data[:-1] for data in
    ↪   historical_data])  # All but last column as features
    labels = np.array([data[-1] for data in historical_data])  #
    ↪   Last column as labels (0: no failure, 1: failure)
    model = RandomForestClassifier(n_estimators=100)
    model.fit(feature_matrix, labels)
    predictions = model.predict_proba(feature_matrix)[:, 1]  #
    ↪   Probability of failure
    return predictions

def resource_allocation(bandwidths, demands):
```

```
'''
Allocate bandwidth based on demands using a simple greedy
↪   strategy.
:param bandwidths: Available bandwidths for each connection.
:param demands: Requested demands from users.
:return: Allocated bandwidths or a message if not enough
↪   resources are available.
'''

allocation = []
for i in range(len(demands)):
    if bandwidths[i] >= demands[i]:
        allocation.append(demands[i])
        bandwidths[i] -= demands[i]   # Reduce the available
        ↪   bandwidth
    else:
        allocation.append(0)   # Not enough bandwidth available
return allocation

# Example Inputs
current_rates = [50, 75, 100, 30]   # Current rates in Mbps
max_network_capacity = 200   # Maximum capacity in Mbps
sensor_data_example = [[0.1, 0.3, 1], [0.4, 0.6, 0], [0.5, 0.5, 1]]
↪   # Example sensor data
labels_example = [0, 1, 1]   # Ground truth labels
historical_maintenance_data = [[1, 2, 0], [2, 1, 1], [2, 3, 1]]   #
↪   Equipment usage and failures
bandwidths_example = [100, 200, 150]   # Available bandwidths
demands_example = [80, 50, 200]   # User demands

# Calculations
adjusted_rates = congestion_control(current_rates,
↪   max_network_capacity)
fault_detection_model = fault_detection(sensor_data_example,
↪   labels_example)
failure_probabilities =
↪   predictive_maintenance(historical_maintenance_data)
allocated_bandwidths = resource_allocation(bandwidths_example,
↪   demands_example)

# Output results
print("Adjusted Rates:", adjusted_rates)
print("Predicted Failure Probabilities:", failure_probabilities)
print("Allocated Bandwidths:", allocated_bandwidths)
```

This code defines four functions:

- `congestion_control` adjusts the data rates of connections to avoid network congestion.
- `fault_detection` trains a Support Vector Classifier for detecting network faults based on sensor data.
- `predictive_maintenance` estimates probabilities of equipment

failure using historical maintenance data with a Random Forest Classifier.

- `resource_allocation` allocates bandwidths based on user demands using a greedy strategy.

The example inputs demonstrate how to use these functions, showcasing adjustments to network rates, predictions of failure probabilities, and the results of bandwidth allocations.

Chapter 20

AI in Sports

Performance Analytics and Player Optimization

In the field of sports, the application of Artificial Intelligence (AI) techniques has gained significant attention in recent years. In this chapter, we focus on the use of AI for performance analytics and player optimization. AI-enabled systems provide valuable insights and assist in decision-making processes to enhance athletic performance and team strategies.

1 Performance Analytics

Performance analytics involve the collection and analysis of a wide range of data to evaluate and understand an athlete's performance. AI techniques, such as machine learning and statistical modeling, are utilized to extract meaningful patterns and insights from vast amounts of data.

One key aspect of performance analytics is player tracking. Advanced sensing technologies, such as GPS trackers and wearable devices, provide real-time data on an athlete's movements, speed, and heart rate during practice or competition. By applying AI algorithms, this data can be analyzed to identify performance trends, measure athletic abilities, and inform training strategies.

Another important area of performance analytics is game analysis. AI systems can analyze video footage of games to identify patterns, assess player actions, and evaluate team strategies. These systems employ computer vision techniques, such as object detection and tracking, to recognize players and their movements. By combining this visual information with other data sources, such as player statistics and game outcomes, AI models can provide deeper insights into game dynamics and player performance.

2 Player Optimization

Player optimization involves using AI techniques to maximize an athlete's potential and enhance performance in specific areas. AI algorithms can analyze individual player data, identify strengths and weaknesses, and recommend personalized training programs.

One application of player optimization is injury prediction and prevention. By analyzing historical injury data, player workload, and other relevant factors, AI models can identify injury-prone players and suggest strategies to reduce the risk of injuries. Furthermore, AI systems can monitor player movements in real-time to detect unusual patterns that may indicate a potential injury. This information can be used to make timely decisions, such as substituting an at-risk player or altering training routines.

Another area of player optimization is skill development. AI models can analyze player performance data and provide personalized coaching recommendations to enhance specific skills. For example, data on shooting accuracy and shot selection can be used to identify areas for improvement and suggest practice drills. Similarly, AI algorithms can analyze player movement patterns to optimize running techniques or improve agility.

3 Team Strategies

AI techniques also play a crucial role in optimizing team strategies and decision-making processes. By analyzing data from multiple sources, AI models can provide coaches and teams with valuable insights and recommendations.

One area of team strategy optimization is opponent analysis. AI systems can analyze historical data of game outcomes, player statistics, and team strategies to identify patterns and tendencies. This information can be used to develop effective game plans and counter-strategies for specific opponents. AI algorithms can also simulate game scenarios to determine the optimal strategies in different situations.

Another important aspect of team strategy optimization is lineup optimization. By analyzing player performance data and considering factors such as player compatibility and chemistry, AI models can suggest optimal lineups for specific game situations. These models can take into account various factors, including player skill levels, playing styles, and match-up advantages.

Furthermore, AI techniques can assist in game-time decision-making. Real-time data on player performance, opponent strategies, and game dynamics can be analyzed to provide coaches with timely recommendations. For example, AI algorithms can suggest substitutions, strategic plays, or adjustments to defensive or offensive formations based on the current game situation.

In summary, AI techniques enable performance analytics, player optimization, and team strategy optimization in the realm of sports. By analyzing large volumes of data, AI systems provide athletes, coaches, and teams with valuable insights to enhance performance, reduce injuries, and optimize team strategies. The integration of AI in sports has the potential to revolutionize athletic performance and improve decision-making processes on and off the field."'latex

Python Code Snippet

Below is a Python code snippet that implements performance analytics and player optimization algorithms in sports. The code includes functionality for player tracking, injury prediction, and game strategy optimization.

```python
import numpy as np
import pandas as pd

def analyze_player_performance(data):
    '''
    Analyzes player performance data to compute various metrics.
    :param data: DataFrame containing player tracking data.
    :return: Dictionary of performance metrics.
    '''
    average_speed = data['speed'].mean()
    max_speed = data['speed'].max()
    distance_covered = data['distance'].sum()
    heart_rate_avg = data['heart_rate'].mean()

    return {
        'average_speed': average_speed,
        'max_speed': max_speed,
        'distance_covered': distance_covered,
```

```python
        'average_heart_rate': heart_rate_avg
    }


def predict_injury_risk(player_data, workload_factor):
    '''
    Predicts injury risk based on player data and workload factors.
    :param player_data: Dictionary with attributes indicating player
    ↪    history.
    :param workload_factor: Measure of player workload during
    ↪    training/games.
    :return: Boolean indicating injury risk.
    '''
    injury_history = player_data['injury_history']
    max_workload = player_data['max_workload']

    if workload_factor > (0.8 * max_workload) and injury_history:
        return True  # High risk of injury

    return False  # Low risk of injury


def optimize_team_strategy(opponent_data, team_data):
    '''
    Optimize team strategy based on opponent and team performance
    ↪    data.
    :param opponent_data: DataFrame containing opponent performance
    ↪    statistics.
    :param team_data: DataFrame containing team performance
    ↪    statistics.
    :return: Suggested optimal strategy.
    '''
    opponent_average = opponent_data.mean()
    team_average = team_data.mean()

    if opponent_average['defense'] > team_average['offense']:
        return 'Focus on defensive plays'
    else:
        return 'Focus on offensive strategies'


# Example player tracking data as a DataFrame
player_tracking_data = pd.DataFrame({
    'speed': [5.1, 6.3, 7.2, 5.8, 6.5],
    'distance': [10, 20, 15, 25, 30],
    'heart_rate': [150, 155, 160, 158, 162]
})

# Player data for injury prediction
player_data_example = {
    'injury_history': True,
    'max_workload': 100  # Assume maximum workload is 100
    ↪    unspecified units
```

143

```
}

# Example opponent and team performance data
opponent_stats = pd.DataFrame({
    'defense': [85, 90, 88],
    'offense': [80, 75, 70]
})

team_stats = pd.DataFrame({
    'defense': [75, 80, 82],
    'offense': [90, 92, 93]
})

# Player performance analysis
performance_metrics =
↪   analyze_player_performance(player_tracking_data)

# Injury risk prediction based on workload factor
workload_factor = 85  # Current workload
injury_risk = predict_injury_risk(player_data_example,
↪   workload_factor)

# Optimize team strategy
optimal_strategy = optimize_team_strategy(opponent_stats.mean(),
↪   team_stats.mean())

# Output results
print("Performance Metrics:", performance_metrics)
print("Injury Risk:", "High" if injury_risk else "Low")
print("Optimal Strategy:", optimal_strategy)
```

This code defines three functions:

- `analyze_player_performance` analyzes player tracking data to compute performance metrics such as average speed and distance covered.
- `predict_injury_risk` predicts the injury risk of a player based on their workload and injury history.
- `optimize_team_strategy` provides recommendations for team strategies based on opponent and team performance data.

The provided example calculates player performance metrics, assesses injury risk, and suggests an optimal team strategy based on statistical analysis. "'

Chapter 21

AI in Automotive

Introduction

The field of Artificial Intelligence (AI) has witnessed remarkable advancements in recent years, revolutionizing various industries. In this chapter, we delve into the realm of automotive engineering and discuss the profound impact of AI technologies on this domain. AI has been instrumental in enhancing autonomous driving capabilities, optimizing vehicle performance, and improving overall transportation systems.

1 Autonomous Driving Technologies

Autonomous driving has emerged as one of the most transformative applications of AI in the automotive industry. It involves the development of vehicles capable of navigating and making decisions without human intervention. This technology relies on sophisticated AI algorithms, including computer vision, machine learning, and sensor fusion techniques.

Self-driving vehicles are equipped with a variety of sensors, such as cameras, radar systems, LiDAR, and ultrasonic sensors, to perceive their surroundings. These sensors collect vast amounts of data, which is processed in real-time using AI algorithms. Through computer vision techniques, the vehicles can detect and classify objects, recognize traffic signs and signals, and accurately estimate distances to obstacles.

Machine learning plays a crucial role in autonomous driving systems, enabling vehicles to learn from large datasets and make informed decisions. Reinforcement learning algorithms allow vehicles to navigate complex environments and learn optimal driving maneuvers through trial and error. Additionally, deep learning models, such as convolutional neural networks (CNNs), are used for object recognition, lane detection, and path planning.

2 Predictive Maintenance and Diagnostics

Another significant application of AI in the automotive industry is predictive maintenance and diagnostics. By employing AI techniques, vehicles can monitor their own condition and detect potential faults or malfunctions before they lead to serious issues. This proactive approach helps reduce downtime, repair costs, and enhances overall safety.

AI algorithms can analyze sensory data collected from various vehicle components and systems, such as the engine, transmission, brakes, and sensors, to identify patterns indicative of impending failures or degradation. Machine learning models can learn from historical data to predict the remaining useful life of critical components, such as batteries or engine parts. This information enables proactive maintenance planning, allowing for timely component replacements or repairs, thereby minimizing unexpected breakdowns.

Furthermore, AI-based diagnostics systems can analyze error codes, performance data, and sensor readings to identify the root cause of malfunctions or abnormal behavior. Diagnostic algorithms can provide real-time alerts to the driver or generate detailed reports for service technicians, facilitating efficient troubleshooting and repair procedures.

3 AI in Automotive Design and Testing

AI technologies have also significantly impacted the design and testing phases of automotive engineering. Traditionally, the design and development of vehicles involve extensive prototyping, testing, and validation processes, which are both time-consuming and expensive. However, AI techniques offer alternative approaches that expedite these processes.

In the domain of vehicle design, AI algorithms can assist engineers in creating optimized designs for specific performance criteria. Optimization algorithms, such as genetic algorithms or particle swarm optimization, can explore a vast design space by iteratively generating and evaluating different vehicle configurations. By incorporating performance objectives and constraints, AI-based optimization methods can rapidly converge to near-optimal solutions.

Moreover, AI techniques enable virtual testing and simulation of vehicle performance, increasing the efficiency of the validation process. By constructing accurate physical models and using AI algorithms for simulation, engineers can predict vehicle behavior under various driving conditions, assess safety measures, and identify potential design flaws without the need for extensive physical prototypes. This virtual testing approach helps reduce costs, shorten development cycles, and enhances overall vehicle reliability.

4 Customer Experience and Personalization

AI technologies have the potential to enhance the overall customer experience by enabling personalized features and advanced driver assistance systems (ADAS). Machine learning algorithms process data from various sources, including vehicle sensors, user preferences, and external information, to provide personalized recommendations and optimized driving experiences.

AI algorithms can learn from historical user data to anticipate individual preferences and adjust vehicle settings, such as seat position, climate control, or entertainment options, automatically. By integrating driver profiling with AI models, vehicles can proactively adapt to user preferences, creating a more comfortable and personalized driving experience.

Additionally, ADAS systems utilize AI algorithms to enhance safety and driving assistance features. These systems leverage sensor data, such as camera images and radar readings, in conjunction with machine learning algorithms to detect and identify potential hazards, assist with parking maneuvers, or provide collision avoidance warnings. The integration of AI enhances the accuracy and reliability of these systems, promoting safer driving conditions.

Conclusion

The automotive industry has been profoundly transformed by the integration of AI technologies. From autonomous driving capabilities to predictive maintenance, AI algorithms have enabled vehicles to become smarter, safer, and more efficient. These advancements have not only improved the driving experience for consumers but also paved the way for future innovations in intelligent transportation systems. As AI continues to evolve, we can expect further breakthroughs in automotive engineering, ushering in an era of intelligent and sustainable mobility.

Python Code Snippet

Below is a Python code snippet that implements key algorithms and formulas related to autonomous driving, predictive maintenance, and AI-based vehicle optimization as discussed in this chapter.

```python
import numpy as np
from sklearn.linear_model import LinearRegression
import matplotlib.pyplot as plt

def object_detection(sensor_data):
    '''
    Simulate object detection using LiDAR sensor data.
    :param sensor_data: Array of distance measurements from LiDAR
    ↪ sensors.
    :return: Detected objects and their distances.
    '''
    detected_objects = []
    for distance in sensor_data:
        if distance < 10:  # Assume any object within 10 meters is
        ↪ detected
            detected_objects.append(distance)
    return detected_objects

def predictive_maintenance(maintenance_data):
    '''
    Predict remaining useful life (RUL) of a vehicle component using
    ↪ linear regression.
    :param maintenance_data: A 2D numpy array where the first column
    ↪ is operating hours and the second column is failure status.
    :return: Predicted RUL for the component.
    '''
    X = maintenance_data[:, 0].reshape(-1, 1)  # Operating hours
    y = maintenance_data[:, 1]  # Failure status (1: failed, 0:
    ↪ operational)

    model = LinearRegression()
    model.fit(X, y)

    # Predicting RUL based on operating hours
    operating_hours = np.array([[100]])  # Example: predicting for
    ↪ 100 hours of operation
    rul_prediction = model.predict(operating_hours)
```

```
    return rul_prediction[0]

def vehicle_design_optimization(initial_design_parameters):
    '''
    Optimize vehicle design parameters using a simple optimization
    ↪   algorithm.
    :param initial_design_parameters: List of initial design
    ↪   parameters (e.g., weight, aerodynamics).
    :return: Optimized design parameters.
    '''
    # Define a simple optimization function that minimizes weight
    ↪   while maximizing aerodynamics (example only)
    def optimization_function(params):
        weight, aerodynamics = params
        return weight / aerodynamics  # Aim to minimize this ratio

    from scipy.optimize import minimize
    result = minimize(optimization_function,
    ↪   initial_design_parameters)

    return result.x

# Example usage of the functions
# 1. Object Detection
sensor_data = [5, 12, 3, 16, 8]  # Example LiDAR distance readings
detected_objects = object_detection(sensor_data)
print("Detected Objects Distances:", detected_objects)

# 2. Predictive Maintenance
maintenance_data = np.array([[120, 0], [150, 1], [180, 0], [200,
↪   1]])  # Columns: [hours, failure status]
predicted_rul = predictive_maintenance(maintenance_data)
print("Predicted Remaining Useful Life (RUL):", predicted_rul)

# 3. Vehicle Design Optimization
initial_design_parameters = [1500, 0.3]  # Weight in kg,
↪   aerodynamics coefficient
optimized_params =
↪   vehicle_design_optimization(initial_design_parameters)
print("Optimized Design Parameters:", optimized_params)
```

This code defines three functions:

- `object_detection` simulates object detection using distance measurements from LiDAR sensors.
- `predictive_maintenance` implements a linear regression model to predict the remaining useful life (RUL) of vehicle components based on maintenance data.
- `vehicle_design_optimization` uses a simple optimization algorithm to minimize weight while maximizing aerodynamics in vehi-

cle design.

The provided example demonstrates the functionality of these algorithms by detecting objects from sensor data, predicting RUL from maintenance history, and optimizing vehicle design parameters.

Chapter 22

AI in Aerospace and Aviation

Introduction

The integration of Artificial Intelligence (AI) in the aerospace and aviation industry has revolutionized various aspects of aircraft design, operation, and maintenance. In this chapter, we explore the profound impact of AI technologies in this domain. Specifically, we delve into the applications of AI in predictive maintenance, flight optimization, autonomous systems, and personalized customer experiences.

1 Predictive Maintenance and Diagnostics

One of the critical challenges in aerospace and aviation is ensuring the safety and reliability of aircraft. Traditional maintenance practices often involve reactive procedures or periodic inspections, which can be time-consuming and inefficient. However, AI techniques have emerged as powerful tools for implementing predictive maintenance and diagnostics systems.

Predictive maintenance utilizes machine learning algorithms to analyze sensor data collected from various aircraft components. By monitoring parameters such as engine performance, vibration levels, and temperature, AI models can detect patterns and anomalies indicative of potential failures or degradation. These models enable operators to predict the remaining useful life of critical components, allowing for timely maintenance actions. Consequently, unexpected downtime and maintenance costs are reduced, ensuring the continuous airworthiness of the aircraft.

Furthermore, AI algorithms can analyze flight data, including parameters recorded by onboard sensors, to diagnose potential faults or malfunctions. By comparing data collected during normal operations with historical datasets, these algorithms can detect deviations from expected behavior and identify the root causes of issues. Such diagnostic systems enable prompt troubleshooting and accurate repair recommendations, minimizing the impact on aircraft performance and reducing maintenance turnaround times.

2 Flight Optimization and Fuel Efficiency

Efficient flight operations play a vital role in reducing fuel consumption, operating costs, and environmental impact. AI technologies offer significant opportunities to optimize flight routes, enhance navigation systems, and improve fuel efficiency.

AI algorithms can analyze vast amounts of flight data, weather conditions, and historical performance metrics to develop optimized flight plans. Through machine learning techniques, these algorithms can identify patterns and relationships between various parameters and determine the most efficient routes and altitudes for specific flight segments. For example, by considering wind patterns and air traffic conditions, AI models can suggest route adjustments that minimize fuel consumption and flight time.

Furthermore, autopilot systems utilizing AI can maintain precise control of the aircraft, ensuring optimal performance parameters. By continuously monitoring and adjusting engine thrust, flight control surfaces, and other variables, these AI systems maximize fuel efficiency, reduce emissions, and minimize wear and tear on aircraft components. Additionally, AI algorithms enable predictive models for fuel consumption, allowing pilots to optimize their fuel loads and adapt flight plans according to changing conditions.

3 Autonomous and Unmanned Systems

AI technologies have made significant contributions to the development of autonomous and unmanned systems in aerospace and aviation. These systems have the potential to revolutionize various applications, including surveillance, cargo transportation, search and rescue operations, and even passenger transportation.

Unmanned aerial vehicles (UAVs), also known as drones, utilize AI algorithms to navigate autonomously and perform specific tasks. These algorithms process data from various onboard sensors, such as cameras, radar systems, and LiDAR, to accurately perceive the environment and avoid obstacles. By implementing machine learning models, these systems can improve their performance over time, enabling increasingly complex missions.

Autonomous systems also play a crucial role in air traffic management. By utilizing AI technologies, such as reinforcement learning and multi-agent systems, aircraft can optimize their routing decisions based on real-time air traffic conditions. These AI-driven systems help minimize congestion, increase airspace capacity, and enhance safety in increasingly complex and crowded airspace.

4 Customer Experience and Personalization

AI technologies have also transformed the customer experience in aerospace and aviation. Through personalized services and enhanced onboard experiences, airlines and operators can differentiate themselves and provide added value to passengers.

AI algorithms can analyze passenger data, including preferences, flight history, and personal information, to tailor services, such as seat selection, meal choices, and in-flight entertainment options. By utilizing machine learning models, airlines can predict individual passenger preferences and offer personalized experiences, providing a higher level of comfort and satisfaction.

Furthermore, AI-powered chatbots and virtual assistants have become increasingly common in aviation. These conversational AI systems can address passenger inquiries, assist with flight bookings, provide real-time flight information, and offer personalized recommendations for travel-related services. By leveraging natural language processing algorithms and machine learning models, these virtual assistants enhance customer support while reducing operational costs.

Conclusion

AI technologies have revolutionized the aerospace and aviation industry by enabling predictive maintenance, flight optimization, autonomous systems, and personalized customer experiences. The integration of AI algorithms and models has enhanced safety, reduced operational costs, increased fuel efficiency, and improved passenger satisfaction. As AI continues to advance, we can expect further advancements in autonomous systems, air traffic management, and personalized services, all of which will contribute to the transformation of the aerospace and aviation sector.

Python Code Snippet

Below is a Python code snippet that demonstrates important algorithms and calculations mentioned in the chapter on AI in Aerospace and Aviation, particularly focusing on predictive maintenance and flight optimization.

```python
import numpy as np
from sklearn.ensemble import RandomForestRegressor
import pandas as pd

# Function to preprocess sensor data
def preprocess_data(sensor_data):
    '''
    Preprocess the sensor data for model training.
    :param sensor_data: DataFrame containing raw sensor data.
    :return: Cleaned and normalized DataFrame.
    '''
    # Fill missing values
    sensor_data.fillna(method='ffill', inplace=True)
    # Normalize data
    normalized_data = (sensor_data - sensor_data.min()) /
    ↪ (sensor_data.max() - sensor_data.min())
    return normalized_data

# Function to train a predictive maintenance model
def train_predictive_model(features, labels):
    '''
    Train a Random Forest model for predictive maintenance.
    :param features: Feature set for the model.
    :param labels: Labels indicating the remaining useful life.
    :return: Trained Random Forest model.
    '''
    model = RandomForestRegressor(n_estimators=100, random_state=42)
    model.fit(features, labels)
    return model

# Function to calculate fuel efficiency
def calculate_fuel_efficiency(distance, fuel_used):
    '''
    Calculate the fuel efficiency of a flight.
    :param distance: Distance traveled in kilometers.
```

```
    :param fuel_used: Fuel consumed in liters.
    :return: Fuel efficiency in kilometers per liter.
    '''
    efficiency = distance / fuel_used
    return efficiency

# Sample sensor data for training predictive maintenance model
data = {
    'engine_temp': [150, 152, 153, 155, 158, 160, 162, 165, 166,
    ↪   170],
    'vibration': [0.01, 0.015, 0.014, 0.012, 0.013, 0.02, 0.021,
    ↪   0.022, 0.025, 0.03],
    'oil_temp': [75, 76, 77, 78, 80, 82, 83, 85, 86, 88],
    'remaining_life': [100, 95, 90, 85, 80, 75, 70, 65, 60, 55]  #
    ↪   Life expectancy in hours
}

# Convert data to DataFrame
sensor_data = pd.DataFrame(data)

# Preprocess the sensor data
normalized_data = preprocess_data(sensor_data)

# Split features and labels
features = normalized_data[['engine_temp', 'vibration',
↪   'oil_temp']].values
labels = normalized_data['remaining_life'].values

# Train predictive maintenance model
predictive_model = train_predictive_model(features, labels)

# Sample distance and fuel used for fuel efficiency calculation
sample_distance = 1500  # kilometers
sample_fuel_used = 300  # liters

# Calculate fuel efficiency
fuel_efficiency = calculate_fuel_efficiency(sample_distance,
↪   sample_fuel_used)

# Output results
print("Predicted Remaining Useful Life:",
↪   predictive_model.predict([[165, 0.025, 85]]), "hours")
print("Fuel Efficiency:", fuel_efficiency, "km/liter")
```

This code defines three functions:

- `preprocess_data` processes the sensor data by filling missing values and normalizing the data.
- `train_predictive_model` trains a Random Forest model to predict the remaining useful life of aircraft components based on sensor data.

- `calculate_fuel_efficiency` computes the fuel efficiency of a flight based on distance traveled and fuel consumed.

The provided example shows how to preprocess data, train a predictive maintenance model, and calculate the fuel efficiency for an aircraft, subsequently printing the results.

Chapter 23

AI in Public Services

In this chapter, we explore the applications of Artificial Intelligence (AI) in public services. AI technologies have the potential to revolutionize various aspects of government operations and citizen services. We will focus on the use of AI for predictive analytics in public safety, AI-driven urban planning and development, smart city initiatives, AI-driven citizen services and support, and data analysis for policy-making.

Predictive Analytics for Public Safety

Ensuring public safety is a top priority for government agencies. AI technologies, particularly predictive analytics, can greatly enhance their ability to prevent and respond to potential threats and emergencies. By analyzing large volumes of historical data, such as crime reports, emergency calls, and social media posts, AI models can identify patterns and trends, helping law enforcement agencies predict areas at higher risk of criminal activities or identify potential hotspots for accidents or public disturbances.

Mathematical modeling plays a critical role in predicting public safety incidents. One commonly used technique is the application of statistical prediction models, such as regression analysis or time series analysis. By identifying relevant predictors, such as demographic data, weather conditions, or previous incidents, these models can estimate the likelihood of future incidents occurring. For example, a regression model could be employed to predict the number of accidents in a given area based on factors like population density, road conditions, and previous accident rates. Such predictions can help public safety agencies allocate resources more effectively, contributing to proactive crime prevention and emergency response strategies.

AI in Urban Planning and Development

Effective urban planning and development are paramount to ensure sustainable and livable cities. AI technologies offer valuable tools for analyzing and modeling urban environments, and for developing strategies to optimize resource allocation and improve the quality of urban services.

One application of AI in urban planning is the use of machine learning algorithms to analyze large-scale urban datasets, including satellite imagery, traffic flow data, and public transportation records. These algorithms can identify patterns and relationships within the data, providing insights into various urban phenomena such as traffic congestion, energy consumption patterns, or air quality changes. Mathematical models, such as clustering or regression analysis, can be applied to understand the impact of different factors on urban development and support decision-making processes.

Additionally, optimization algorithms play a crucial role in urban planning. For example, the traveling salesman problem (TSP), a well-known optimization problem, can be utilized to determine the best routes for waste collection or public transportation. By minimizing travel distances or maximizing resource utilization, these algorithms can lead to more efficient and cost-effective urban planning solutions.

Smart City Initiatives

In recent years, the concept of smart cities has gained prominence, leveraging AI technologies to create cities that are connected, sustainable, and efficient. Smart city initiatives involve integrating various data sources, Internet of Things (IoT) devices, and AI algorithms to improve the quality of urban life and enhance the delivery of public services.

Mathematics plays a crucial role in smart city applications. For instance, predictive analytics models are used to optimize energy consumption by analyzing historical data and predicting demand patterns. Time series analysis, regression models, or deep learning algorithms can be employed to forecast future energy needs, facilitating efficient resource allocation and reducing energy waste.

Furthermore, optimization algorithms are utilized to optimize traffic flow, reduce congestion, and improve transportation systems. By incorporating real-time data into mathematical models, cities can dynamically adjust traffic signal timings or reroute vehicles to minimize travel time and maximize efficiency.

AI-driven Citizen Services and Support

Citizen services and support are vital functions of public services. AI technologies can enhance citizen engagement and streamline administrative processes, improving the accessibility and responsiveness of government agencies to citizen needs.

Chatbots and virtual assistants powered by AI algorithms are commonly used in citizen services. These AI systems employ natural language processing techniques to understand citizen inquiries and provide automated responses or route requests to the appropriate departments. By leveraging machine learning models, chatbots can learn from past interactions and improve their understanding of citizen inquiries over time.

Moreover, AI technologies can be employed for citizen sentiment analysis by analyzing social media data, citizen feedback, or survey responses. Sentiment analysis algorithms enable government agencies to gain insights into public opinions and sentiments, aiding in decision-making processes and the design of citizen-centric services.

Data Analysis for Policy-making

Mathematics and statistical analysis play a crucial role in data-driven policy-making. Government agencies can utilize AI algorithms and statistical models to analyze large datasets and gain insights into social, economic, and environmental factors.

One such application is the analysis of government census data or surveys. By employing statistical techniques, such as regression analysis or hypothesis testing, policymakers can identify relationships between various factors, such as education levels, income distribution, or healthcare access, and implement evidence-based policies to address societal challenges.

Furthermore, mathematical models, like optimization algorithms or game theory, can be employed to analyze complex policy problems. For example, an optimization algorithm could be used to allocate resources for disaster response or healthcare facilities to maximize coverage or minimize response time.

In summary, the application of AI in public services has the potential to greatly improve public safety, enhance urban planning and development, enable smart city initiatives, streamline citizen services, and support data-driven policy-making. Leveraging mathematical modeling, statistical analysis, and optimization techniques, government agencies can harness the power of AI to create more efficient, responsive, and sustainable societies."'latex

Python Code Snippet

Below is a Python code snippet that implements various important equations and algorithms mentioned in this chapter, focusing on predictive analytics for public safety, urban planning, and citizen services.

```python
import numpy as np
import pandas as pd
from sklearn.linear_model import LinearRegression
from sklearn.cluster import KMeans
from sklearn.metrics import mean_squared_error
from sklearn.preprocessing import StandardScaler

def predictive_policing_model(data):
    '''
    Predict areas with high crime risk using linear regression based
    ↪ on historical data.
    :param data: DataFrame containing historical crime data.
    :return: Predicted risk values for different areas.
    '''
    # Features and target variable
    X = data[['population_density', 'previous_incidents',
    ↪ 'income_level']]
    y = data['crime_rate']

    # Train a linear regression model
    model = LinearRegression()
    model.fit(X, y)

    # Predict crime rate for the training data
    predictions = model.predict(X)
    return predictions
```

```python
def urban_planning_analysis(satellite_data):
    '''
    Analyze urban patterns using KMeans clustering on satellite
    ↪ data.
    :param satellite_data: DataFrame containing features extracted
    ↪ from satellite imagery.
    :return: Cluster labels for each data point.
    '''

    scaler = StandardScaler()
    scaled_data = scaler.fit_transform(satellite_data)

    kmeans = KMeans(n_clusters=5, random_state=42)
    kmeans.fit(scaled_data)
    return kmeans.labels_

def sentiment_analysis(feedback_data):
    '''
    Analyze citizen sentiments from feedback data.
    :param feedback_data: DataFrame containing citizen feedback.
    :return: Sentiment score for the feedback.
    '''

    from textblob import TextBlob

    feedback_data['sentiment'] =
    ↪ feedback_data['comments'].apply(lambda x:
    ↪ TextBlob(x).sentiment.polarity)
    return feedback_data[['comments', 'sentiment']]

# Example Usage:
# Generating mock crime data
data = pd.DataFrame({
    'population_density': [1000, 2000, 1500, 2500, 3000],
    'previous_incidents': [5, 15, 10, 20, 30],
    'income_level': [30000, 50000, 40000, 60000, 70000],
    'crime_rate': [30, 60, 45, 80, 100]
})

# Predict public safety incidents
predicted_crime_rates = predictive_policing_model(data)
print("Predicted Crime Rates:", predicted_crime_rates)

# Mock satellite imagery data for urban planning
satellite_data = pd.DataFrame({
    'green_space_ratio': [0.4, 0.2, 0.3, 0.1, 0.5],
    'traffic_density': [250, 1200, 700, 900, 300],
})

# Analyze urban planning
cluster_labels = urban_planning_analysis(satellite_data)
print("Urban Planning Clusters:", cluster_labels)

# Mock citizen feedback data for sentiment analysis
feedback_data = pd.DataFrame({
```

161

```
    'comments': [
        "Great services but can improve public transport.",
        "Very satisfied with the city's cleanliness.",
        "Need better parking facilities.",
        "City is beautiful but very congested.",
    ]
})

# Analyze citizen sentiment
sentiment_scores = sentiment_analysis(feedback_data)
print("Citizen Sentiment Analysis:\n", sentiment_scores)
```

This code defines three functions:

- `predictive_policing_model` predicts potential crime rates using linear regression on features extracted from historical crime data.
- `urban_planning_analysis` clusters urban data using KMeans to identify patterns in satellite imagery.
- `sentiment_analysis` assesses citizen feedback sentiments using the TextBlob library.

The provided examples demonstrate the application of these functions to generate predictions regarding public safety, urban planning, and sentiment analysis of citizen feedback, with printed results showcasing their respective outputs. "'

Chapter 24

AI in Security

The field of security, encompassing various domains such as video surveillance, cybersecurity, identity verification, and threat detection, plays a fundamental role in maintaining the safety and integrity of individuals, organizations, and nations. Artificial Intelligence (AI) has emerged as a powerful tool in enhancing security measures, providing advanced capabilities for anomaly detection, automated decision-making, and predictive analysis. In this chapter, we explore the application of AI in security, delving into areas such as video surveillance and anomaly detection, cybersecurity threat detection, AI in identity verification and authentication, predictive analytics for security incident prevention, and automated decision-making in security protocols.

Video Surveillance and Anomaly Detection

Video surveillance is a critical component of security systems, involving the capture and analysis of visual information to monitor and identify potential threats or suspicious activities. AI technologies, coupled with computer vision algorithms, have significantly improved the effectiveness of video surveillance by automating the detection of anomalies and unusual behavior.

One commonly used approach in video surveillance is the application of deep learning algorithms, particularly convolutional neural networks (CNNs), to analyze video streams in real-time. By training these networks on large labeled datasets, such as videos of normal activities and known anomalies, the AI models can learn to recognize and flag unusual behavior. Moreover, recurrent neural networks (RNNs) can be employed to capture temporal dependencies in video sequences, enabling the detection of abnormal activities that span multiple frames.

In terms of mathematics, these deep learning algorithms perform complex computations involving matrix multiplications, convolutions, and non-linear activations. By optimizing the weight parameters and biases of the neural networks through techniques like gradient descent, these models learn to represent and distinguish normal and abnormal patterns in video data. The use of mathematical models also extends to the analysis of motion patterns, optical flow algorithms, and background subtraction techniques to preprocess the video streams and identify areas of interest for anomaly detection.

Cybersecurity Threat Detection

With the increasing reliance on digital technologies, the importance of robust cybersecurity measures cannot be overstated. AI techniques are proving to be valuable assets in the fight against cyber threats, aiding in the identification and prevention of malicious activities, such as cybersecurity attacks, fraud attempts, and data breaches.

One application of AI in cybersecurity is the use of anomaly detection algorithms to identify deviations from normal usage patterns in network traffic or user behavior. By leveraging techniques such as statistical analysis, machine learning, or deep learning, these models can identify suspicious activities that may indicate a cybersecurity threat. For instance, clustering algorithms, such as k-means or DBSCAN, can be employed to group similar network connections or user behavior, allowing the identification of outliers that signify potential attacks.

Furthermore, neural networks and other machine learning algorithms can be trained on large datasets of known cyber threats to classify incoming network traffic or user actions as legitimate or malicious. These models can detect patterns that may not be obvious to traditional rule-based systems, enabling the detection of sophisticated attacks or zero-day vulnerabilities.

AI in Identity Verification and Authentication

Identity verification and authentication are crucial components of security protocols, ensuring that only authorized individuals gain access to restricted resources or sensitive information. AI technologies can enhance these processes by incorporating biometric authentication, facial recognition, and behavioral analysis algorithms.

One application of AI in identity verification is the use of facial recognition algorithms to match an individual's face to a pre-registered template. These algorithms employ deep learning architectures, such as siamese networks or deep metric learning, to extract unique facial features and compare them against a database of known individuals. Face detection algorithms, such as Haar cascades or deep learning-based detectors, are employed to localize and align faces in images or video streams.

Additionally, behavioral analysis algorithms can be used to detect unusual patterns in user interactions or access attempts. By leveraging machine learning techniques, these models can learn the typical behavior of individuals and detect deviations that may indicate unauthorized access or fraudulent activity. For example, an AI model could learn the usual typing speed and patterns of a user and flag any significant deviations as potential security threats.

Mathematically, these AI algorithms utilize complex computations involving image preprocessing, feature extraction, and distance or similarity calculations. Various mathematical techniques, such as linear algebra, optimization, and statistical modeling, are employed to train these models on labeled datasets and optimize their performance.

Predictive Analytics for Security Incident Prevention

Predictive analytics is a powerful tool in preemptively identifying and preventing security incidents. By analyzing historical data, AI models can uncover hidden patterns and relationships, enabling the prediction of potential security threats or vulnerabilities.

One common approach in predictive analytics for security is the analysis of log files and event data, utilizing machine learning algorithms to detect anomalies or patterns that may lead to security incidents. By training these models on historical data, they can learn to recognize known attack patterns or precursor events that often precede security breaches. Techniques such as sequential pattern mining, time series analysis, or recurrent neural networks can be employed to capture temporal relationships and dependencies within the data, facilitating the detection of suspicious activities or sequences of events.

Moreover, predictive analytics can be utilized to forecast probabilities of specific security incidents occurring, such as cyber attacks, unauthorized access attempts, or equipment failure. By leveraging techniques such as regression analysis, time-series forecasting, or Bayesian networks, AI models can estimate the likelihood of future incidents based on relevant predictors and historical data. These predictions allow security professionals to allocate resources effectively and implement proactive security measures.

Automated Decision-Making in Security Protocols

AI technologies are increasingly being employed for automated decision-making in security protocols, enabling real-time responses to security threats and reducing human response time. By utilizing machine learning algorithms, these systems can learn from historical data, identify patterns, and make informed decisions with minimal human intervention.

One application of AI in automated decision-making is the use of anomaly detection algorithms to trigger automated responses to security events. For instance, if an intrusion is detected in a network, an AI-driven security system can automatically isolate the affected part of the network, block suspicious IP addresses, or alert security personnel. Reinforcement learning techniques can also be employed to train AI models to make optimal decisions based on the current security state and the desired security objectives.

Mathematically, these decision-making systems employ optimization algorithms, game theory, or reinforcement learning techniques to determine the most appropriate response. By modeling the security system as a game between the defender and attacker, these AI systems can learn optimal strategies and dynamically adapt to evolving threats.

In conclusion, the application of AI in security brings forth advanced capabilities for video surveillance and anomaly detection, cybersecurity threat detection, identity verification and authentication, predictive analytics for security incident prevention, and automated decision-making in security protocols. Leveraging mathematical models, machine learning algorithms, and complex computations, AI technologies contribute to enhancing security measures and safeguarding individuals, organizations, and nations against potential threats.

Python Code Snippet

Below is a comprehensive Python code snippet that implements important algorithms and mathematical principles discussed in the chapter. This snippet includes functions for video surveillance anomaly detection, a cybersecurity anomaly detection system, an identity verification system using facial recognition, and basic predictive analytics for security incident prevention.

```python
import numpy as np
import cv2
from sklearn.ensemble import IsolationForest
from sklearn.preprocessing import StandardScaler
from sklearn.metrics.pairwise import cosine_similarity

# Function to detect anomalies in video surveillance
def detect_anomalies(video_path):
    '''
    Perform anomaly detection on video using background subtraction.
    :param video_path: Path to the video file.
    :return: List of anomalous frames.
    '''
    cap = cv2.VideoCapture(video_path)
    backSub = cv2.createBackgroundSubtractorMOG2()
    anomalies = []

    while True:
        ret, frame = cap.read()
        if not ret:
            break
        fg_mask = backSub.apply(frame)
        if np.sum(fg_mask) > 5000:  # Anomaly threshold
            anomalies.append(frame)

    cap.release()
    return anomalies


# Function for cybersecurity event anomaly detection
```

```python
def cybersecurity_anomaly_detection(data):
    '''
    Detect anomalies in network traffic data.
    :param data: 2D numpy array of network traffic features.
    :return: Indices of anomalous events.
    '''
    scaler = StandardScaler()
    data_scaled = scaler.fit_transform(data)
    model = IsolationForest(contamination=0.05)  # 5% expected as
    ↪   anomalies
    model.fit(data_scaled)
    anomalies = np.where(model.predict(data_scaled) == -1)[0]
    return anomalies


# Function for facial recognition to verify identity
def verify_identity(face_encoding, known_face_encodings,
↪   known_face_names):
    '''
    Verify identity using facial recognition.
    :param face_encoding: Encoding of the face to verify.
    :param known_face_encodings: List of known face encodings.
    :param known_face_names: List of corresponding known face names.
    :return: Identified name or None if unknown.
    '''
    similarities = cosine_similarity([face_encoding],
    ↪   known_face_encodings)
    max_index = np.argmax(similarities)
    if similarities[0][max_index] > 0.6:  # Similarity threshold
        return known_face_names[max_index]
    return None


# Predictive analytics to forecast potential security incidents
def predict_security_incidents(event_data):
    '''
    Simple predictive analytics for security incident forecasting.
    :param event_data: 2D numpy array of historical security events.
    :return: Predicted likelihood of future incidents.
    '''
    # Using a naive approach to calculate mean incidents ratio
    total_events = len(event_data)
    if total_events == 0:
        return 0
    incident_count = np.sum(event_data)
    return incident_count / total_events  # Ratio of incidents


# Example Usage:

# Path to video for anomaly detection
video_path = 'surveillance_video.mp4'
```

168

```python
# Simulated network traffic data for anomaly detection
network_data = np.random.rand(100, 5)  # 100 samples, 5 features

# Known faces encoding (this would come from a facial recognition
↪  library)
known_face_encodings = np.random.rand(5, 128)  # Simulated
known_face_names = ['Alice', 'Bob', 'Charlie', 'David', 'Eve']

# Example face encoding to verify
face_encoding_to_verify = np.random.rand(128)

# Event data for predictive analytics
event_data = np.array([1, 0, 1, 1, 0, 0, 1])

# Detect anomalies in video
anomalous_frames = detect_anomalies(video_path)
print(f"Number of anomalous frames detected:
↪  {len(anomalous_frames)}")

# Detect cybersecurity anomalies
anomalous_events = cybersecurity_anomaly_detection(network_data)
print(f"Indices of anomalous events detected:
↪  {anomalous_events.tolist()}")

# Verify identity
identified_name = verify_identity(face_encoding_to_verify,
↪  known_face_encodings, known_face_names)
print(f"Identified Name: {identified_name if identified_name else
↪  'Unknown'}")

# Predict security incidents
incident_probability = predict_security_incidents(event_data)
print(f"Likelihood of future incidents: {incident_probability:.2f}")
```

This code defines several functions:

- `detect_anomalies` analyzes video frames for significant deviations from background activity to detect unusual behavior.
- `cybersecurity_anomaly_detection` applies isolation forest methodology to identify anomalies in network traffic data.
- `verify_identity` uses facial recognition encodings to verify identities based on similarity thresholds.
- `predict_security_incidents` performs simple predictive analytics to assess the likelihood of future security incidents based on historical data.

The provided example shows how to utilize these functions for video surveillance, cybersecurity assessments, identity verification, and predictive analytics in a security context.

Chapter 25

AI in Music and Sound

1 AI-Driven Music Composition and Production

The integration of AI in music composition and production has revolutionized the creative process. By employing machine learning algorithms, deep neural networks, and generative models, AI systems can generate original music compositions in various styles and genres.

One notable approach is the use of recurrent neural networks (RNNs) to create music with long-term dependencies. A popular RNN variant, the long short-term memory (LSTM) network, can capture sequential patterns in music and generate coherent musical phrases. The network is trained on large datasets of musical compositions to learn the underlying structure and style. By sampling from the learned distributions, AI models can generate new compositions with a similar style.

Additionally, generative adversarial networks (GANs) have been employed to produce highly realistic music. GANs consist of a generator and a discriminator network competing against each other. The generator aims to create original music that the discriminator cannot distinguish from human-composed music. Through an adversarial training process, GANs can create authentic and novel musical pieces across various genres.

2 Personalized Music Recommendations

AI has transformed the way music is recommended to listeners by leveraging techniques such as collaborative filtering and content-based filtering. Collaborative filtering analyzes the preferences and behaviors of users with similar musical tastes to generate personalized recommendations. This approach identifies patterns in user interaction with music, such as track playcounts or favorited songs, and recommends similar music based on these patterns.

Content-based filtering, on the other hand, focuses on the characteristics of the music itself. By considering features like tempo, key, melody, and instrumentation, AI algorithms can identify similarities between songs and recommend tracks that align with a listener's preferences.

To enhance music recommendations, deep learning models such as convolutional neural networks (CNNs) and transformer models have been employed. CNNs can extract intricate features from audio signals, enabling a more nuanced analysis of musical compositions. Transformer models, known for their success in natural language processing tasks, can handle sequential data, such as song playlists, and generate accurate recommendations based on this sequential information.

3 Analysis of Listener Behavior and Preferences

AI techniques enable comprehensive analysis of listener behavior and preferences, aiding in the development of more targeted music experiences. By leveraging machine learning algorithms, clustering techniques, and natural language processing, AI algorithms can uncover patterns and insights from vast amounts of user-generated data.

Sentiment analysis techniques, for instance, can determine the emotions associated with music based on user reviews, comments, or social media posts. This information can be utilized to understand user preferences and tailor recommendations accordingly.

Moreover, AI models can analyze user behavior and listening patterns to identify trends and predict future music preferences. By considering factors such as time of day, location, previous listening history, and context, AI algorithms can anticipate a listener's mood or specific music preferences during different situations.

4 Automated Sound Design

AI algorithms have been applied to automate sound design processes, leading to greater efficiency and creativity. By utilizing deep learning, generative models, and audio synthesis techniques, AI systems can automatically generate and manipulate sound elements for creative purposes, including film, animation, and video game production.

One approach to automated sound design is the use of variational autoencoders (VAEs). VAEs learn latent representations of sound samples, allowing for the generation of novel sounds by sampling from the learned representations. This method enables the creation of unique sound effects tailored to specific contexts.

Additionally, AI models can analyze audio signals to separate sources and enhance audio quality. Source separation algorithms employ techniques like non-negative matrix factorization and deep neural networks to isolate individual instruments or vocals from mixed audio recordings. This enables remixing, audio cleanup, and creative sound manipulation.

In conclusion, AI has transformed the music and sound industry by enabling AI-driven music composition and production, personalized music recommendations, analysis of listener behavior and preferences, and automated sound design. Through the integration of machine learning algorithms and deep neural networks, AI systems bring new possibilities to the creation, consumption, and manipulation of music and sound.

5 Mathematical Equations:

The underlying mathematical concepts that enable AI-driven music and sound applications are vital to their implementation. Here, we present some equations employed in the discussed AI techniques:

Long Short-Term Memory (LSTM) Network:

The LSTM network consists of gating mechanisms that control the flow of information within a neural network cell:

$$f_t = \sigma(W_f \cdot [h_{t-1}, x_t] + b_f)$$

$$i_t = \sigma(W_i \cdot [h_{t-1}, x_t] + b_i)$$

$$c_t = f_t \circ c_{t-1} + i_t \circ \tanh(W_c \cdot [h_{t-1}, x_t] + b_c)$$

$$o_t = \sigma(W_o \cdot [h_{t-1}, x_t] + b_o)$$

$$h_t = o_t \circ \tanh(c_t)$$

Where f_t represents the forget gate, i_t the input gate, c_t the cell state, o_t the output gate, h_t the hidden state, x_t the input at time t, W_f, W_i, W_c, W_o the weight matrices, and b_f, b_i, b_c, b_o the bias vectors.

Generative Adversarial Networks (GANs):

The GAN framework consists of two competing neural networks, a generator (G) and a discriminator (D):

$$\min_G \max_D V(D, G) = \mathbb{E}_{x \sim p_{\text{data}}(x)}[\log D(x)] + \mathbb{E}_{z \sim p_z(z)}[\log(1 - D(G(z)))]$$

Where $p_{\text{data}}(x)$ represents the data distribution, $p_z(z)$ the noise distribution, $G(z)$ the generated sample, and $D(x)$ the discriminator output for sample x.

Convolutional Neural Networks (CNNs):

Convolutional neural networks use convolutional layers to capture spatial relationships in audio signals:

$$x_i' = x_i + \sum_{j=0}^{n-1} W_j x_{i+j}$$

Where x_i represents the input at index i, W_j the filter weights, and x_i' the output after convolution.

Transformer Models:

Transformer models employ self-attention mechanisms and multi-head attention to process sequential data:

$$\text{Attention}(Q, K, V) = \text{softmax}\left(\frac{QK^T}{\sqrt{d_k}}\right)V$$

Where Q represents the queries, K the keys, and V the values.

These equations illustrate the mathematical foundations behind the discussed AI applications in the field of music and sound. Through the effective utilization of these mathematical concepts, AI systems can dramatically impact the creative process, listener experience, and sound production.

Python Code Snippet

Below is a Python code snippet that implements the important algorithms and mathematical equations mentioned in the chapter, including LSTM and GANs for AI-driven music composition and production, personalized music recommendations using CNNs, and transformer models.

```python
import numpy as np
import keras
from keras.layers import LSTM, Dense, Input, Embedding, Conv2D,
↪   Flatten, Dropout
from keras.models import Model
from sklearn.model_selection import train_test_split
from keras.layers import MultiHeadAttention

# LSTM for Music Composition
def create_lstm_model(input_shape):
    '''
    Create and compile an LSTM model for music composition.
    :param input_shape: Shape of the input data.
    :return: Compiled LSTM model.
    '''
    model = keras.Sequential()
    model.add(LSTM(128, input_shape=input_shape,
    ↪   return_sequences=True))
    model.add(Dropout(0.2))
    model.add(LSTM(128))
    model.add(Dense(256, activation='relu'))
    model.add(Dense(1, activation='sigmoid'))   # Binary
    ↪   classification for simplicity
    model.compile(loss='binary_crossentropy', optimizer='adam',
    ↪   metrics=['accuracy'])
    return model

# GANs for Music Generation
def create_gan_model(generator, discriminator):
    '''
    Create a GAN model by combining generator and discriminator.
    :param generator: Generator model of the GAN.
    :param discriminator: Discriminator model of the GAN.
    :return: Combined GAN model.
    '''
    discriminator.trainable = False
    model = keras.Sequential()
    model.add(generator)
    model.add(discriminator)
    model.compile(loss='binary_crossentropy', optimizer='adam')
    return model

# CNN for Personalized Music Recommendation
```

```python
def create_cnn_model(input_shape):
    '''
    Create and compile a CNN model for music recommendations.
    :param input_shape: Shape of the input data.
    :return: Compiled CNN model.
    '''
    input_layer = Input(shape=input_shape)
    x = Conv2D(32, (3, 3), activation='relu')(input_layer)
    x = Flatten()(x)
    x = Dense(64, activation='relu')(x)
    x = Dropout(0.5)(x)
    output_layer = Dense(10, activation='softmax')(x)  # 10 classes
    ↪    for recommendation
    model = Model(inputs=input_layer, outputs=output_layer)
    model.compile(loss='categorical_crossentropy', optimizer='adam',
    ↪    metrics=['accuracy'])
    return model

# Transformer Model for Music Recommendation
def create_transformer_model(num_classes):
    '''
    Create and compile a Transformer model for music
    ↪    recommendations.
    :param num_classes: Number of output classes.
    :return: Compiled Transformer model.
    '''
    inputs = Input(shape=(None, 64))  # Sequence of vectors
    attention_output = MultiHeadAttention(num_heads=2,
    ↪    key_dim=64)(inputs, inputs)
    x = keras.layers.GlobalAveragePooling1D()(attention_output)
    x = Dense(64, activation='relu')(x)
    outputs = Dense(num_classes, activation='softmax')(x)
    model = Model(inputs=inputs, outputs=outputs)
    model.compile(loss='categorical_crossentropy', optimizer='adam',
    ↪    metrics=['accuracy'])
    return model

# Example usage
if __name__ == "__main__":
    # Dummy data
    X_train_lstm = np.random.random((1000, 10, 64))  # 1000 samples,
    ↪    10 time steps, 64 features
    y_train_lstm = np.random.randint(2, size=(1000, 1))  # Binary
    ↪    labels for LSTM

    # Create LSTM Model
    lstm_model = create_lstm_model((10, 64))
    lstm_model.fit(X_train_lstm, y_train_lstm, epochs=10,
    ↪    batch_size=32)

    # Dummy data for GANs
    generator_model = keras.Sequential([
        Dense(128, activation='relu', input_dim=100),
```

```
    Dense(256, activation='relu'),
    Dense(512, activation='sigmoid'),
])

discriminator_model = keras.Sequential([
    Dense(512, activation='relu', input_shape=(512,)),
    Dense(256, activation='relu'),
    Dense(1, activation='sigmoid'),
])

gan_model = create_gan_model(generator_model,
↪    discriminator_model)

# Dummy data for CNN
X_recommendation = np.random.random((1000, 64, 64, 1))   # 1000
↪    samples, 64x64 images
y_recommendation = np.random.randint(10, size=(1000,))   # 10
↪    classes for recommendation
y_recommendation = keras.utils.to_categorical(y_recommendation,
↪    num_classes=10)

# Create CNN Model
cnn_model = create_cnn_model((64, 64, 1))
cnn_model.fit(X_recommendation, y_recommendation, epochs=10,
↪    batch_size=32)

# Transformer Model Example
transformer_model = create_transformer_model(num_classes=10)
transformer_model.summary()
```

This code provides implementations for three essential AI applications referenced in the chapter:

- create_lstm_model builds and compiles an LSTM model for music composition.
- create_gan_model combines a generator and discriminator model to form a GAN for music generation.
- create_cnn_model defines and compiles a CNN model for personalized music recommendations.
- create_transformer_model constructs a Transformer model for handling music data sequences.
The example runs demonstrate how to create these models, fit them on dummy data, and highlight the architecture of the Transformer model.

Chapter 26

AI in Renewable Energy

1 Optimizing Solar and Wind Energy Production

The optimization of solar and wind energy production is a critical aspect of the renewable energy industry. AI techniques play a significant role in maximizing the efficiency and output of these renewable energy sources. By leveraging mathematical models and algorithms, AI can aid in addressing the inherent variability and uncertainty associated with solar and wind energy generation.

One approach involves using AI algorithms to optimize the placement and tracking of solar panels. By analyzing geographic data, weather patterns, and solar irradiance, AI can determine the most suitable locations for solar panels and the optimal angles for capturing sunlight. This optimization not only improves energy generation but also reduces installation costs and maintenance.

Similarly, AI algorithms can optimize the positioning and operation of wind turbines. By analyzing wind speed, direction, and turbulence data, AI models can determine the most efficient orientation and configuration of wind turbines. This optimization ensures that wind energy is harnessed effectively and minimizes the risk of structural damage due to turbulent wind conditions.

2 Predictive Maintenance of Renewable Energy Assets

The maintenance of renewable energy assets, such as solar panels and wind turbines, is crucial for their long-term performance and cost-efficiency. AI techniques, particularly predictive maintenance models, aid in optimizing maintenance schedules and reducing unexpected failures.

With the help of AI, historical data on the condition and performance of renewable energy assets can be analyzed to identify patterns and early warning signs of potential issues. Machine learning algorithms, such as support vector machines (SVMs) and random forests, can be trained on this data to predict the maintenance needs and remaining useful life of equipment accurately. By performing maintenance tasks proactively, renewable energy operators can minimize downtime, optimize resource allocation, and reduce operational costs.

3 Grid Integration and Load Balancing with AI

Integrating renewable energy sources into the existing power grid presents several challenges, including grid stability and load balancing. AI techniques offer solutions to these challenges by enabling accurate predictions of renewable energy generation, demand forecasting, and optimal load balancing strategies.

AI algorithms can analyze historical energy generation and consumption data to identify consumption patterns and forecast renewable energy generation. By combining these insights with techniques like machine learning, time series analysis, and neural networks, AI models can predict future energy generation and demand with high accuracy. These predictions enable grid operators to manage and optimize energy distribution effectively, ensuring a stable and reliable power supply.

Furthermore, AI-based load balancing algorithms can optimize the distribution of energy from renewable sources by dynamically adjusting energy flows and coordinating energy storage systems. By intelligently balancing energy supply and demand, AI algorithms can help reduce reliance on non-renewable energy sources during periods of high demand, contributing to a more sustainable and efficient grid infrastructure.

4 AI in Energy Storage Management

Energy storage is a key component in maximizing the utilization and efficiency of renewable energy sources. AI techniques play a crucial role in optimizing energy storage systems, such as batteries, pumped hydro storage, and compressed air energy storage.

AI algorithms can analyze historical energy generation and demand data to determine optimal energy storage capacities and time-of-use pricing strategies. Machine learning models can learn patterns in energy supply and demand, weather conditions, and market prices to make intelligent decisions on when to charge, discharge, or store energy in the most cost-effective manner.

Additionally, AI models can optimize the control algorithms for energy storage systems, minimizing energy losses and maximizing the lifespan of the storage infrastructure. Reinforcement learning techniques, such as Q-learning and deep Q-networks, can autonomously learn optimal control policies for energy storage devices in response to changing energy market conditions.

5 Economic Forecasting for Renewable Investments

Investing in renewable energy projects requires accurate economic forecasting to assess project viability, mitigate risks, and attract financing. AI techniques, in conjunction with mathematical modeling and statistical analysis, enable accurate economic forecasting for renewable energy investments.

AI models can analyze various factors, including energy market prices, government policies, project costs, and regulatory frameworks, to assess the financial feasibility of renewable energy projects. Machine learning algorithms, such as regression analysis and time series forecasting, can identify patterns in historical data and predict future energy market trends, enabling better decision-making for project developers and potential investors.

Furthermore, AI techniques can evaluate the economic impact of integrating renewable energy into the existing energy systems. Computational models, informed by AI algorithms, can simulate different scenarios and assess the cost-effectiveness of renewable energy integration at the local, regional, or national scales. These assessments provide valuable insights for policymakers, utilities, and investors in planning and implementing renewable energy projects.

In conclusion, AI techniques offer significant benefits in optimizing renewable energy production, maintenance, grid integration, energy storage management, and economic forecasting. Through the utilization of mathematical models, machine learning algorithms, and predictive analytics, AI enables the efficient and sustainable utilization of renewable energy sources, contributing to a more environmentally friendly and economically viable energy landscape."'latex

Python Code Snippet

Below is a Python code snippet that implements key algorithms and calculations related to optimizing renewable energy production, predictive maintenance, grid integration, energy storage management, and economic forecasting.

```python
import numpy as np
import pandas as pd
from sklearn.ensemble import RandomForestRegressor
from sklearn.metrics import mean_squared_error
from datetime import timedelta

def optimize_solar_panel_placement(solar_data):
    '''
    Optimizes the placement and angle of solar panels based on
    ↪  geographic data and weather patterns.
    :param solar_data: DataFrame containing solar radiation and
    ↪  geographic data.
    :return: Optimal location and angle for solar panel placement.
    '''
    # Assuming solar_data has columns 'location', 'irradiance',
    ↪  'angle'
    best_location =
    ↪  solar_data.loc[solar_data['irradiance'].idxmax()]
    return best_location['location'], best_location['angle']

def predict_maintenance NEEDS(history_data):
    '''
    Predicts maintenance needs using historical asset performance
    ↪  data.
    :param history_data: DataFrame of historical data including
    ↪  performance metrics.
    :return: Predicted maintenance needs.
    '''
    X = history_data.drop(['maintenance_needed'], axis=1)
    y = history_data['maintenance_needed']

    model = RandomForestRegressor()
    model.fit(X, y)
```

```python
    predictions = model.predict(X)
    return predictions

def load_balancing(predicted_demand, predicted_supply):
    '''
    Balances load by adjusting supply and demand predictions.
    :param predicted_demand: Array of predicted demand values.
    :param predicted_supply: Array of predicted supply values.
    :return: Adjusted supply and demand arrays.
    '''
    adjustment = np.maximum(predicted_supply - predicted_demand, 0)
    return predicted_supply - adjustment, predicted_demand +
    ↪   adjustment

def optimize_energy_storage(storage_data):
    '''
    Optimizes energy storage management based on generation and
    ↪   consumption patterns.
    :param storage_data: DataFrame containing energy generation and
    ↪   consumption data.
    :return: Recommendations for charging and discharging.
    '''
    recommendations = []
    for index, row in storage_data.iterrows():
        if row['generation'] > row['consumption']:
            recommendations.append('Charge')
        else:
            recommendations.append('Discharge')
    return recommendations

def economic_forecasting(investment_data):
    '''
    Forecast economic viability of renewable projects using
    ↪   historical data.
    :param investment_data: DataFrame containing historical market
    ↪   data.
    :return: Forecasted economic viability score.
    '''
    X = investment_data.drop(['project_viability'], axis=1)
    y = investment_data['project_viability']

    model = RandomForestRegressor()
    model.fit(X, y)

    forecast = model.predict(X)
    return forecast

# Sample Data Preparation
solar_data = pd.DataFrame({
    'location': ['A', 'B', 'C'],
    'irradiance': [5.4, 6.2, 4.6],
    'angle': [30, 45, 60]
})
```

```
history_data = pd.DataFrame({
    'performance_metric1': [1, 2, 3],
    'performance_metric2': [4, 5, 6],
    'maintenance_needed': [0, 1, 0]
})

storage_data = pd.DataFrame({
    'generation': [15, 10, 8],
    'consumption': [10, 11, 7]
})

investment_data = pd.DataFrame({
    'energy_market_price': [100, 150, 200],
    'project_cost': [1000, 2000, 3000],
    'project_viability': [1, 0, 1]
})

# Execute Functions
optimal_location, optimal_angle =
↪  optimize_solar_panel_placement(solar_data)
predicted_maintenance = predict_maintenance_NEEDS(history_data)
new_supply, new_demand = load_balancing(np.array([10, 12, 15]),
↪  np.array([12, 14, 10]))
storage_recommendations = optimize_energy_storage(storage_data)
economic_forecast = economic_forecasting(investment_data)

# Output Results
print("Optimal Solar Panel Location:", optimal_location)
print("Optimal Solar Panel Angle:", optimal_angle)
print("Predicted Maintenance Needs:", predicted_maintenance)
print("Adjusted Supply:", new_supply)
print("Adjusted Demand:", new_demand)
print("Storage Recommendations:", storage_recommendations)
print("Economic Forecast:", economic_forecast)
```

This code defines five functions:

- `optimize_solar_panel_placement` identifies the best location and angle for solar panels based on irradiance.
- `predict_maintenance_NEEDS` predicts future maintenance requirements using historical performance data.
- `load_balancing` adjusts energy supply and demand based on predictions.
- `optimize_energy_storage` provides recommendations for energy storage management.
- `economic_forecasting` predicts the economic viability of renewable energy projects based on market trends.

The provided example executes these functions and prints out the results for each, aiding in the management and optimization of renewable energy operations. " '

Chapter 27

AI in Renewable Energy

1 Optimizing Solar and Wind Energy Production

Renewable energy, including solar and wind energy, plays a pivotal role in combating climate change and reducing dependence on fossil fuels. However, the inherent variability and uncertainty associated with solar and wind energy generation present challenges for achieving optimal energy production. In this section, we explore how Artificial Intelligence (AI) techniques can be applied to optimize the production of solar and wind energy.

To optimize solar energy production, AI algorithms can determine the best placement and tracking of solar panels. By analyzing geographic data, weather patterns, and solar irradiance, we can mathematically model the relationship between panel orientation and sunlight absorption.

$$\text{Optimal Location, Angle for Solar Panels} =$$

$$\arg\max_{\text{location,angle}} (\text{Solar Irradiance(location, angle)})$$

Similarly, AI algorithms can optimize the positioning and operation of wind turbines. By analyzing wind speed, direction, and turbulence data, we can mathematically model the efficiency of wind turbines. These mathematical models, combined with AI algorithms, enable us to determine the most efficient orientation and configuration of wind turbines.

2 Predictive Maintenance of Renewable Energy Assets

Effective maintenance of renewable energy assets, such as solar panels and wind turbines, is vital to ensure their long-term performance and cost-efficiency. Traditional maintenance schedules can be suboptimal, leading to unforeseen failures and increased costs. In this section, we discuss how AI techniques, specifically predictive maintenance models, can enhance the maintenance of renewable energy assets.

By leveraging historical data on the condition and performance of renewable energy assets, AI algorithms can identify patterns and early warning signs of potential issues. These algorithms, commonly based on machine learning techniques, can then predict the maintenance needs and remaining useful life of the equipment. This prediction enables maintenance tasks to be performed proactively, minimizing downtime, optimizing resource allocation, and reducing costs.

3 Grid Integration and Load Balancing with AI

Integrating renewable energy sources into existing power grids presents challenges related to grid stability and load balancing. Fluctuations in energy generation from renewable sources can cause instability and inadequate supply-demand matching. In this section, we delve into how AI techniques address these challenges by enabling accurate predictions of renewable energy generation, demand forecasting, and optimal load balancing strategies.

AI algorithms analyze historical energy generation and consumption data to identify consumption patterns and forecast renewable energy generation. These predictions, combined with techniques such as machine learning, time series analysis, and neural networks, empower grid operators to effectively manage and optimize energy distribution. Accurate predictions of energy supply and demand enable intelligent load balancing decisions, minimizing reliance on non-renewable energy sources during peak demand periods and contributing to a more sustainable and efficient grid infrastructure.

4 AI in Energy Storage Management

Energy storage systems, such as batteries, play a pivotal role in maximizing the utilization and efficiency of renewable energy sources.

Effective management of energy storage allows for optimal utilization of excess energy during periods of low demand and ensures a stable power supply. AI techniques can enhance energy storage management by optimizing charging and discharging strategies based on energy generation and consumption patterns.

AI algorithms can analyze historical energy generation and demand data to determine the optimal charging and discharging strategies for energy storage systems. By leveraging machine learning models, these algorithms can learn patterns in energy supply and demand, weather conditions, and market prices.

$$\text{Recommendations for Charging and Discharging} =$$

$$\arg\max_{\text{strategy}} \left(\text{Energy Storage Optimization(generation, demand)}\right)$$

These recommendations, combined with real-time data, allow energy storage systems to charge during periods of excess generation and discharge during peak demand, ensuring efficient utilization of renewable energy sources.

5 Economic Forecasting for Renewable Investments

Investing in renewable energy projects requires accurate economic forecasting to assess project viability, mitigate risks, and attract financing. In this section, we explore how AI techniques, in conjunction with mathematical modeling and statistical analysis, enable accurate economic forecasting for renewable energy investments.

AI models analyze various factors, including energy market prices, government policies, project costs, and regulatory frameworks, to assess the financial feasibility of renewable energy projects. By leveraging machine learning algorithms, such as regression analysis and time series forecasting, these models identify patterns in historical data and predict future energy market trends.

$$\text{Forecasted Economic Viability Score} =$$

$$\text{AI-based Model(Energy Market Data, Project Costs)}$$

These economic forecasts provide valuable insights for project developers, potential investors, and policymakers. By evaluating the economic impact of integrating renewable energy into existing energy systems, stakeholders can make informed decisions and foster the transition towards a sustainable energy future.

Python Code Snippet

Below is a comprehensive Python code snippet that implements the important equations and algorithms discussed in the chapter on AI in Renewable Energy, specifically for optimizing solar and wind energy production, predictive maintenance, grid integration, energy storage management, and economic forecasting for renewable investments.

```python
import numpy as np
import pandas as pd
from sklearn.linear_model import LinearRegression
from sklearn.model_selection import train_test_split
import matplotlib.pyplot as plt

def optimal_solar_panel_location(solar_irradiance_data):
    '''
    Determines optimal solar panel location and angle for maximum
    ↪ irradiance.
    :param solar_irradiance_data: DataFrame containing location and
    ↪ irradiance information.
    :return: Optimal location and angle for solar panels.
    '''
    # Assuming solar_irradiance_data contains 'latitude',
    ↪ 'longitude', 'angle', and 'irradiance'
    optimal =
    ↪ solar_irradiance_data.loc[solar_irradiance_data['irradiance']
    .idxmax()]
    return optimal['latitude'], optimal['longitude'],
    ↪ optimal['angle']

def predictive_maintenance(maintenance_data):
    '''
    Predicts maintenance needs based on historical performance data.
    :param maintenance_data: DataFrame containing historical
    ↪ performance and maintenance records.
    :return: Predicted maintenance needs and remaining useful life.
    '''
    # Features and target variable
    X = maintenance_data[['performance_metric', 'age']]
    y = maintenance_data['maintenance_needed']

    # Splitting the dataset
    X_train, X_test, y_train, y_test = train_test_split(X, y,
    ↪ test_size=0.2, random_state=42)

    # Training the model
    model = LinearRegression()
    model.fit(X_train, y_train)
```

```python
    # Making predictions
    predictions = model.predict(X_test)
    return predictions

def grid_integration_prediction(grid_data):
    '''
    Predicts energy generation and demand for optimized grid
    ↪   integration.
    :param grid_data: DataFrame containing historical energy
    ↪   generation and demand data.
    :return: Predicted generation and demand.
    '''
    # Simple linear model for forecasting (could be expanded with
    ↪   more features like time, weather)
    X = grid_data[['previous_generation', 'previous_demand']]
    y_generation = grid_data['current_generation']
    y_demand = grid_data['current_demand']

    # Train-test split
    X_train, X_test, y_gen_train, y_gen_test = train_test_split(X,
    ↪   y_generation, test_size=0.2, random_state=42)
    X_train, X_test, y_demand_train, y_demand_test =
    ↪   train_test_split(X, y_demand, test_size=0.2,
    ↪   random_state=42)

    # Creating models
    gen_model = LinearRegression()
    demand_model = LinearRegression()

    # Fitting models
    gen_model.fit(X_train, y_gen_train)
    demand_model.fit(X_train, y_demand_train)

    # Predicting
    predicted_generation = gen_model.predict(X_test)
    predicted_demand = demand_model.predict(X_test)
    return predicted_generation, predicted_demand

def energy_storage_management(energy_data):
    '''
    Recommends optimal charging and discharging strategy for energy
    ↪   storage.
    :param energy_data: DataFrame containing historical energy
    ↪   generation and demand data.
    :return: Recommendations for charging and discharging.
    '''
    excess_energy = energy_data[energy_data['generation'] >
    ↪   energy_data['demand']]
    shortage_energy = energy_data[energy_data['generation'] <
    ↪   energy_data['demand']]

    charging_recommendations = excess_energy[['generation',
    ↪   'demand']]
```

```python
    discharging_recommendations = shortage_energy[['generation',
    ↪  'demand']]

    return charging_recommendations, discharging_recommendations

def economic_forecasting(market_data):
    '''
    Forecasts the economic viability of renewable energy projects.
    :param market_data: DataFrame containing energy market prices
    ↪  and project costs.
    :return: Forecasted economic viability score.
    '''
    X = market_data[['market_price', 'project_cost']]
    y = market_data['economic_viability']

    # Training and testing
    X_train, X_test, y_train, y_test = train_test_split(X, y,
    ↪  test_size=0.2, random_state=42)

    # Model
    model = LinearRegression()
    model.fit(X_train, y_train)

    # Prediction
    forecast = model.predict(X_test)
    return forecast

# Example DataFrames (replace this with actual data)
solar_irradiance_data = pd.DataFrame({
    'latitude': [34.05, 36.16, 40.71],
    'longitude': [-118.24, -115.15, -74.00],
    'angle': [30, 45, 60],
    'irradiance': [5.67, 6.50, 4.89]
})

maintenance_data = pd.DataFrame({
    'performance_metric': [90, 80, 70, 85, 95],
    'age': [1, 2, 3, 1, 2],
    'maintenance_needed': [0, 1, 1, 0, 0]
})

grid_data = pd.DataFrame({
    'previous_generation': [100, 150, 200],
    'previous_demand': [90, 160, 180],
    'current_generation': [110, 145, 220],
    'current_demand': [95, 155, 190]
})

energy_data = pd.DataFrame({
    'generation': [120, 85, 75, 200],
    'demand': [100, 90, 150, 190]
})
```

```
market_data = pd.DataFrame({
    'market_price': [50, 55, 60],
    'project_cost': [1000, 1200, 1100],
    'economic_viability': [1, 0, 1]
})

# Function calls
optimal_location =
↪  optimal_solar_panel_location(solar_irradiance_data)
predicted_maintenance = predictive_maintenance(maintenance_data)
predicted_gen, predicted_demand =
↪  grid_integration_prediction(grid_data)
charging_recommendations, discharging_recommendations =
↪  energy_storage_management(energy_data)
economic_forecast = economic_forecasting(market_data)

# Output results
print("Optimal Solar Panel Location:", optimal_location)
print("Predicted Maintenance Needs:", predicted_maintenance)
print("Predicted Generation:", predicted_gen)
print("Predicted Demand:", predicted_demand)
print("Charging Recommendations:\n", charging_recommendations)
print("Discharging Recommendations:\n", discharging_recommendations)
print("Economic Forecasting Results:", economic_forecast)
```

This code defines several functions:

- optimal_solar_panel_location determines the best solar panel placement based on irradiance data.
- predictive_maintenance predicts maintenance needs using historical performance data.
- grid_integration_prediction forecasts energy generation and demand for effective grid management.
- energy_storage_management provides recommendations for charging and discharging energy storage systems.
- economic_forecasting assesses the economic viability of renewable energy projects based on market data.

By calling these functions with example DataFrames, the code provides insights into solar panel optimization, maintenance prediction, grid prediction, energy management, and economic forecasting. The results are then printed for review.

Chapter 28

AI in Biotechnology

In this chapter, we explore the applications of Artificial Intelligence (AI) in the field of Biotechnology. Specifically, we delve into the use of AI techniques in drug discovery and development, genomic analysis and personalized medicine, predictive analytics for clinical trials, automated laboratory processes, disease modeling and simulation.

1 Drug Discovery and Development

Drug discovery and development is a complex, time-consuming, and expensive process. AI plays a crucial role in accelerating this process by assisting in the identification of potential drug candidates, optimization of drug properties, and prediction of drug efficacy and safety.

One key area where AI is applied is in virtual screening, where large libraries of molecules are screened in silico to identify potential drug candidates. Machine learning algorithms, such as Support Vector Machines (SVMs) and Random Forests, can be trained on known drug-target interactions to predict the likelihood of a molecule binding to a specific target.

Mathematically, this can be represented as:

$$\text{Drug Likelihood} = \text{Machine Learning Model(Molecular Features)}$$

AI techniques also aid in the optimization of drug properties, such as solubility, bioavailability, and toxicity. Through generative models, such as Generative Adversarial Networks (GANs) and

Variational Autoencoders (VAEs), novel drug-like molecules can be generated that adhere to specific structural and physicochemical criteria.

$$\text{Generated Molecules} = \text{Generative Model(Constraints)}$$

Furthermore, AI is employed in predicting the efficacy and safety of drug candidates. Machine learning algorithms analyze and integrate diverse datasets, including genetic, proteomic, and clinical data, to develop predictive models for assessing drug response, side effects, and potential drug-drug interactions.

$$\text{Drug Response} = \text{Machine Learning Model(Patient Features, Drug Features)}$$

2 Genomic Analysis and Personalized Medicine

With the advent of high-throughput sequencing technologies, vast amounts of genomic data are generated, which can be leveraged by AI techniques for various applications in personalized medicine. AI algorithms enable the identification of disease-related genetic variants, interpretation of mutations, and prediction of disease susceptibility.

By applying machine learning algorithms to large-scale genomic datasets, genetic markers associated with particular diseases or drug responses can be identified. This information assists in predicting disease risk or identifying potential therapeutic targets.

$$\text{Disease Risk} = \text{Machine Learning Model(Genetic Variants)}$$

In the realm of precision medicine, AI aids in tailoring medical treatments to individual patients based on their genetic profiles. By integrating genomic data with clinical and epidemiological information, AI algorithms can generate personalized treatment recommendations and predict the response to specific therapies.

$$\text{Treatment Recommendation} =$$

$$\text{Machine Learning Model(Genetic Profile, Clinical Data)}$$

3 Predictive Analytics for Clinical Trials

Clinical trials are crucial for evaluating the safety and efficacy of new drugs. AI techniques are employed to enhance the design and efficiency of clinical trials, optimize patient recruitment, and predict trial outcomes.

Machine learning algorithms analyze historical clinical trial data to identify patterns and predictors of treatment response. This enables the development of predictive models to estimate the likelihood of success for new trials, informing decision-making processes.

$$\text{Trial Success Probability} = \text{Machine Learning Model}(\text{Trial Features})$$

AI algorithms also aid in patient recruitment for clinical trials by identifying potentially eligible participants from diverse data sources. By analyzing healthcare records, genetic data, and social media activity, machine learning models can identify and target specific patient populations, thereby improving recruitment rates and trial efficiency.

4 Automated Laboratory Processes

Laboratory experiments often involve tedious and repetitive tasks. AI techniques, such as robotics and automation, can streamline and optimize these processes, freeing up researchers' time and reducing human error.

Robotic systems equipped with computer vision and machine learning algorithms can autonomously carry out laboratory protocols, including pipetting, sample preparation, and data analysis. These systems can accurately execute experiments, increasing reproducibility and experimental throughput.

5 Disease Modeling and Simulation

AI techniques are employed in disease modeling and simulation to gain insights into disease mechanisms, identify potential drug targets, and optimize treatment strategies.

Using mathematical modeling and simulation techniques, AI algorithms can simulate the progression of diseases, such as cancer or infectious diseases, and predict their response to different therapeutic interventions. By incorporating patient-specific data, these models can assist in personalized treatment planning and optimization.

$$\text{Disease Progression} =$$

$$\text{Mathematical Model(Patient Data, Treatment Strategies)}$$

Additionally, AI algorithms can analyze biological networks, such as protein-protein interaction networks or gene regulatory networks, to identify key molecules or pathways implicated in disease development. These findings aid in the discovery of novel drug targets or the repurposing of existing drugs for new indications.

$$\text{Key Molecules/Pathways} = \text{Graph Analysis(Biological Network)}$$

In conclusion, AI techniques have revolutionized the field of biotechnology by accelerating drug discovery, enabling personalized medicine, enhancing clinical trial design, automating laboratory processes, and facilitating disease modeling and simulation. The integration of AI with biotechnology has the potential to significantly advance healthcare and contribute to the development of innovative therapeutic solutions.

Python Code Snippet

Below is a Python code snippet that implements important equations and algorithms discussed in the chapter on Artificial Intelligence in Biotechnology, specifically for drug discovery, genomic analysis, predictive analytics for clinical trials, automated laboratory processes, and disease modeling and simulation.

```python
import numpy as np
from sklearn.ensemble import RandomForestClassifier
from sklearn.model_selection import train_test_split
from sklearn.metrics import accuracy_score
import pandas as pd

# Drug Discovery and Development - Predict Drug Response
def predict_drug_response(patient_features, drug_features):
    '''
    Predict drug response based on patient and drug features.
    :param patient_features: Array of patient characteristics.
    :param drug_features: Array of drug properties.
    :return: Predicted drug response.
    '''

    model = RandomForestClassifier()
```

```python
    # Assume X_train and y_train are predefined datasets for
    ↪   training
    X_train = np.random.rand(100, 10)  # Mock data
    y_train = np.random.randint(0, 2, 100)  # Binary response
    model.fit(X_train, y_train)

    return model.predict([np.concatenate((patient_features,
    ↪   drug_features))])[0]

# Genomic Analysis - Predict Disease Risk
def predict_disease_risk(genetic_variants):
    '''
    Predict disease risk based on genetic variants.
    :param genetic_variants: Array of genetic variant data.
    :return: Predicted risk level.
    '''
    model = RandomForestClassifier()
    X_train = np.random.rand(100, 10)  # Mock data
    y_train = np.random.randint(0, 2, 100)  # Binary risk
    ↪   classification
    model.fit(X_train, y_train)

    return model.predict([genetic_variants])[0]

# Predictive Analytics for Clinical Trials
def predict_trial_success(trial_features):
    '''
    Predict trial success based on historical trial features.
    :param trial_features: Array of trial characteristics.
    :return: Trial success probability.
    '''
    model = RandomForestClassifier()
    X_train = np.random.rand(100, 10)  # Mock historical trial data
    y_train = np.random.randint(0, 2, 100)  # Success or failure
    model.fit(X_train, y_train)

    return model.predict([trial_features])[0]

# Automated Laboratory Processes - Mock Output Generation
def automated_lab_process():
    '''
    Simulate an automated laboratory process.
    :return: Mock results of the experiment.
    '''
    results = {
        'experiment_id': np.random.randint(1000, 9999),
        'yield': np.random.uniform(0.5, 1.0),  # Random yield
        ↪   between 50% to 100%
        'error_margin': np.random.uniform(0.01, 0.1)  # Random error
        ↪   margin
    }
    return results
```

```
# Disease Modeling and Simulation
def simulate_disease_progression(patient_data,
↪   treatment_strategies):
    '''
    Simulate disease progression based on patient data and treatment
    ↪   strategies.
    :param patient_data: Array of patient-specific information.
    :param treatment_strategies: Array of treatment strategies.
    :return: Simulated disease progression metric.
    '''
    # Simplified simulation: Just a linear combination for
    ↪   demonstration
    progression_score = np.dot(patient_data, treatment_strategies)
    return progression_score

# Example usage
# Input data
patient_features = np.random.rand(5)   # Mock patient features
drug_features = np.random.rand(5)   # Mock drug features
genetic_variants = np.random.rand(10)   # Mock genetic variant data
trial_features = np.random.rand(5)   # Mock trial features
patient_data = np.random.rand(5)   # Mock patient data for simulation
treatment_strategies = np.random.rand(5)   # Mock treatment
↪   strategies

# Calculations
drug_response = predict_drug_response(patient_features,
↪   drug_features)
disease_risk = predict_disease_risk(genetic_variants)
trial_success = predict_trial_success(trial_features)
lab_results = automated_lab_process()
disease_progression = simulate_disease_progression(patient_data,
↪   treatment_strategies)

# Output results
print("Predicted Drug Response:", drug_response)
print("Predicted Disease Risk:", disease_risk)
print("Trial Success Probability:", trial_success)
print("Automated Lab Results:", lab_results)
print("Simulated Disease Progression Score:", disease_progression)
```

This code defines five functions:

- `predict_drug_response` predicts the response to a drug based
on patient and drug features using a Random Forest classifier.
- `predict_disease_risk` estimates the risk of a disease based on
genetic variants through another Random Forest model.
- `predict_trial_success` evaluates the likelihood of success for a
clinical trial using historical data.
- `automated_lab_process` simulates automated laboratory exper-

iments and generates mock results.

- `simulate_disease_progression` models the progression of a disease based on patient data and treatment strategies.

The provided example demonstrates how to use these functions to make predictions and generate outputs relevant to biotechnology, drug discovery, and personalized medicine.

Chapter 29

AI in Mining

Mining is a vital industry that contributes to economic growth by extracting valuable minerals and resources from the earth. As mining operations continue to expand and become more complex, the integration of Artificial Intelligence (AI) techniques has emerged as a key driver for optimizing safety, efficiency, and productivity.

1 Predictive Maintenance of Mining Equipment

The maintenance of mining equipment is crucial for ensuring the smooth operation of mining operations. AI techniques, particularly predictive maintenance, can help identify potential equipment failures before they occur, thereby minimizing downtime and reducing maintenance costs.

By analyzing sensor data collected from mining equipment, machine learning algorithms can detect patterns and anomalies that indicate equipment degradation or imminent failure. This allows for proactive maintenance, as maintenance teams can address issues before they lead to costly breakdowns.

2 Geological Data Analysis and Resource Detection

Geological data analysis plays a fundamental role in mining operations, as it aids in identifying potential mineral deposits and optimizing resource extraction. AI algorithms can efficiently process large volumes of geological data, such as geophysical surveys, drilling data, and geological maps, to identify promising areas for further exploration.

Machine learning techniques, such as clustering and classification algorithms, can identify patterns and correlations in geological datasets. This enables geologists to pinpoint areas with high mineral potential, streamlining the exploration process and reducing the time and costs associated with traditional manual methods.

3 Autonomous Mining Vehicles and Machinery

AI-driven autonomous vehicles and machinery are transforming the mining industry by enhancing operational efficiency, safety, and productivity. Autonomous vehicles, such as self-driving trucks and robotic drilling rigs, can navigate mining sites and perform tasks without human intervention.

These autonomous systems leverage AI algorithms, including computer vision, sensor fusion, and machine learning, to perceive their surroundings, make decisions, and execute tasks. By removing the need for human operators in hazardous or repetitive tasks, autonomous mining vehicles improve safety and increase productivity.

4 Worker Safety and Risk Management

Safety is a top priority in the mining industry, and AI techniques contribute significantly to improving worker safety and risk management. AI algorithms can analyze real-time sensor data, such as gas concentrations, noise levels, and temperature, to detect potential hazards and provide early warnings to miners.

By integrating data from various sources, including environmental sensors, wearable devices, and surveillance systems, AI systems can monitor worker behavior and identify potential safety risks, such as fatigue, improper equipment usage, or non-compliance with safety protocols.

5 Supply Chain Optimization in Mining Operations

AI techniques enable efficient supply chain management in mining operations by optimizing inventory management, logistics, and production planning. Machine learning algorithms can forecast demand based on historical data, market trends, and external factors, allowing mining companies to optimize inventory levels and reduce costs.

AI algorithms can also optimize transportation and logistics by predicting the most efficient routes for mineral transportation, considering factors such as distance, road conditions, and traffic. This helps reduce transportation costs and ensure timely delivery of minerals to processing plants or end customers.

In conclusion, the integration of Artificial Intelligence (AI) in the mining industry brings remarkable benefits, including predictive maintenance of mining equipment, geological data analysis for resource detection, autonomous mining vehicles and machinery, worker safety and risk management, and supply chain optimization. By harnessing the power of AI, mining companies can improve operational efficiency, maximize resource extraction, and enhance safety standards, contributing to sustainable and responsible mining practices.

Python Code Snippet

Below is a Python code snippet that implements predictive maintenance for mining equipment, geological data analysis, and autonomous vehicle navigation. This example demonstrates the core algorithms and calculations described in the chapter.

```python
import numpy as np
import pandas as pd
from sklearn.model_selection import train_test_split
from sklearn.ensemble import RandomForestClassifier
from sklearn.metrics import accuracy_score
import joblib

# Predictive Maintenance Code

def predict_equipment_failure(sensor_data):
    '''
    Predict the likelihood of equipment failure using a trained
    ↪   model.
    :param sensor_data: DataFrame containing sensor readings.
    :return: Prediction of failure (1 for failure, 0 for no
    ↪   failure).
    '''
    model = joblib.load('equipment_failure_model.pkl')  # Load a
    ↪   pre-trained model
    return model.predict(sensor_data)
```

```python
# Example sensor data for prediction (replace with actual sensor
↪    data)
sensor_data_example = pd.DataFrame({
    'temperature': [75, 80, 90],
    'vibration': [0.05, 0.15, 0.2],
    'pressure': [40, 42, 35]
})

predictions = predict_equipment_failure(sensor_data_example)
print("Predicted Equipment Failures:", predictions)

# Geological Data Analysis Code

def analyze_geological_data(geological_data):
    '''
    Analyze geological data to identify areas with high mineral
    ↪    potential.
    :param geological_data: DataFrame containing geological
    ↪    features.
    :return: Identified regions with potential resources.
    '''
    # Simple clustering model to segment the data
    from sklearn.cluster import KMeans
    kmeans = KMeans(n_clusters=3)  # Assume 3 clusters for
    ↪    demonstration
    geological_data['cluster'] = kmeans.fit_predict(geological_data)
    return geological_data.groupby('cluster').mean()

# Example geological data for analysis
geological_data_example = pd.DataFrame({
    'feature1': np.random.rand(10),
    'feature2': np.random.rand(10),
    'feature3': np.random.rand(10)
})

geological_analysis_results =
↪    analyze_geological_data(geological_data_example)
print("Geological Analysis Results:\n", geological_analysis_results)

# Autonomous Vehicle Navigation Code

def autonomous_vehicle_navigation(obstacle_data):
    '''
    Navigate an autonomous vehicle based on obstacle data.
    :param obstacle_data: DataFrame containing obstacle positions.
    :return: Optimal path for navigation.
    '''
    # Simple heuristic for pathfinding (A* or Dijkstra's not
    ↪    implemented for simplicity)
    path = []
    for index, row in obstacle_data.iterrows():
        if row['distance_to_vehicle'] > 5:  # Arbitrary safe
        ↪    distance
```

201

```
                path.append((row['x'], row['y']))
        return path

# Example obstacle data (replace with actual data)
obstacle_data_example = pd.DataFrame({
    'x': np.random.randint(0, 10, 5),
    'y': np.random.randint(0, 10, 5),
    'distance_to_vehicle': np.random.uniform(1, 10, 5)
})

optimal_path = autonomous_vehicle_navigation(obstacle_data_example)
print("Optimal Path for Navigation:", optimal_path)
```

This code includes the following functions:

- `predict_equipment_failure` loads a trained model and predicts equipment failure based on sensor readings.
- `analyze_geological_data` processes geological data to assess mineral potential using clustering techniques.
- `autonomous_vehicle_navigation` determines the optimal path for an autonomous vehicle while avoiding obstacles.

The example shows how to use these functions with synthetic input data, demonstrating their application in mining operations.

Chapter 30

AI in Pharmaceuticals

In this chapter, we delve into the applications of Artificial Intelligence (AI) in the field of pharmaceuticals. The integration of AI techniques in pharmaceutical research and development has shown immense potential for accelerating drug discovery, optimizing patient outcomes, and improving overall healthcare. We explore key areas where AI is making significant strides, including drug formulation and optimization, predictive modeling for patient outcomes, AI in regulatory compliance, automated data management in clinical trials, and AI-driven supply chain for pharmaceutical distribution.

1   Drug Formulation and Optimization

One of the key challenges in the pharmaceutical industry is developing safe and effective drug formulations. AI, coupled with computational models, provides a promising avenue for predicting and optimizing drug properties. By utilizing machine learning algorithms and molecular simulations, researchers can predict the behavior of drug molecules, including their solubility, stability, and absorption rates.

The Quantitative Structure-Activity Relationship (QSAR) is a prominent technique used in drug design and optimization. This approach involves developing mathematical models to correlate the structural features of drug molecules with their biological activities. QSAR models can be utilized to predict the efficacy, toxicity, and pharmacokinetic properties of potential drug candidates, aiding in the selection of promising leads for further development.

2 Predictive Modeling for Patient Outcomes

Personalized medicine aims to tailor medical treatment to individual patients based on their genetic information, medical history, and other factors. AI plays a pivotal role in predictive modeling for patient outcomes, enabling healthcare providers to make better-informed decisions and optimize treatment plans.

Machine learning algorithms can analyze large-scale datasets, including electronic health records, genomic information, and clinical outcomes, to identify patterns and correlations. By learning from historical data, these models can generate predictions about patient responses to specific treatments, disease progression, and potential adverse events. Such insights facilitate personalized treatment strategies, such as selecting the most suitable drug or dosage for individual patients, improving patient care and overall treatment outcomes.

3 AI in Regulatory Compliance

The pharmaceutical industry operates within a stringent regulatory framework, ensuring the safety and efficacy of drugs before they reach the market. AI tools can assist in various aspects of regulatory compliance, including automating the analysis of regulatory documents, adverse event reporting, and ensuring compliance with Good Clinical Practice (GCP) guidelines.

Natural Language Processing (NLP) techniques enable the efficient extraction, analysis, and interpretation of relevant information from vast amounts of unstructured regulatory text, such as drug labels and clinical trial protocols. This aids regulatory professionals in navigating complex regulatory requirements and expediting the drug approval process.

4 Automated Data Management in Clinical Trials

Clinical trials are critical for evaluating the safety and efficacy of new drugs. However, managing and analyzing the vast amount of data generated during these trials pose significant challenges. AI-based solutions can automate data management processes, improving efficiency, accuracy, and reducing manual errors.

Machine learning algorithms can assist in data extraction, annotation, and cleaning, ensuring high data quality and reducing the time-consuming task of manual data curation. Additionally, AI techniques can analyze and integrate data from various sources, such as electronic health records, patient-reported outcomes, and laboratory data, enabling faster and more comprehensive analysis of clinical trial results.

5 AI-driven Supply Chain for Pharmaceutical Distribution

Efficient supply chain management is crucial to ensure the timely and safe distribution of pharmaceutical products. AI can optimize various aspects of the pharmaceutical supply chain, including demand forecasting, inventory management, and logistics optimization.

Predictive analytics techniques, such as time series forecasting and machine learning algorithms, can forecast demand based on historical data, external factors (e.g., disease outbreaks), and market trends. This allows pharmaceutical companies to optimize inventory levels, reducing stock-outs and overstocking.

AI algorithms can optimize transportation and logistics operations by determining optimal routes, considering factors like transportation costs, delivery schedules, and perishable product requirements. This aids in achieving faster and more cost-effective distribution, while adhering to strict regulatory guidelines for product integrity and safety.

In conclusion, AI is revolutionizing the pharmaceutical industry, with applications in drug formulation and optimization, predictive modeling for patient outcomes, regulatory compliance, automated data management in clinical trials, and supply chain optimization. Leveraging AI techniques enables pharmaceutical researchers and practitioners to make more informed decisions, enhance patient care, and contribute to the development of safer and more effective treatments.

Python Code Snippet

Below is a Python code snippet that demonstrates important equations, formulas, and algorithms relevant to applications of AI in pharmaceuticals as discussed in this chapter.

```python
import numpy as np
from sklearn.model_selection import train_test_split
```

```python
from sklearn.linear_model import LinearRegression
from sklearn.metrics import mean_squared_error
from sklearn.preprocessing import PolynomialFeatures
import pandas as pd

def qsar_model(X, y):
    '''
    Create and evaluate a Quantitative Structure-Activity
    ↪ Relationship (QSAR) model.
    :param X: Features dataset (structural information of
    ↪ compounds).
    :param y: Target variable (biological activity).
    :return: Trained model and mean squared error.
    '''
    # Split the dataset into training and test sets
    X_train, X_test, y_train, y_test = train_test_split(X, y,
    ↪ test_size=0.2, random_state=42)

    # Create a Linear Regression model
    model = LinearRegression()
    model.fit(X_train, y_train)

    # Predict on the test set
    predictions = model.predict(X_test)

    # Calculate the mean squared error
    mse = mean_squared_error(y_test, predictions)
    return model, mse


def predict_patient_outcome(patient_data, model):
    '''
    Predict patient outcome using a trained model.
    :param patient_data: New patient features for prediction.
    :param model: Trained predictive model.
    :return: Predicted patient outcome.
    '''
    outcome = model.predict(patient_data)
    return outcome


def automate_data_management(data):
    '''
    Automate data cleaning for clinical trials data.
    :param data: Raw clinical trial data.
    :return: Cleaned and formatted data.
    '''
    # Drop rows with missing values
    cleaned_data = data.dropna()

    # Reset index after cleaning
    cleaned_data.reset_index(drop=True, inplace=True)
    return cleaned_data
```

```python
def optimize_supply_chain(demand_forecast, inventory_levels):
    '''
    Optimize inventory levels based on demand forecasts.
    :param demand_forecast: Predicted demand for products.
    :param inventory_levels: Current inventory levels.
    :return: Adjusted inventory levels.
    '''
    optimized_inventory = demand_forecast - inventory_levels
    # Ensure we do not suggest negative inventory
    return np.maximum(optimized_inventory, 0)


# Example usage
# Define some example data for QSAR modeling
X = pd.DataFrame({
    'logP': [1.2, 2.1, 0.5, 1.8, 2.4],
    'MW': [200, 250, 180, 300, 310]  # Molecular weight
})
y = pd.Series([0.8, 0.9, 0.5, 0.7, 0.6])  # Biological activity

# Create and evaluate QSAR model
qsar_model_trained, qsar_mse = qsar_model(X, y)
print("QSAR Model Mean Squared Error:", qsar_mse)

# Predict patient outcome (example data)
new_patient_data = np.array([[1.5, 220]])  # Example patient
↪  features
predicted_outcome = predict_patient_outcome(new_patient_data,
↪  qsar_model_trained)
print("Predicted Patient Outcome:", predicted_outcome)

# Sample raw clinical trial data
raw_data = pd.DataFrame({
    'Subject': [1, 2, 3, None, 5],
    'Age': [34, 45, None, 29, 41],
    'Outcome': ['Improved', 'Improved', 'Neutral', 'Worse', None]
})

# Automate data management
cleaned_data = automate_data_management(raw_data)
print("Cleaned Clinical Trial Data:\n", cleaned_data)

# Optimize supply chain example
demand_forecast = np.array([50, 60, 80])
inventory_levels = np.array([40, 50, 90])
optimized_inventory = optimize_supply_chain(demand_forecast,
↪  inventory_levels)
print("Optimized Inventory Levels:", optimized_inventory)
```

This code defines several important functions:

- `qsar_model` creates a QSAR model utilizing linear regression and evaluates its performance through mean squared error.
- `predict_patient_outcome` predicts the outcome for a new patient based on the trained QSAR model.
- `automate_data_management` cleans clinical trial data by removing rows with missing values.
- `optimize_supply_chain` adjusts inventory levels based on demand forecasts, ensuring no negative inventory levels.

The provided example demonstrates the creation of a QSAR model, prediction of a patient outcome, cleaning of clinical data, and optimization of inventory levels based on demand forecasts.

Chapter 31

AI in Telecommunications Infrastructure

In this chapter, we delve into the applications of Artificial Intelligence (AI) in the field of telecommunications infrastructure. The integration of AI techniques in telecommunications has shown immense potential for optimizing network management, enhancing customer service, ensuring security, and personalizing services and content. We explore key areas where AI is making significant strides, including network optimization and management, AI-driven customer service and support, predictive analytics for network issues, personalization of services and content, and fraud detection and prevention.

1   Network Optimization and Management

Telecommunications companies manage vast networks that transmit voice, data, and video signals. AI plays a crucial role in optimizing and managing these networks, ensuring efficient operation and high-quality service delivery.

One prominent application is in network load balancing and optimization. AI algorithms, such as reinforcement learning, can continually analyze network conditions, traffic patterns, and resource usage to dynamically adjust network configurations. These algorithms determine the optimal routing and allocation of network resources, maximizing data throughput and minimizing latency.

AI is also instrumental in fault detection and resolution. By continuously monitoring network performance and analyzing real-time data, AI algorithms can detect abnormalities and identify potential network issues. This enables proactive troubleshooting, minimizing downtime, and improving overall network reliability.

2 AI-driven Customer Service and Support

Providing excellent customer service is crucial for telecommunications companies to maintain customer satisfaction and loyalty. AI-driven customer service solutions, such as chatbots and virtual assistants, are becoming increasingly prevalent in the industry.

Chatbots leverage natural language processing (NLP) techniques to understand and respond to customer inquiries. These bots interact with customers through text or speech, providing support, answering common questions, and assisting with basic troubleshooting. By automating routine customer interactions, chatbots can handle a large volume of inquiries simultaneously, reducing wait times and improving customer service efficiency.

Virtual assistants take customer interactions a step further by integrating with various systems and databases. They can access customer records, account information, and service status, allowing them to provide more personalized and accurate assistance. Virtual assistants can perform tasks such as changing service plans, scheduling appointments, or resolving technical issues.

3 Predictive Analytics for Network Issues

AI techniques, such as machine learning and data analytics, are invaluable in predicting and preventing network issues. By analyzing historical network data, AI algorithms can identify patterns and anomalies, enabling proactive measures to mitigate potential problems.

Predictive analytics models can identify network congestion points, hardware failures, or software vulnerabilities that may lead to service disruptions. By forecasting network traffic and resource utilization, these models help telecommunications companies allocate resources effectively and prevent network overload.

The application of AI in root cause analysis is another vital aspect of network issue prevention. AI algorithms can analyze vast amounts of data, including network logs and diagnostic information, to identify the underlying causes of network errors or service degradations. By addressing root causes promptly, telecommunications companies can minimize the impact on customer experience and reduce troubleshooting time.

4   Personalization of Services and Content

With the increasing availability of digital services, personalization has become a crucial factor in telecommunications. AI techniques enable service providers to deliver customized offerings, tailored to individual customer preferences and needs.

Machine learning algorithms analyze vast amounts of customer data, including usage patterns, preferences, and past behavior. By processing this data, AI models can predict customer preferences, anticipate future needs, and offer targeted recommendations. For example, service providers can offer personalized content suggestions, tailored service bundles, or promotions based on customers' viewing habits or usage patterns.

Personalization extends beyond content recommendations. AI can also personalize service features such as user interfaces, pricing plans, or interactive voice response systems, catering to individual preferences and delivering a more user-friendly experience.

5   Fraud Detection and Prevention

Detecting and preventing fraudulent activities is critical in telecommunications, where unauthorized usage or breaches can lead to significant financial losses. AI plays a significant role in fraud detection and prevention, leveraging advanced analytics and machine learning techniques.

AI algorithms can analyze large-scale data, including call records, transaction data, and customer behavior patterns, to identify anomalous or suspicious activities. By establishing models of normal customer behavior, AI can detect deviations that may indicate fraudulent activity, such as SIM card cloning, account takeovers, or premium rate service abuse.

Real-time monitoring and analysis enable telecommunications companies to promptly detect and respond to potential security breaches. AI algorithms can trigger alerts when suspicious patterns or unusual activities are identified, enabling immediate action to mitigate risks.

In conclusion, AI is revolutionizing the telecommunications industry, with applications in network optimization and management, AI-driven customer service and support, predictive analytics for network issues, personalization of services and content, and fraud detection and prevention. Leveraging AI techniques enables telecommunications companies to enhance network performance, improve customer satisfaction, ensure network security, and deliver personalized services to meet evolving customer demands. Certainly! Below is the comprehensive Python code snippet based on the important equations and algorithms discussed in the chapter on AI in Telecommunications Infrastructure. This code includes functions for network load balancing, fault detection, predictive analytics, personalization of services, and fraud detection.

Python Code Snippet

Below is a Python code snippet that implements various algorithms relevant to telecommunications infrastructure.

```python
import numpy as np
import pandas as pd
from sklearn.ensemble import RandomForestClassifier
from sklearn.metrics import classification_report
from sklearn.model_selection import train_test_split
from sklearn.preprocessing import StandardScaler

def network_load_balancing(traffic_data, resource_capacity):
    '''
    Optimize network resource allocation based on traffic data.
    :param traffic_data: List of current traffic loads on each
    ↪   network segment.
    :param resource_capacity: Total capacity of network resources
    ↪   available.
    :return: Optimized resource allocation.
    '''

    total_traffic = np.sum(traffic_data)
    allocation = [(load / total_traffic) * resource_capacity for
    ↪   load in traffic_data]
    return allocation

def fault_detection(network_metrics):
    '''
    Detect network faults based on performance metrics.
    :param network_metrics: DataFrame containing metrics like
    ↪   latency, packet loss, etc.
    :return: List of boolean flags indicating fault status for each
    ↪   segment.
```

```python
    '''
    threshold_latency = 100   # ms
    threshold_packet_loss = 0.05   # 5%
    faults = (network_metrics['latency'] > threshold_latency) |
    ↪ (network_metrics['packet_loss'] > threshold_packet_loss)
    return faults.tolist()

def predictive_analytics(data, target_variable):
    '''
    Predict future outcomes based on historical data using Random
    ↪ Forest.
    :param data: DataFrame containing features for prediction.
    :param target_variable: Column name of the target variable to
    ↪ predict.
    :return: Classification report of the model performance.
    '''
    X = data.drop(columns=[target_variable])
    y = data[target_variable]
    X_train, X_test, y_train, y_test = train_test_split(X, y,
    ↪ test_size=0.2, random_state=42)
    scaler = StandardScaler()
    X_train = scaler.fit_transform(X_train)
    X_test = scaler.transform(X_test)

    model = RandomForestClassifier(n_estimators=100,
    ↪ random_state=42)
    model.fit(X_train, y_train)
    predictions = model.predict(X_test)

    report = classification_report(y_test, predictions)
    return report

def personalize_service(user_data):
    '''
    Personalize service offerings based on user preferences.
    :param user_data: Dictionary containing user preferences and
    ↪ history.
    :return: Recommended services.
    '''
    recommended_services = []
    if user_data['streaming'] > 10:
        recommended_services.append('Premium Streaming Package')
    if user_data['data_usage'] > 50:
        recommended_services.append('Unlimited Data Plan')
    return recommended_services

def fraud_detection(transactions):
    '''
    Detect fraudulent transactions based on patterns.
    :param transactions: DataFrame of transaction records.
    :return: List of boolean flags indicating potential fraud.
    '''
    # Assume features include amount, time, location, etc.
```

213

```python
    model = RandomForestClassifier()  # A simple model for example
    ↪ purposes
    features = transactions.drop('is_fraud', axis=1)
    model.fit(features, transactions['is_fraud'])

    predictions = model.predict(features)
    return predictions.tolist()


# Example Data Inputs
traffic_data_example = [100, 200, 150, 250]  # Current traffic on
↪ network segments
resource_capacity_example = 1000  # Total capacity available

network_metrics_example = pd.DataFrame({
    'latency': [90, 110, 80, 150],  # in ms
    'packet_loss': [0.02, 0.07, 0.01, 0.06]  # as a fraction
})

historical_data_example = pd.DataFrame({
    'feature1': [1, 2, 3, 4],
    'feature2': [4, 3, 2, 1],
    'target': [0, 1, 0, 1]
})

user_preferences_example = {'streaming': 15, 'data_usage': 60}

transactions_example = pd.DataFrame({
    'amount': [100, 150, 200, 300],
    'time': [1, 2, 3, 4],
    'location': ['loc1', 'loc2', 'loc1', 'loc3'],
    'is_fraud': [0, 1, 0, 0]  # Labels for training
})

# Calculation Example
optimized_allocation = network_load_balancing(traffic_data_example,
↪ resource_capacity_example)
fault_status = fault_detection(network_metrics_example)
predictive_report = predictive_analytics(historical_data_example,
↪ 'target')
personalized_service = personalize_service(user_preferences_example)
fraud_predictions = fraud_detection(transactions_example)

# Output results
print("Optimized Resource Allocation:", optimized_allocation)
print("Fault Status:", fault_status)
print("Predictive Analytics Report:\n", predictive_report)
print("Personalized Service Recommendations:", personalized_service)
print("Fraud Detection Predictions:", fraud_predictions)
```

This code defines several functions:

- `network_load_balancing` optimizes network resource allocation based on current traffic data.
- `fault_detection` detects network faults by analyzing performance metrics.
- `predictive_analytics` applies machine learning to predict future network issues.
- `personalize_service` recommends services tailored to user preferences.
- `fraud_detection` identifies potentially fraudulent transactions using a machine learning model.

The provided example executes these functions with sample data and prints the results of the operations, showcasing the application of AI in telecommunications.

Chapter 32

AI in Automation of Financial Processes

In this chapter, we delve into the applications of Artificial Intelligence (AI) in automating financial processes. As a mathematics PhD with expertise in the intersection of finance and AI, we provide a comprehensive analysis of the various ways AI can enhance and streamline financial operations. Specifically, we focus on the areas of robotic process automation, AI-driven reconciliation and accounting, predictive analytics for financial planning, fraud detection and compliance management, and AI in financial reporting and analysis.

Robotic Process Automation in Finance

Definition: Robotic Process Automation (RPA) refers to the use of software robots or bots to automate repetitive and rule-based tasks in financial processes.

Robotic Process Automation (RPA) is revolutionizing finance by automating mundane and time-consuming tasks, such as data entry, data extraction, reconciliations, and reporting. By implementing RPA, financial institutions can enhance operational efficiency, reduce errors, and improve overall process accuracy.

RPA can be employed in various financial domains, including accounts payable and receivable, general ledger, regulatory reporting, and financial statement preparation. The bots are designed to mimic human actions, interacting with different systems, databases, and applications to perform tasks at scale and with heightened accuracy.

Some key benefits of RPA in finance include:

- Improved Accuracy: RPA eliminates the potential for human errors, ensuring accurate data entry and reducing the need for manual reconciliations.

- Time and Cost Savings: Bots can process tasks much faster than humans, resulting in significant time savings and ultimately reducing costs for financial institutions.

- Scalability: RPA allows organizations to easily scale their operations by deploying additional bots to handle increased volumes of work without significant additional costs.

- Auditability and Compliance: RPA logs all transactions performed, enabling a transparent and auditable process. It also helps ensure compliance with regulatory requirements by automating the enforcement of internal controls.

Equation demonstrates how RPA can improve operational efficiency by automating a reconciliation process:

$$\text{Time Saved} = (\text{Time taken by humans to complete the process} -$$
$$\text{Time taken by bots to complete the process}) \times$$
$$\text{Number of reconciliations}$$

AI-driven Reconciliation and Accounting

Definition: AI-driven reconciliation and accounting processes involve the use of machine learning and AI techniques to automate complex matching and verification tasks in financial operations.

Reconciliation is a critical process in finance to ensure the accuracy and consistency of financial records across different systems. Traditionally, reconciliation can be a time-consuming and error-prone task, particularly in large financial institutions.

AI-driven reconciliation automates the matching and verification of financial data by leveraging machine learning algorithms. These algorithms can learn from historical reconciliation patterns, identify discrepancies, and accurately match large volumes of transactions.

The reconciliation process is often performed through three key steps:

1. Data Extraction: AI algorithms extract relevant financial transaction data from various sources, such as bank statements, invoices, and ledgers.

2. Data Matching: The algorithm compares the extracted data with corresponding records in other systems, such as the general ledger, to identify discrepancies or exceptions.

3. Exception Handling: AI-driven systems distinguish between normal and exceptional cases. Exceptions, if any, are flagged for manual review and corrective action.

By automating the reconciliation and accounting process, organizations can achieve the following benefits:

- Enhanced Accuracy: AI algorithms can accurately match and verify records, reducing errors and minimizing manual intervention.

- Time Savings: Automation significantly reduces the time required for the reconciliation process, allowing financial professionals to focus on value-added tasks.

- Scalability: AI-driven systems can handle larger volumes of transactions, enabling organizations to manage increased workflows without sacrificing accuracy or efficiency.

Predictive Analytics for Financial Planning

Definition: Predictive analytics in financial planning involves the use of statistical modeling and machine learning techniques to forecast future financial outcomes based on historical data and relevant factors.

Predictive analytics enables financial institutions to make informed decisions based on data-driven insights. By analyzing historical data, identifying patterns, and predicting future outcomes, organizations can optimize financial planning, budgeting, and resource allocation.

Financial planning areas where predictive analytics is commonly employed include revenue forecasting, expense prediction, cash flow analysis, and investment portfolio modeling. Machine learning algorithms can learn from historical trends, external market factors, and key influencers to generate accurate predictions.

Equation 32.1 represents an example of a time series forecasting model commonly used in financial planning, where y_t denotes the value of the target variable at time t, and x_t represents the relevant explanatory variables:

$$y_t = f(x_t, x_{t-1}, x_{t-2}, ..., x_{t-k}) + \epsilon_t \qquad (32.1)$$

In Equation 32.1, $f(\cdot)$ represents the underlying relationship between the variables, while ϵ_t is the random error term. The model captures the historical dependencies between the target variable and explanatory variables to forecast future values.

The benefits of employing predictive analytics in financial planning include:

- Improved Accuracy: Predictive models provide more accurate forecasts than traditional methods, enabling organizations to make more precise financial decisions.

- Scenario Planning: By leveraging predictive models, organizations can simulate various scenarios to assess the impact of potential business decisions on financial outcomes.

- Risk Assessment: Predictive analytics can identify potential risks and uncertainties by analyzing historical data and detecting anomalies or deviations from expected patterns.

Fraud Detection and Compliance Management

Definition: Fraud detection and compliance management involve the use of AI techniques to identify and prevent fraudulent activities, as well as ensure compliance with regulatory requirements.

Fraud detection in finance is a vital area where AI can play a significant role. By applying machine learning algorithms to analyze large volumes of data, financial institutions can detect and prevent fraudulent transactions, identity theft, and other illegal activities.

AI-driven fraud detection systems use advanced analytics to identify patterns, anomalies, and suspicious behaviors that indicate potential fraud. These systems continuously learn from new data to enhance their accuracy and adapt to evolving fraud patterns.

Compliance management is another critical aspect of financial operations. Financial institutions must comply with regulatory requirements, such as anti-money laundering (AML) and know-your-customer (KYC) regulations. AI enables the automation of compliance monitoring, ensuring adherence to these regulations while minimizing manual intervention.

The application of AI in fraud detection and compliance management brings several benefits, such as:

- Early Fraud Detection: AI algorithms can detect fraudulent activities in real-time, minimizing financial losses and reputational damage.

- Reduced False Positives: AI systems can improve accuracy in fraud detection by reducing false positives, thereby decreasing the number of legitimate transactions incorrectly flagged as fraudulent.

- Regulatory Compliance: AI automates compliance workflows, ensuring consistent adherence to regulatory requirements and reducing the risk of penalties or non-compliance.

AI in Financial Reporting and Analysis

Definition: AI in financial reporting and analysis involves the use of machine learning and natural language processing techniques to automate the generation of financial reports and extract insights from large volumes of financial data.

Traditional financial reporting and analysis can be a laborious task, often requiring significant manual effort to compile, analyze, and interpret data. AI offers solutions to automate these processes, allowing for more efficient, accurate, and timely financial reporting and analysis.

AI systems can extract relevant information from various sources, such as financial statements, corporate filings, news articles, and economic indicators. By analyzing this data, AI algorithms can identify important trends, detect anomalies, and provide valuable insights for decision-making.

Additionally, AI can automate report generation by leveraging natural language processing techniques. It can extract data, analyze financial narratives, and summarize key findings, facilitating the production of comprehensive reports in a fraction of the time required by manual processes.

The advantages of AI in financial reporting and analysis include:

- Time Savings: AI automates data extraction, analysis, and report generation processes, allowing financial professionals to focus on higher-value tasks.

- Data-driven Insights: AI algorithms analyze large volumes of financial data to identify important trends, outliers, and relationships, providing valuable insights for decision-making.

- Improved Accuracy: AI systems reduce the potential for human errors and biases in financial reporting, resulting in more reliable and consistent analyses.

In conclusion, AI has significant implications for automating financial processes. Through robotic process automation, reconciliation and accounting, predictive analytics, fraud detection and compliance management, and financial reporting and analysis, AI enhances operational efficiency, accuracy, and decision-making in the financial domain. As a mathematics PhD with expertise in both finance and AI, it is clear that the integration of AI techniques in financial processes has the potential to transform the industry and revolutionize how financial institutions operate.

Python Code Snippet

Below is a Python code snippet that implements the equations and algorithms discussed in the chapter on AI in Automation of Financial Processes.

```
import pandas as pd
import numpy as np

def calculate_rpa_time_saved(time_human, time_bot,
    num_reconciliations):
    '''
```

```
    Calculate the time saved by using RPA for a reconciliation
    ↪    process.
    :param time_human: Time taken by humans to complete the process
    ↪    (in hours).
    :param time_bot: Time taken by bots to complete the process (in
    ↪    hours).
    :param num_reconciliations: Number of reconciliations performed.
    :return: Total time saved (in hours).
    '''
    return (time_human - time_bot) * num_reconciliations

def ai_driven_reconciliation(transactions, records):
    '''
    Perform AI-driven reconciliation by matching transactions with
    ↪    records.
    :param transactions: DataFrame containing transactions.
    :param records: DataFrame containing records for matching.
    :return: DataFrame of matched transactions and any
    ↪    discrepancies.
    '''
    matched = pd.merge(transactions, records, how='inner',
    ↪    on='transaction_id')
    discrepancies = transactions.merge(records, how='outer',
    ↪    on='transaction_id', indicator=True).query('_merge !=
    ↪    "both"')
    return matched, discrepancies

def predictive_financial_model(data, target_var, explanatory_vars):
    '''
    Fit a predictive model for financial forecasting.
    :param data: DataFrame containing historical financial data.
    :param target_var: Column name of the target variable.
    :param explanatory_vars: List of column names of explanatory
    ↪    variables.
    :return: Fitted model and predictions.
    '''
    from sklearn.model_selection import train_test_split
    from sklearn.linear_model import LinearRegression

    X = data[explanatory_vars]
    y = data[target_var]

    X_train, X_test, y_train, y_test = train_test_split(X, y,
    ↪    test_size=0.2, random_state=42)

    model = LinearRegression()
    model.fit(X_train, y_train)
    predictions = model.predict(X_test)

    return model, predictions

def detect_fraud(transactions):
    '''
```

```
    Identify potential fraudulent transactions using a machine
    ↪  learning model.
    :param transactions: DataFrame containing transaction data.
    :return: DataFrame of flagged transactions.
    '''

    from sklearn.ensemble import IsolationForest

    model = IsolationForest(contamination=0.01)
    transactions['anomaly'] =
    ↪  model.fit_predict(transactions[['amount',
    ↪  'transaction_type']])

    return transactions[transactions['anomaly'] == -1]

# Example Data for RPA
time_taken_by_humans = 5   # Time taken by humans in hours
time_taken_by_bots = 0.5   # Time taken by bots in hours
number_of_reconciliations = 100

# Calculate time saved using RPA
time_saved = calculate_rpa_time_saved(time_taken_by_humans,
↪  time_taken_by_bots, number_of_reconciliations)
print("Time saved by RPA:", time_saved, "hours")

# Example Data for AI-driven Reconciliation
transactions_data = {
    'transaction_id': [1, 2, 3, 4, 5],
    'amount': [100, 200, 300, 400, 500]
}
records_data = {
    'transaction_id': [4, 5, 6, 7],
    'amount': [400, 500, 600, 700]
}
transactions_df = pd.DataFrame(transactions_data)
records_df = pd.DataFrame(records_data)
matched, discrepancies = ai_driven_reconciliation(transactions_df,
↪  records_df)

print("Matched Transactions:\n", matched)
print("Discrepancies:\n", discrepancies)

# Example Data for Predictive Financial Model
financial_data = {
    'revenue': [1000, 1500, 2000, 2500, 3000],
    'expenses': [800, 900, 1200, 2000, 1800],
    'profit': [200, 600, 800, 500, 1200]
}
financial_df = pd.DataFrame(financial_data)

# Fit a predictive financial model
model, predictions = predictive_financial_model(financial_df,
↪  'profit', ['revenue', 'expenses'])
print("Predictions of Profit:", predictions)
```

```
# Example Transactions for Fraud Detection
fraud_transactions_data = {
    'transaction_id': [1, 2, 3, 4, 5],
    'amount': [100, 1500, 300, 400, 100000],
    'transaction_type': ['purchase', 'withdrawal', 'purchase',
    ↪ 'withdrawal', 'withdrawal']
}
fraud_transactions_df = pd.DataFrame(fraud_transactions_data)

# Detect potential fraud
flagged_transactions = detect_fraud(fraud_transactions_df)
print("Flagged Fraudulent Transactions:\n", flagged_transactions)
```

This code snippet implements several important functions relevant to the chapter:

- `calculate_rpa_time_saved` calculates the total time saved by using robotic process automation for reconciliation.
- `ai_driven_reconciliation` matches financial transactions with records and identifies discrepancies.
- `predictive_financial_model` fits a predictive model to forecast financial outcomes based on historical data.
- `detect_fraud` uses anomaly detection to identify potentially fraudulent transactions.

The example demonstrates the application of these functions, providing insights into automation and AI's role in enhancing financial processes and reducing manual effort.

Chapter 33

AI in Travel and Tourism

The application of Artificial Intelligence (AI) in the field of travel and tourism has transformed the industry, revolutionizing various aspects from customer experience to operational efficiency. In this chapter, we will explore the different ways AI technologies are utilized in travel and tourism, providing expert insight into each area.

Predictive Analytics for Demand Forecasting

One of the most significant challenges in the travel and tourism industry is predicting demand accurately. AI-driven predictive analytics play a crucial role in forecasting future demand patterns based on historical data, external factors, and trends. These predictive models provide valuable insights that assist travel agencies and service providers in optimizing their offerings and resources.

To forecast demand, various mathematical and statistical techniques, such as time series analysis and machine learning algorithms, are employed. These models analyze historical booking data, past travel patterns, and other influencing factors such as seasonality, holidays, weather conditions, and economic indicators. The forecasting process typically involves capturing dependencies between time periods to predict future demand.

A common mathematical model used for demand forecasting is

the autoregressive integrated moving average (ARIMA) model. In its simplest form, the ARIMA(p, d, q) model predicts future values by combining three components: autoregression (AR), differencing (I), and moving average (MA). The parameters (p, d, q) represent the number of autoregressive, difference, and moving average terms, respectively.

The ARIMA model estimates future demand by regressing the current demand on past values and taking into account seasonality and other factors. The model equations for ARIMA(p, d, q) can be represented in LaTeX as follows:

$$(1-\phi_1 L-\phi_2 L^2-\ldots-\phi_p L^p)(1-L)^d Y_t = (1+\theta_1 L+\theta_2 L^2+\ldots+\theta_q L^q)\epsilon_t$$

where Y_t denotes the demand at time t, L is the lag operator (often represented as $L^d Y_t = Y_t - Y_{t-d}$ for differencing), and ϵ_t represents the error term.

By leveraging predictive analytics, travel and tourism companies can anticipate demand fluctuations, optimize pricing strategies, allocate resources efficiently, and enhance overall operational planning.

Personalized Travel Recommendations and Itineraries

AI-based recommendation systems have become an integral part of the travel and tourism industry. These systems leverage machine learning algorithms, collaborative filtering, and natural language processing to provide personalized travel recommendations and itineraries to individual customers.

Recommendation engines analyze user preferences, historical travel data, past behavior, as well as information from similar users to generate personalized suggestions. The process typically involves creating a user profile based on explicit feedback (e.g., ratings, reviews) and implicit information (e.g., search history, click-through rate). This data is then used to train machine learning models that predict the user's preferences and make tailored recommendations.

Latent factor models, such as matrix factorization, are commonly used in recommendation systems. These models represent users and items (e.g., destinations, hotels, activities) as latent factors in a low-dimensional space. The model equations can be expressed as:

$$R \approx P \cdot Q^T$$

where R is the user-item rating matrix, P represents the user-factor matrix, and Q denotes the item-factor matrix. The dot product between P and Q^T estimates the ratings for unseen user-item pairs.

By leveraging AI-driven personalized recommendations, travel companies can enhance customer satisfaction, improve engagement, and increase cross-selling and upselling opportunities.

Chatbots for Customer Inquiries

The deployment of chatbots in the travel and tourism industry has significantly transformed customer service operations. AI-powered chatbots automate customer inquiries, provide instant responses, and offer personalized assistance, enhancing the overall customer experience.

Chatbots leverage natural language processing (NLP) techniques to analyze and understand customer queries, enabling them to provide relevant and accurate responses. These systems utilize machine learning algorithms trained on vast amounts of data to improve conversation quality and understand user intent.

A commonly employed NLP technique for chatbot development is the use of recurrent neural networks (RNNs) with long short-term memory (LSTM) units. These models can capture the sequential dependencies in natural language and generate appropriate responses.

The equations for the LSTM units in an RNN can be expressed as follows:

$$f_t = \sigma(W_f \cdot [h_{t-1}, x_t] + b_f)$$
$$i_t = \sigma(W_i \cdot [h_{t-1}, x_t] + b_i)$$
$$g_t = \tanh(W_c \cdot [h_{t-1}, x_t] + b_c)$$
$$o_t = \sigma(W_o \cdot [h_{t-1}, x_t] + b_o)$$
$$c_t = f_t \odot c_{t-1} + i_t \odot g_t$$
$$h_t = o_t \odot \tanh(c_t)$$

where f_t represents the forget gate, i_t denotes the input gate, g_t represents the candidate activation, o_t denotes the output gate, c_t represents the cell state, and h_t denotes the hidden state at time t. W_f, W_i, W_c, and W_o represent weight matrices, b_f, b_i, b_c, and b_o represent bias vectors, and $\odot$ represents element-wise multiplication.

Chatbots streamline customer interactions, enable 24/7 service, and reduce response times, contributing to overall customer satisfaction and loyalty.

AI in Travel Logistics and Booking Systems

AI technologies have greatly transformed travel logistics and booking systems, improving efficiency and optimizing the overall travel experience. By leveraging AI algorithms and data-driven insights, travel companies can simplify operations, enhance customer satisfaction, and streamline travel logistics.

AI in travel logistics involves optimizing aspects such as travel routes, transportation schedules, and accommodation planning. Machine learning algorithms can analyze historical data on travel patterns, traffic congestion, flight delays, and other relevant factors to generate optimized itineraries and suggest the most efficient travel routes.

The application of AI in travel booking systems facilitates personalized recommendations, real-time availability updates, and pricing optimization. By analyzing large volumes of historical booking data, search patterns, and market trends, AI algorithms can offer the most suitable options to customers, deliver real-time pricing information, and dynamically adjust prices based on factors such as demand and availability.

Additionally, AI technologies enable automated data handling, streamlining the booking process, and reducing administrative burdens. By automating tasks such as data entry, reservation management, and payment processing, travel companies can focus on personalized customer service and higher-value tasks.

In conclusion, the integration of AI technologies in the travel and tourism industry has had a significant impact on various areas, from demand forecasting to personalized recommendations and chatbot assistance. By leveraging predictive analytics, recommendation systems, NLP algorithms, and optimization models, travel companies can enhance operational efficiency, provide personalized customer experiences, and optimize travel logistics and booking processes. As a mathematics PhD with expertise in AI, it is clear that AI has become a fundamental tool in the travel and tourism industry, driving innovation and transforming the way travel services are offered and experienced.

Python Code Snippet

Below is a comprehensive Python code snippet that implements the important equations and algorithms discussed in the chapter, including demand forecasting using the ARIMA model, personalized travel recommendations utilizing matrix factorization, and a chatbot utilizing LSTM-based natural language processing.

```python
import numpy as np
import pandas as pd
import statsmodels.api as sm
from sklearn.decomposition import NMF

# Function for ARIMA model forecasting
def arima_forecasting(data, order):
    '''
    Perform ARIMA forecasting.
    :param data: Time series data.
    :param order: Tuple of (p, d, q) parameters for the ARIMA model.
    :return: Forecasted values.
    '''
    model = sm.tsa.ARIMA(data, order=order)
    model_fit = model.fit()
    forecast = model_fit.forecast(steps=5)  # Forecasting next 5
    ↪    periods
    return forecast

# Example time series data for demand forecasting
demand_data = pd.Series([150, 160, 170, 155, 165, 185, 160])  #
↪  Historical demand data
arima_order = (1, 1, 1)  # ARIMA(p, d, q) order
forecasted_demand = arima_forecasting(demand_data, arima_order)
print("Forecasted Demand (ARIMA):", forecasted_demand)

# Function for matrix factorization in personalized recommendations
def recommend_items(user_item_matrix, n_components=2):
    '''
    Generate recommendations based on matrix factorization.
    :param user_item_matrix: User-item ratings matrix.
    :param n_components: Number of factors.
    :return: User and item factor matrices.
    '''
    nmf = NMF(n_components=n_components)
    user_factors = nmf.fit_transform(user_item_matrix)
    item_factors = nmf.components_
```

229

```
    return user_factors, item_factors

# Example user-item rating matrix
ratings_matrix = np.array([[5, 3, 0, 1],
                           [4, 0, 0, 1],
                           [1, 1, 0, 5],
                           [1, 0, 0, 4],
                           [0, 1, 5, 4]])
user_factors, item_factors = recommend_items(ratings_matrix,
↪  n_components=2)
print("User Factors:\n", user_factors)
print("Item Factors:\n", item_factors)

# Function for chatbot implementation using LSTM
def chatbot_response(input_sequence):
    '''
    Simulated response for a chatbot using a sequence input.
    :param input_sequence: Input sequence to the chatbot.
    :return: Simulated response.
    '''
    # In a real application, this would involve a trained LSTM model
    response_dict = {
        "Hello": "Hi! How can I assist you today?",
        "Book a flight": "Sure! Where would you like to fly?",
        "Help": "I'm here to help you with travel queries.",
    }
    return response_dict.get(input_sequence, "I'm sorry, I didn't
↪  understand that.")

# Simulating chatbot interaction
user_input = "Book a flight"
response = chatbot_response(user_input)
print("Chatbot Response:", response)
```

This code defines three key functions:

- arima_forecasting implements the ARIMA model to forecast future demand based on historical time series data.
- recommend_items uses matrix factorization to analyze user-item ratings and generate personalized recommendations.
- chatbot_response simulates a simple chatbot that provides responses based on user input.

The provided example demonstrates forecasting demand using the ARIMA model, generating personalized recommendations from a user-item rating matrix, and simulating a chatbot interaction for travel inquiries.

Chapter 34

AI in Aerospace Engineering

Aerospace engineering plays a critical role in the design, development, and utilization of aircraft and spacecraft. With the advent of Artificial Intelligence (AI), various applications have emerged in the field, revolutionizing aerospace engineering and bringing about significant advancements. In this chapter, we will delve into the ways in which AI is being employed in aerospace engineering, providing expert insight into each area.

Design Optimization and Simulation

The design and optimization of aerospace systems are essential to ensure efficiency, safety, and performance. AI techniques have been instrumental in enhancing the design process and reducing development time.

One application of AI in aerospace design is the utilization of genetic algorithms (GAs). GAs mimic the process of natural selection and evolution to find optimal solutions to complex problems. In the context of aerospace engineering, GAs can be employed to optimize parameters such as airfoil shapes, wing geometries, and propulsion system configurations. By iteratively evolving a population of potential solutions and applying selection and mutation operators, GAs can identify optimal designs that meet predefined objectives, such as minimizing drag or maximizing lift.

Another area where AI is applied is in the simulation of aerospace systems. AI techniques, including machine learning and neural networks, can be trained on vast amounts of data generated from flight simulations, wind tunnel experiments, and real flight data. These trained models can then predict the behavior and performance of aerospace systems under various operating conditions. By leveraging these simulations, engineers can refine designs, assess the impact of different parameters, and optimize system performance.

Predictive Maintenance and Diagnostics

Efficient operations and maintenance are crucial in the aerospace industry to ensure safety and minimize downtime. AI plays a vital role in predictive maintenance and diagnostics by monitoring the health of aerospace systems, detecting anomalies, and predicting failures before they occur.

With AI, engineers can develop models that analyze sensor data from aircraft or spacecraft, ranging from temperature and pressure measurements to vibration patterns. These models use techniques such as machine learning and deep learning to identify normal system behavior and detect deviations that may indicate potential faults or failures. By continuously monitoring the health of various components, AI algorithms can predict maintenance requirements, enabling proactive maintenance scheduling and minimizing the risk of unplanned downtime.

Moreover, AI techniques can be employed to diagnose the root causes of faults or failures in aerospace systems. By combining historical data, system models, physics-based simulations, and AI algorithms, engineers can identify the underlying issues contributing to malfunctions. This diagnostic capability helps streamline troubleshooting, minimize repair time, and optimize maintenance procedures.

Autonomous Flight and Navigation Systems

AI has been instrumental in the development of autonomous flight and navigation systems, enabling advanced capabilities and enhancing safety in aerospace operations.

In autonomous flight, AI algorithms analyze sensor data, such as radar, lidar, and camera inputs, to understand the environment and make real-time decisions. Reinforcement learning techniques can be employed to train autonomous flight systems by providing rewards or penalties based on the system's actions. This iterative learning process allows the system to optimize its behavior and make intelligent decisions, such as route planning, obstacle avoidance, and landing maneuvers.

Navigation systems in aerospace engineering benefit from AI algorithms capable of processing large amounts of data and providing precise positioning and guidance. Global Navigation Satellite Systems (GNSS) combined with AI techniques enable accurate navigation, even in challenging environments where signals may be weak or blocked. AI algorithms can integrate data from various sensors, such as GNSS, inertial measurement units (IMUs), and vision systems, to enhance positioning accuracy and provide reliable navigation information.

AI in Mission Planning and Execution

Mission planning and execution in aerospace engineering involve complex decision-making processes that require considering various constraints, objectives, and uncertainties. AI techniques are employed to optimize mission planning, enhance situational awareness, and enable adaptive decision-making.

In mission planning, AI algorithms can generate optimal routes, plan fuel-efficient trajectories, and allocate resources efficiently. Genetic algorithms and other optimization techniques can optimize these mission planning processes, taking into account factors such as payload requirements, fuel consumption, weather conditions, and airspace restrictions. By leveraging AI, aerospace engineers can identify suitable mission profiles that maximize operational effectiveness while considering various constraints.

During mission execution, AI techniques enable adaptive decision-making based on real-time data and evolving scenarios. Machine learning algorithms can analyze the state of the aircraft or spacecraft, assess external factors such as weather conditions, and make autonomous decisions to ensure mission success and safety. These algorithms can adjust flight parameters, modify trajectories, and optimize operations in response to changing conditions, enhancing the efficiency and effectiveness of aerospace missions.

In conclusion, the integration of AI technologies in aerospace engineering has revolutionized the field, offering new opportunities for design optimization, predictive maintenance, autonomous systems, and adaptive decision-making. By leveraging AI algorithms, aerospace engineers can enhance the efficiency, safety, and performance of aircraft and spacecraft, paving the way for advanced aerospace technologies of the future. As a Mathematics PhD with expertise in AI, it is clear that AI is transforming aerospace engineering, enabling the development of more efficient and intelligent aerospace systems.

Python Code Snippet

Below is a Python code snippet that implements some key algorithms and formulas mentioned in the chapter, including genetic algorithms for design optimization, predictive maintenance using machine learning, and basic autonomous flight decision-making.

```python
import numpy as np
from sklearn.ensemble import RandomForestClassifier
from sklearn.model_selection import train_test_split
from sklearn.metrics import accuracy_score

# Genetic Algorithm for Design Optimization
def genetic_algorithm(population_size, generations, mutation_rate,
↪  objective_function):
    '''
    This function implements a simple genetic algorithm.
    :param population_size: Number of individuals in the population.
    :param generations: Number of generations for evolution.
    :param mutation_rate: Probability of mutation for an individual.
    :param objective_function: Function to optimize.
    :return: Best individual found.
    '''
    # Generate initial random population
    population = np.random.rand(population_size, 2)  # Assume 2D
    ↪  parameter space

    for _ in range(generations):
        # Evaluate fitness
        fitness = np.apply_along_axis(objective_function, 1,
        ↪  population)

        # Select parents based on fitness
        selected_indices =
        ↪  np.random.choice(np.arange(population_size),
        ↪  size=population_size // 2, p=fitness/fitness.sum())
        parents = population[selected_indices]

        # Crossover to create next generation
```

```python
        children = []
        for i in range(len(parents)):
            for j in range(i + 1, len(parents)):
                crossover_point = np.random.randint(2)   # Assuming
                ↪  2D parameters
                child =
                ↪  np.concatenate((parents[i][:crossover_point],
                ↪  parents[j][crossover_point:]))
                children.append(child)

        # Mutation
        for i in range(len(children)):
            if np.random.rand() < mutation_rate:
                mutation = np.random.normal(0, 0.1,
                ↪  size=children[i].shape)
                children[i] += mutation
                children[i] = np.clip(children[i], 0, 1)   # Ensure
                ↪  boundaries

        population = np.vstack((parents, children))

    best_individual =
    ↪  population[np.argmax(np.apply_along_axis(objective_function,
    ↪  1, population))]
    return best_individual

def example_objective_function(parameters):
    '''
    Example of an objective function to minimize.
    :param parameters: Parameters to evaluate.
    :return: Negative value to maximize (as an example).
    '''
    return -1 * (parameters[0]**2 + parameters[1]**2)   #
    ↪  Optimization to minimize the distance from origin

# Predictive Maintenance using Machine Learning
def train_predictive_model(X, y):
    '''
    Train a predictive maintenance model using Random Forest.
    :param X: Features (sensor data).
    :param y: Labels (status: normal or fault).
    :return: Trained model.
    '''
    X_train, X_test, y_train, y_test = train_test_split(X, y,
    ↪  test_size=0.2, random_state=42)
    model = RandomForestClassifier()
    model.fit(X_train, y_train)

    # Predicting on test set
    predictions = model.predict(X_test)
    accuracy = accuracy_score(y_test, predictions)
    print("Model accuracy:", accuracy)
    return model
```

235

```
# Autonomous Flight Decision Making
def make_flight_decision(sensor_data):
    '''
    Simple function to make flight decisions based on sensor data.
    :param sensor_data: Array of sensor input data.
    :return: Decision to execute.
    '''

    if sensor_data[0] < 100:   # Example condition (e.g., altitude)
        return "Ascend"
    elif sensor_data[0] > 200:
        return "Descend"
    else:
        return "Maintain Altitude"

# Example usage
best_design = genetic_algorithm(population_size=100, generations=50,
↪    mutation_rate=0.1,
↪    objective_function=example_objective_function)
print("Best design parameters found:", best_design)

# Example data for predictive maintenance
X_data = np.random.rand(100, 5)   # Simulated sensor data
y_labels = np.random.choice([0, 1], size=100)   # Simulated labels: 0
↪    = normal, 1 = fault
trained_model = train_predictive_model(X_data, y_labels)

# Example sensor data for decision making
sensor_inputs = np.array([150])   # Example sensor data input
flight_decision = make_flight_decision(sensor_inputs)
print("Flight decision:", flight_decision)
```

This code defines several functions:

- genetic_algorithm implements a genetic algorithm for design optimization based on an objective function.
- example_objective_function is a simple function used to evaluate the designs produced by the genetic algorithm.
- train_predictive_model trains a machine learning model for predictive maintenance using a Random Forest classifier.
- make_flight_decision evaluates sensor data inputs and makes decisions for autonomous flight operations.

The provided example illustrates how to find the best design parameters using a genetic algorithm, train a predictive maintenance model, and make basic flight decisions based on sensor data.

Chapter 35

AI in Industrial Design

In the realm of industrial design, artificial intelligence (AI) has emerged as a powerful tool, revolutionizing various aspects of the design process. By harnessing AI techniques, designers can optimize their processes, enhance product functionality, and create innovative and efficient solutions. In this chapter, we will delve into the applications of AI in industrial design, providing expert insight into each area.

AI-driven Product Design and Prototyping

AI is transforming the way products are designed and developed, enabling designers to explore a broader design space and optimize designs efficiently. By leveraging machine learning algorithms and generative design techniques, AI-driven product design automates and streamlines the traditional design process.

Generative design algorithms utilize optimization methods and design constraints to iteratively generate and evaluate design alternatives. By considering factors such as material properties, manufacturing constraints, and performance requirements, AI algorithms can efficiently explore a vast solution space and produce optimized designs. This approach allows designers to quickly evaluate and compare multiple design iterations, leading to improved product performance and reduced development time.

AI-driven product design also incorporates prototyping techniques that employ rapid manufacturing technologies such as 3D printing. By integrating AI algorithms with these technologies, designers can automate the prototyping process and quickly produce physical prototypes. This acceleration enables designers to validate their design concepts, conduct testing, and gather feedback early in the design iteration, saving time and resources.

Predictive Analytics for Market Trends

Predicting and understanding market trends is a crucial aspect of industrial design, facilitating the development and launch of successful products. AI techniques, including machine learning and data analytics, enable designers to extract valuable insights from large volumes of market data, providing a competitive edge.

Machine learning algorithms can analyze historical market data, including customer preferences, sales figures, and market trends, to identify patterns and make predictions. By utilizing regression models, classification algorithms, and time series analysis, designers can forecast demand, identify emerging trends, and make data-driven decisions regarding product features, pricing, and marketing strategies.

Furthermore, sentiment analysis, a natural language processing (NLP) technique, can be employed to analyze customer feedback, reviews, and social media sentiments. By understanding customer preferences, perceptions, and pain points, designers can gain valuable insights into product improvements, identify new market opportunities, and enhance the overall user experience.

Automated Testing and Iteration

The testing and iteration phase is vital in industrial design to ensure product performance, reliability, and compliance with standards. AI techniques offer automation and optimization capabilities that simplify and enhance the testing process.

AI algorithms can automate various aspects of product testing, including analysis of simulation data, sensor measurements, and physical prototypes. By leveraging machine learning techniques, these algorithms can identify potential design flaws, predict failure modes, and recommend design modifications. This enables designers to address issues early in the development process, reducing the cost and time associated with physical testing.

Moreover, AI algorithms can optimize the design iteration process by intelligently exploring design alternatives based on simulation results and user feedback. By employing techniques such as reinforcement learning and evolutionary algorithms, designers can navigate the design space more effectively and discover innovative solutions. This automation and optimization of the design iteration process enable designers to create high-performing, reliable, and cost-effective products.

Customization and Personalization in Design

In today's market, consumers increasingly demand personalized and customized products tailored to their unique needs and preferences. AI techniques allow designers to deliver customization and personalization at scale, providing individualized experiences to customers.

AI algorithms can analyze customer data, such as demographics, behavior, and purchase history, to understand individual preferences and generate customized design recommendations. These algorithms leverage techniques such as collaborative filtering, content-based filtering, and deep learning to match customer preferences with design attributes. By incorporating these personalized design elements, designers can create products that resonate with customers on a personal level, increasing customer satisfaction and loyalty.

Furthermore, AI-powered design tools enable users to engage directly in the design process, offering interactive interfaces and parametric design capabilities. Users can personalize product attributes, modify design parameters, and visualize the customized product in real-time. This co-creation process enhances user engagement, fosters creativity, and ensures that the final product meets individual requirements.

Supply Chain Optimization in Industrial Design

Efficient supply chain management is critical for industrial design, ensuring timely production, cost-effectiveness, and sustainability.

AI techniques facilitate supply chain optimization by analyzing large-scale data, optimizing logistics, and minimizing inefficiencies.

Machine learning algorithms can analyze historical supply chain data, including inventory levels, manufacturing lead times, and transportation costs, to identify patterns and optimize resource allocation. These algorithms can predict demand, optimize production schedules, and recommend inventory levels, minimizing waste and optimizing resource utilization.

Furthermore, AI techniques enable intelligent logistics management by considering factors such as transportation routes, carrier selection, and delivery schedules. Optimization algorithms can determine the most cost-effective routes, minimize shipping delays, and reduce carbon footprints, promoting sustainability in industrial design operations.

In conclusion, the integration of AI techniques in industrial design offers significant opportunities to enhance the design process, optimize product functionality, and deliver personalized experiences to customers. By leveraging AI algorithms, designers can overcome traditional constraints, unlock innovative design solutions, and streamline the entire product development lifecycle. As a Mathematics PhD with expertise in AI, it is evident that AI is revolutionizing industrial design, paving the way for more efficient and creative product development approaches.

Python Code Snippet

Below is a Python code snippet that demonstrates various algorithms and formulas relevant to industrial design, including generative design optimization, predictive analytics, automated testing, and customization.

```python
import numpy as np
import pandas as pd
from sklearn.linear_model import LinearRegression
from sklearn.metrics import mean_squared_error

def generative_design(objective_function, constraints,
    num_iterations=1000):
    '''
    Simulate generative design optimization.
    :param objective_function: Function to minimize.
    :param constraints: Constraints on the design variables.
    :param num_iterations: Number of iterations for optimization.
    :return: Optimal design variable values and the objective value.
```

```
    '''
    best_design = None
    best_value = float('inf')

    for _ in range(num_iterations):
        design = np.random.uniform(constraints[0], constraints[1])
        value = objective_function(design)
        if value < best_value:
            best_value = value
            best_design = design

    return best_design, best_value

def predict_market_trends(data):
    '''
    Predict market trends using linear regression.
    :param data: DataFrame containing historical sales data.
    :return: Predictions for future sales.
    '''
    X = np.array(data['month']).reshape(-1, 1)
    y = np.array(data['sales']).reshape(-1, 1)

    model = LinearRegression()
    model.fit(X, y)

    future_months = np.array([[i] for i in range(len(data),
    ↪   len(data) + 12)])  # Next 12 months
    predictions = model.predict(future_months)

    return predictions.flatten()

def automated_testing(simulated_data, threshold):
    '''
    Analyze simulated data to identify potential design flaws.
    :param simulated_data: Array of simulation results.
    :param threshold: Threshold for failure.
    :return: List of indices where failures occurred.
    '''
    failure_indices = np.where(simulated_data > threshold)[0]
    return failure_indices.tolist()

def customize_product(customer_data):
    '''
    Provide customizations based on customer preferences.
    :param customer_data: List of customer attributes.
    :return: Customized product recommendations.
    '''
    customizations = []
    for customer in customer_data:
        if customer['preference'] == 'eco-friendly':
            customizations.append({'color': 'green', 'material':
            ↪   'recycled'})
        else:
```

241

```
            customizations.append({'color': 'standard', 'material':
            ↪  'standard'})
        return customizations

# Example usage
# Generative Design
constraints = [0, 1]  # A design variable range
def objective_function(x):
        return (x - 0.5) ** 2  # Example: minimize distance from 0.5

optimal_design, optimal_value =
↪  generative_design(objective_function, constraints)
print("Optimal Design:", optimal_design, "Objective Value:",
↪  optimal_value)

# Predict Market Trends
historical_data = pd.DataFrame({
        'month': range(1, 25),
        'sales': np.random.randint(100, 200, size=24)
})
predictions = predict_market_trends(historical_data)
print("Predicted Sales for Next 12 Months:", predictions)

# Automated Testing
simulated_results = np.random.random(100)  # Example simulation
↪  data
failure_list = automated_testing(simulated_results, 0.8)
print("Failure Indices:", failure_list)

# Customize Product
customer_info = [{'preference': 'eco-friendly'}, {'preference':
↪  'standard'}]
recommendations = customize_product(customer_info)
print("Customization Recommendations:", recommendations)
```

This code includes several functions:

- `generative_design` simulates a generative design optimization process.
- `predict_market_trends` utilizes linear regression to forecast future sales based on historical data.
- `automated_testing` identifies potential design flaws by analyzing simulation data.
- `customize_product` generates product customization options based on customer preferences.

The example demonstrates the use of AI techniques in industrial design, showcasing optimization, prediction, testing, and personalization functionalities. "'

Chapter 36

AI in Electrical Engineering

In this chapter, we will explore the applications of Artificial Intelligence (AI) techniques in the field of Electrical Engineering. AI has emerged as a powerful tool, revolutionizing various aspects of electrical engineering, including power systems optimization, electric vehicle design, semiconductor manufacturing, and energy-efficient systems. As a Mathematics PhD with expertise in AI, I will provide expert insight into the applications and mathematical foundations behind these AI-driven advancements.

Optimizing Power Systems and Grid Management

AI techniques play a crucial role in optimizing power systems, improving their efficiency, stability, and reliability. By leveraging machine learning and optimization algorithms, electrical engineers can tackle key challenges, such as load balancing, energy forecasting, and grid management.

One key application is load forecasting, where AI algorithms utilize historical load data, weather patterns, and other relevant factors to predict future power demands. Time series analysis, regression models, and deep learning techniques enable accurate load forecasting, facilitating optimal resource allocation and reducing peak demand fluctuations.

Moreover, AI algorithms can optimize power generation and distribution systems by minimizing transmission losses, voltage fluctuations, and optimizing energy flow. Techniques such as optimal power flow (OPF) and economic dispatch (ED) utilize mathematical optimization to allocate power generation resources efficiently, considering factors like generation costs, demand, and transmission constraints.

Predictive Maintenance of Electrical Infrastructure

AI techniques, such as machine learning and data analytics, play a vital role in the predictive maintenance of electrical infrastructure, ensuring reliable operation, minimizing downtime, and reducing maintenance costs. By leveraging historical operational data, sensor measurements, and maintenance records, AI algorithms can identify potential equipment failures and recommend maintenance actions.

Machine learning algorithms, including decision trees, support vector machines (SVM), and neural networks, can effectively process sensor data to detect anomalies and predict equipment failures. By analyzing patterns and deviations from normal behavior, these algorithms can issue warnings and schedule maintenance actions proactively.

Additionally, AI algorithms can optimize maintenance scheduling by considering factors such as equipment criticality, cost, and availability of resources. Through techniques like reinforcement learning and genetic algorithms, optimal maintenance strategies can be determined, minimizing costs and maximizing equipment availability.

Smart Grid Technology

Smart grid technology is revolutionizing the electrical power distribution system, facilitating efficient energy management, reducing carbon emissions, and improving system reliability. AI plays a crucial role in enabling various components of the smart grid, including advanced metering infrastructure, demand response, and distributed energy resources.

One important aspect is demand response, where AI algorithms enable consumers to modify their electricity consumption based on real-time price signals or grid conditions. By leveraging techniques like reinforcement learning and optimization algorithms, AI-equipped smart grids can dynamically adjust electricity prices and incentivize load shifting, facilitating grid stability and reducing peak demand.

Furthermore, AI algorithms can optimize the integration of distributed energy resources (DERs), such as solar panels and wind turbines, into the grid. By considering variables like weather patterns, electricity prices, and demand forecasts, these algorithms can intelligently control DERs, optimizing their output and minimizing the reliance on traditional power sources.

AI in Electric Vehicle Design

AI techniques are revolutionizing the design and optimization of electric vehicles (EVs), enhancing their performance, range, and charging efficiency. By leveraging AI algorithms, electrical engineers can address fundamental challenges like battery management, charging infrastructure optimization, and powertrain design.

Battery management systems (BMS) are critical for EV performance and longevity. AI techniques, including machine learning and estimation algorithms, enable accurate state-of-charge (SOC) and state-of-health (SOH) predictions, optimizing battery usage and prolonging battery life.

Additionally, AI algorithms can optimize charging infrastructure placement, considering factors like travel patterns, charging demand, and energy grid constraints. By employing techniques like clustering analysis and optimization algorithms, engineers can determine optimal locations for charging stations, ensuring convenient access and minimizing infrastructure costs.

Moreover, AI plays a crucial role in powertrain design optimization. By utilizing techniques like reinforcement learning and simulation-based design, engineers can optimize powertrain components, such as motors, inverters, and energy management systems, improving overall vehicle efficiency and range.

Energy-Efficient Systems and Solutions

AI techniques are increasingly used to design and optimize energy-efficient systems, ensuring sustainable and environmentally friendly solutions. Electrical engineers can utilize AI algorithms to reduce energy consumption, optimize system performance, and minimize carbon footprints.

Advanced control algorithms, such as model predictive control (MPC) and fuzzy logic control, enable real-time optimization of energy-consuming systems, like heating, ventilation, and air conditioning (HVAC) systems. These algorithms consider variables such as occupancy, temperature, and electricity prices to dynamically adjust system parameters, maximizing energy efficiency while maintaining user comfort.

Another application is the design optimization of energy-efficient circuits and systems. AI algorithms, such as genetic algorithms and evolutionary strategies, can explore large design spaces to identify optimal circuit topologies, component values, and energy-saving techniques. By optimizing power consumption at the circuit level, overall system efficiency can be significantly improved.

In conclusion, AI plays a vital role in various domains of electrical engineering, revolutionizing power systems optimization, predictive maintenance, electric vehicle design, and energy-efficient systems. By leveraging AI techniques, engineers can tackle complex challenges, optimize energy utilization, and contribute to sustainability in the field of electrical engineering.Certainly! Below is a comprehensive Python code snippet that illustrates key equations and algorithms mentioned in the chapter related to AI applications in electrical engineering. This code includes examples of load forecasting, predictive maintenance, and optimization in smart grid technology.

Python Code Snippet

Below is a Python code snippet that showcases key algorithms and formulas for optimizing power systems, predictive maintenance of electrical infrastructure, and energy-efficient systems.

```python
import numpy as np
from sklearn.linear_model import LinearRegression
from sklearn.ensemble import RandomForestRegressor
from sklearn.metrics import mean_squared_error
```

246

```python
# Load Forecasting using Linear Regression
def load_forecasting(X_train, y_train, X_test):
    '''
    Predict future load using linear regression.
    :param X_train: Features for training (historical data).
    :param y_train: Load demand for training.
    :param X_test: Features for testing (future data).
    :return: Predicted load.
    '''
    model = LinearRegression()
    model.fit(X_train, y_train)
    predictions = model.predict(X_test)
    return predictions


# Predictive Maintenance using Random Forest
def equipment_failure_prediction(X, y):
    '''
    Predict potential equipment failures using random forest.
    :param X: Features including sensor data.
    :param y: Labels (failure or not).
    :return: Random forest classifier.
    '''
    model = RandomForestRegressor()
    model.fit(X, y)
    return model


# Function to calculate optimal power flow (OPF) using gradient
↪   descent
def optimal_power_flow(demand, generation_capacity,
↪   max_iterations=100):
    '''
    Optimize power flow considering demand and generation capacity.
    :param demand: Electricity demand.
    :param generation_capacity: Available generation capacity.
    :param max_iterations: Maximum iterations for convergence.
    :return: Optimal power output from generators.
    '''
    generation_output = np.ones_like(demand) * (generation_capacity
    ↪   / len(demand))  # Initial guess
    for _ in range(max_iterations):
        adjustment = (demand - generation_output).mean()
        generation_output += adjustment
    return generation_output.clip(0, generation_capacity)  #
    ↪   Constraint on generation capacity


# Example Inputs Data
# Historical load data
X_train = np.array([[1, 0], [2, 1], [3, 3], [4, 2]])  # Features
↪   (e.g., time, temperature)
```

```
y_train = np.array([100, 150, 200, 250])  # Corresponding load
↪   demand
X_test = np.array([[5, 3]])  # Future features for prediction

# Predict future load
predicted_load = load_forecasting(X_train, y_train, X_test)
print("Predicted Load: ", predicted_load)

# Sample sensor data for predictive maintenance
sensor_data = np.array([[1, 50], [2, 30], [1, 60], [2, 20]])
failure_labels = np.array([0, 1, 0, 1])  # 0: No failure, 1: Failure

# Train equipment failure prediction model
failure_model = equipment_failure_prediction(sensor_data,
↪   failure_labels)

# Example of optimal power flow calculation
demand = np.array([100, 150, 200, 250])  # Load demand
generation_capacity = 300  # Total generation capacity

optimal_generation = optimal_power_flow(demand, generation_capacity)
print("Optimal Generation Output: ", optimal_generation)
```

This code defines several key functions:

- load_forecasting predicts future electricity load using a linear regression model based on historical data.
- equipment_failure_prediction applies a random forest approach to predict potential equipment failures from sensor data.
- optimal_power_flow manages power flow optimization within a predefined generation capacity using a simple iterative approach.

The provided example uses historical data for load prediction, trains a predictive maintenance model for equipment failures, and computes optimal power generation outputs based on demand and capacity constraints, printing the results accordingly.

Chapter 37

AI in Civil Engineering

Predictive Analytics for Infrastructure Maintenance

In civil engineering, the maintenance of infrastructure is of utmost importance to ensure safety and longevity. Artificial Intelligence (AI) techniques, such as predictive analytics, play a crucial role in identifying potential issues and optimizing maintenance strategies.

Predictive analytics utilizes historical data, sensor measurements, and simulation models to predict the degradation and performance of infrastructure components. By analyzing patterns and correlations, engineers can estimate the remaining useful life of structures, such as bridges or buildings, and make informed decisions regarding maintenance activities.

One common approach for predicting infrastructure degradation is the use of regression models. By considering various factors, such as environmental conditions, traffic loads, and material properties, engineers can formulate regression equations to estimate degradation rates and anticipate future maintenance needs.

Smart City Planning and Management

The concept of smart cities incorporates AI techniques to optimize urban planning, development, and resource management. By leveraging data from various sources, including sensors, social media, and public records, AI algorithms can provide valuable insights for decision-making.

AI plays a crucial role in optimizing transportation systems and mitigating traffic congestion. Through techniques like machine learning and optimization algorithms, engineers can analyze real-time traffic data to identify congestion patterns, optimize traffic signal timings, and predict demand for future planning.

Moreover, AI algorithms can enhance energy management in smart cities by optimizing power distribution, load balancing, and demand response. By considering factors like weather conditions, energy prices, and user preferences, these algorithms can optimize energy consumption, reduce peak demand, and facilitate the integration of renewable energy sources.

AI-Driven Construction Project Management

Managing construction projects involves complex tasks such as scheduling, resource allocation, and risk assessment. AI techniques can improve efficiency and reduce costs in construction project management by optimizing these processes.

AI algorithms, including machine learning and optimization techniques, can automatically generate construction schedules and optimize resource allocation. By considering factors such as project scope, resource availability, and constraints, these algorithms can generate efficient schedules that minimize project duration and cost.

Furthermore, AI can assist in risk assessment and mitigation strategies. By analyzing historical project data, AI algorithms can identify potential risks and predict their impact on project schedules and costs. This enables proactive risk management and the development of contingency plans to minimize project delays and cost overruns.

Safety Monitoring and Incident Prediction

Maintaining safety in construction sites is crucial to prevent accidents and ensure worker well-being. AI techniques, such as computer vision and sensor data analysis, can enhance safety monitoring and predict potential incidents.

Computer vision algorithms can analyze video feeds from construction sites to detect unsafe conditions, such as workers not wearing appropriate protective equipment or violations of safety protocols. By leveraging image recognition and object detection techniques, these algorithms can issue real-time alerts and reminders to ensure compliance with safety standards.

Sensor data analysis is another vital aspect of safety monitoring in construction. By analyzing data from sensors installed on equipment or within construction materials, AI algorithms can identify potential hazards, such as equipment malfunctions or structural weaknesses. Predictive analytics can then be used to forecast potential incidents and plan preventive actions.

AI-Driven Optimization of Geotechnical Solutions

Geotechnical engineering involves analyzing the behavior of soil and rock in engineering projects. AI techniques can optimize geotechnical solutions, such as foundation design, slope stability analysis, and excavation planning.

Machine learning algorithms can leverage historical geotechnical data, including soil samples, rock properties, and project outcomes, to predict the behavior of soil and make informed decisions regarding foundation design. These algorithms can identify correlations between soil properties and project performance, enabling engineers to optimize designs for specific soil conditions.

Furthermore, AI can assist in slope stability analysis by considering factors such as soil composition, rainfall patterns, and slope geometry. By simulating various scenarios and analyzing data, AI algorithms can predict potential slope failures and recommend stabilization measures.

AI algorithms can also optimize excavation planning by analyzing geological data and simulating excavation scenarios. By considering factors such as soil strength, groundwater levels, and equipment limitations, these algorithms can optimize excavation strategies to minimize costs, maximize safety, and ensure project efficiency.

In conclusion, AI techniques offer significant potential in civil engineering by enhancing predictive analytics, optimizing construction project management, improving safety monitoring, and optimizing geotechnical solutions. By leveraging AI algorithms, engineers can make informed decisions, optimize resources, and enhance the overall efficiency and sustainability of infrastructure development.

Python Code Snippet

Below is a Python code snippet that implements key algorithms discussed in the chapter regarding predictive analytics for infrastructure maintenance, smart city planning and management, and safety monitoring.

```python
import numpy as np
import pandas as pd
import matplotlib.pyplot as plt
from sklearn.model_selection import train_test_split
from sklearn.linear_model import LinearRegression
from sklearn.metrics import mean_squared_error

# Predictive Analytics for Infrastructure Maintenance
def predict_infrastructure_degradation(data):
    '''
    Predict the degradation of infrastructure components using
    ↪ regression.
    :param data: DataFrame containing historical degradation data
    ↪ and influencing factors.
    :return: Estimated remaining useful life and mean squared error
    ↪ of the model.
    '''

    X = data.drop('degradation', axis=1)  # Features
    y = data['degradation']  # Target variable

    # Splitting the data into training and testing sets
    X_train, X_test, y_train, y_test = train_test_split(X, y,
    ↪ test_size=0.2, random_state=42)

    # Creating a linear regression model
    model = LinearRegression()
    model.fit(X_train, y_train)

    # Predictions and performance evaluation
    predictions = model.predict(X_test)
    mse = mean_squared_error(y_test, predictions)

    return predictions, mse


# Smart City Planning and Management
def optimize_traffic_flow(traffic_data):
    '''
```

```
    Optimize traffic flow in a smart city using traffic data.
    :param traffic_data: DataFrame containing real-time traffic
    ↪   data.
    :return: Suggested traffic signal timings.
    '''
    # Analyze patterns in traffic data (dummy implementation)
    avg_traffic_volume = traffic_data.mean(axis=0)

    # Setting traffic signal timings based on average volumes (dummy
    ↪   logic)
    signal_timings = avg_traffic_volume / avg_traffic_volume.sum() *
    ↪   60  # Seconds per signal phase

    return signal_timings


# Safety Monitoring and Incident Prediction
def detect_unsafe_conditions(video_data):
    '''
    Detect unsafe conditions using image processing on video data.
    :param video_data: Array of images from the construction site.
    :return: List of alerts based on detected unsafe conditions.
    '''
    # Dummy implementation of safety detection (e.g., using CNN)
    alerts = []
    for frame in video_data:
        # Placeholder for real object detection logic
        if np.random.rand() > 0.8:  # Simulates detection of unsafe
        ↪   condition with randomness
            alerts.append("Unsafe condition detected!")
    return alerts


# Sample Usage
if __name__ == "__main__":
    # Simulated data for infrastructure degradation prediction
    historical_data = pd.DataFrame({
        'environmental_condition': np.random.rand(100),
        'traffic_load': np.random.rand(100),
        'material_quality': np.random.rand(100),
        'degradation': np.random.rand(100) * 100  # Degradation
        ↪   percentage
    })

    # Predicting infrastructure degradation
    predictions, mse =
    ↪   predict_infrastructure_degradation(historical_data)
    print("Predicted Degradation:", predictions)
    print("Mean Squared Error:", mse)

    # Simulated traffic data for optimizing flow
    traffic_data = pd.DataFrame({
        'morning_rush': np.random.randint(0, 100, size=50),
```

```
        'midday_traffic': np.random.randint(0, 100, size=50),
        'evening_rush': np.random.randint(0, 100, size=50)
})

# Optimizing traffic flow
traffic_signal_timings = optimize_traffic_flow(traffic_data)
print("Optimized Traffic Signal Timings (seconds):",
↪  traffic_signal_timings)

# Simulated video data for safety monitoring
video_data = [np.random.rand(224, 224, 3) for _ in range(10)]  #
↪  Simulated frames

# Detecting unsafe conditions
safety_alerts = detect_unsafe_conditions(video_data)
print("Safety Alerts:", safety_alerts)
```

In this code, we define three functions:

- `predict_infrastructure_degradation` creates a predictive model for infrastructure degradation using regression techniques based on historical data.
- `optimize_traffic_flow` suggests optimal traffic signal timings based on average traffic volumes.
- `detect_unsafe_conditions` simulates the detection of unsafe conditions in a construction environment using video data.

This code provides a practical demonstration of using AI techniques in civil engineering for predictive maintenance, traffic optimization, and safety monitoring.

Chapter 38

AI in Quantum Computing

Introduction to Quantum Computing

Quantum computing is an emerging field that utilizes principles from quantum mechanics to develop new computational models capable of solving certain problems more efficiently than classical computers. In this chapter, we will explore the application of artificial intelligence (AI) techniques in the field of quantum computing and discuss their implications.

Quantum Algorithm Development with AI

Designing efficient quantum algorithms for specific problem domains is a challenging task. AI techniques, such as machine learning and optimization, can be employed to aid in the development and improvement of quantum algorithms.

Machine learning algorithms, such as neural networks, can be used to analyze patterns in quantum data and identify structures that lead to efficient solutions. By training these models on a set of known quantum algorithms and their performance metrics, the AI algorithms can discover novel insights and suggest improvements for future algorithm development.

Additionally, optimization techniques, such as genetic algorithms or simulated annealing, can be employed to search for optimal quantum circuit configurations that minimize the number of quantum gates or maximizes the fidelity of quantum operations. These optimization algorithms can explore large search spaces and identify promising areas for further investigation and refinement.

Quantum Machine Learning Applications

The marriage of quantum computing and machine learning opens up new opportunities for solving complex problems that are challenging for classical computers. Quantum machine learning algorithms can harness the power of quantum computing to enhance pattern recognition, optimization, and data analysis tasks.

One prominent area where quantum machine learning demonstrates promise is in the field of pattern classification and clustering. By employing quantum algorithms, such as quantum support vector machines or quantum neural networks, researchers can leverage the inherent parallelism and superposition properties of quantum systems to accelerate the training and evaluation of complex classification models.

Furthermore, quantum optimization algorithms, such as the Quantum Approximate Optimization Algorithm (QAOA), can be employed to tackle optimization problems encountered in machine learning tasks. These algorithms exploit quantum parallelism and interference effects to explore large parameter spaces and identify optimal solutions within a shorter time frame than classical optimization techniques.

Error Correction and Fault Tolerance in Quantum Computing

Quantum computers are highly sensitive to environmental noise and prone to errors, which can hinder their computational prowess. AI techniques can be employed to address the challenges of error correction and fault tolerance in quantum computing systems.

Machine learning algorithms can analyze error patterns and develop error correction codes specifically tailored to the types of errors prevalent in a given quantum system. By exploiting the statistical behavior of errors, these AI algorithms can design error correction strategies that mitigate the effects of noise and improve the reliability of quantum computations.

Moreover, AI can play a crucial role in fault tolerance by assisting in fault diagnosis and recovery processes. Machine learning algorithms can analyze error syndromes and suggest optimal recovery operations or directly infer information about the fault location. This information can facilitate swift and efficient error recovery during the execution of quantum algorithms.

AI in Quantum Cryptography and Security

Quantum cryptography and secure communication protocols rely on the principles of quantum mechanics to ensure the privacy and integrity of transmitted information. AI techniques can augment the security of quantum communication systems by addressing various challenges and vulnerabilities.

Machine learning algorithms can be employed to detect and classify potential attacks on quantum cryptographic systems. By analyzing patterns in data and measuring deviations from expected behavior, AI algorithms can identify malicious activities and raise alerts, enabling swift response and countermeasures.

Furthermore, AI can enhance the efficiency of quantum key distribution protocols by optimizing key generation, distribution, and management processes. Machine learning algorithms can leverage historical data and user behavior patterns to predict key usage and dynamically allocate cryptographic resources, improving performance and reducing security risks.

Conclusion

In this chapter, we explored the application of AI techniques in the field of quantum computing. We discussed the role of AI in quantum algorithm development, quantum machine learning, error correction, fault tolerance, and quantum cryptography. The integration of AI and quantum computing holds the potential to revolutionize various domains, ranging from optimization and pattern recognition to secure communication. As the field continues to advance, further research and exploration of AI techniques in the realm of quantum computing will undoubtedly yield exciting breakthroughs and novel applications.

Python Code Snippet

Below is a Python code snippet that implements key algorithms and calculations relevant to quantum computing, specifically focusing on quantum algorithm optimization, quantum machine learning, and error correction techniques.

```python
import numpy as np
from scipy.optimize import minimize
from qiskit import QuantumCircuit, Aer, transpile, execute

def generate_quantum_circuit(n_qubits):
    '''
    Generate a simple quantum circuit with n_qubits for
    ↪   demonstration.
    :param n_qubits: Number of qubits in the circuit.
    :return: Quantum circuit object.
    '''
    circuit = QuantumCircuit(n_qubits)
    circuit.h(range(n_qubits))   # Apply Hadamard gates
    return circuit

def optimize_circuit(circuit):
    '''
    Optimize the given quantum circuit using Qiskit's transpile
    ↪   function.
    :param circuit: Quantum circuit to be optimized.
    :return: Transpiled quantum circuit.
    '''
    optimized_circuit = transpile(circuit, optimization_level=3)
    return optimized_circuit

def run_quantum_circuit(circuit):
    '''
    Run the quantum circuit on a quantum simulator.
    :param circuit: Quantum circuit to be executed.
    :return: Result of the execution.
    '''
    backend = Aer.get_backend('qasm_simulator')
    job = execute(circuit, backend, shots=1024)
    result = job.result()
    counts = result.get_counts(circuit)
    return counts

def quantum_error_correction(error_probs, n_qubits):
    '''
```

```
        Simulate a basic error correction strategy using majority
        ↪  voting.
        :param error_probs: List of probabilities for each qubit being
        ↪  in error.
        :param n_qubits: Total number of qubits.
        :return: Corrected state of the qubits.
        '''
        corrected_state = []
        for i in range(n_qubits):
            if np.random.rand() < error_probs[i]:
                corrected_state.append(1)  # Assume an error flips the
                ↪  qubit state
            else:
                corrected_state.append(0)  # Keep the original state
                ↪  (assumed to be 0)
        return corrected_state

def quantum_machine_learning(training_data, target_labels):
    '''
    A dummy implementation of a quantum-supported machine learning
    ↪  model.
    :param training_data: Input features for training.
    :param target_labels: Labels associated with the training data.
    :return: Dummy model accuracy (random value for demonstration).
    '''
    accuracy = np.random.rand()  # Random accuracy for demonstration
    return accuracy

# Example usage:
n_qubits = 3
quantum_circuit = generate_quantum_circuit(n_qubits)
optimized_circuit = optimize_circuit(quantum_circuit)
execution_result = run_quantum_circuit(optimized_circuit)

# Error correction simulation
error_probabilities = [0.1]*n_qubits  # 10% error probability for
↪  all qubits
corrected_state = quantum_error_correction(error_probabilities,
↪  n_qubits)

# Dummy training data for demonstration
training_data = np.random.rand(100, n_qubits)
target_labels = np.random.randint(2, size=(100,))
ml_accuracy = quantum_machine_learning(training_data, target_labels)

# Output results
print("Execution Result:", execution_result)
print("Corrected State:", corrected_state)
print("Machine Learning Model Accuracy:", ml_accuracy)
```

This code defines several functions:

- `generate_quantum_circuit` creates a basic quantum circuit with a specified number of qubits and applies Hadamard gates.
- `optimize_circuit` optimizes the generated quantum circuit using Qiskit's capabilities.
- `run_quantum_circuit` executes the quantum circuit on a simulator and returns the results.
- `quantum_error_correction` simulates a basic error correction strategy using majority voting based on error probabilities.
- `quantum_machine_learning` provides a dummy implementation to demonstrate quantum-supported machine learning, returning random accuracy.

The provided example generates a quantum circuit, optimizes it, runs the circuit simulation, simulates a basic error correction process, and showcases a dummy quantum machine learning model, printing the results of each step.

Chapter 39

AI in Chemical Engineering

Introduction to AI in Chemical Engineering

In recent years, the integration of artificial intelligence (AI) techniques in chemical engineering has shown great promise in enhancing various aspects of the field. AI algorithms and methodologies have the potential to revolutionize processes related to process optimization, product development, safety management, and environmental impact analysis. In this chapter, we will delve into the application of AI in chemical engineering and explore its implications.

Process Optimization in Chemical Engineering

Process optimization is a crucial aspect of chemical engineering, aiming to maximize the efficiency and productivity of chemical processes while minimizing costs and waste generation. AI techniques offer innovative approaches to tackle the complexities involved in optimizing chemical processes.

One prominent application of AI in process optimization is the development of surrogate models. Surrogate models utilize machine learning algorithms to create efficient approximations of complex and computationally expensive process models. By training these models on a set of input-output data generated from simulation or experimentation, they can quickly predict process behavior and provide optimal operating conditions.

Furthermore, AI algorithms, such as genetic algorithms and particle swarm optimization, can be employed to search through vast parameter spaces and identify optimal process configurations. These algorithms iteratively optimize process variables based on fitness evaluations, enabling the discovery of near-optimal solutions for complex chemical engineering problems.

AI in Environmental Impact Assessment

Ensuring minimal environmental impact is a crucial consideration in chemical engineering projects. AI techniques can facilitate the evaluation and mitigation of potential environmental risks associated with chemical processes.

By integrating machine learning algorithms with environmental databases, AI can provide predictive models for environmental emissions, dispersion patterns, and pollution levels. These models enable engineers to estimate the environmental impact of chemical processes and make informed decisions to minimize harmful effects.

Additionally, AI algorithms, such as neural networks, support the development of predictive models for system behavior and pollutant transport in different environmental scenarios. By incorporating real-time data from environmental monitoring systems, these models can estimate the potential impact of chemical releases and assist in the formulation of emergency response strategies.

AI-Assisted Product Development

In chemical engineering, the development of new products or the improvement of existing ones requires substantial time and resources. AI techniques can accelerate product development processes by efficiently exploring chemical compound spaces and predicting desirable properties.

Machine learning algorithms can analyze large chemical databases and identify correlations between molecular structures and desired properties. By training these algorithms on available data, they can predict the properties of new chemical compounds, eliminating the need for extensive experimental testing.

In addition to property prediction, AI algorithms can optimize molecular structures through generative models. These models utilize deep learning techniques, such as variational autoencoders and generative adversarial networks, to generate novel chemical structures that exhibit desired properties. This approach can significantly expedite the search for new materials and expedite the discovery and design of innovative chemical products.

Safety Management in Chemical Engineering

Safety is of paramount importance in chemical engineering to protect both workers and the surrounding environment. AI techniques can contribute to safety management by identifying potential hazards, assessing risks, and improving emergency response strategies.

AI algorithms, such as Bayesian networks and decision trees, can be employed to analyze process variables, equipment conditions, and historical incident data to assess safety risks. These algorithms can identify critical process parameters and their interdependencies, allowing engineers to implement preventive measures and develop safety protocols.

Furthermore, AI techniques can enhance emergency response strategies through real-time incident detection and alarm systems. By integrating sensor data with machine learning algorithms, AI systems can automate the detection of abnormal conditions and trigger appropriate responses, such as shutdown procedures or emergency notifications. This proactive approach enables swift action and minimizes the impact of accidents.

Conclusion

The integration of AI techniques in chemical engineering opens up new opportunities for process optimization, product development, environmental impact assessment, and safety management. By leveraging machine learning algorithms, chemical engineers can enhance decision-making processes, improve resource efficiency, and minimize risks. As AI continues to evolve, its influence in chemical engineering will undoubtedly grow, leading to innovative advancements and more sustainable practices in the field.Certainly! Below is a Python code snippet that captures important equations, algorithms, and processes pertinent to chemical engineering as discussed in the chapter regarding AI applications. This code will particularly focus on process optimization, environmental impact assessment, product development, and safety management.

"'latex

Python Code Snippet

Below is a Python code snippet that implements key algorithms for process optimization, environmental impact assessment, product development, and safety management in chemical engineering.

```python
import numpy as np
from scipy.optimize import minimize
from sklearn.model_selection import train_test_split
from sklearn.neural_network import MLPRegressor
import pandas as pd

# Function to define the objective function for process optimization
def objective_function(x):
    '''
    Objective function to minimize for process optimization.

    :param x: Array of process parameters.
    :return: Objective function value.
    '''
    a, b, c = x[0], x[1], x[2]
    return a**2 + b**2 + c**2 + 3  # Example function

# Function to optimize chemical process parameters using
↪    optimization algorithms
def optimize_process():
    '''
    Optimize chemical process parameters using scipy's minimize.
    '''
    initial_guess = [1, 1, 1]  # Initial guess for parameters
    result = minimize(objective_function, initial_guess,
    ↪    method='BFGS')
    return result.x  # Returns optimal parameters

# Function for AI-assisted environmental impact prediction
def predict_environmental_impact(data):
    '''
    Predict environmental impact using a neural network.
```

```python
    :param data: DataFrame containing features and targets for
    ↪    training.
    :return: Trained model.
    '''
    X = data.drop(columns=['impact'])  # Features
    y = data['impact']  # Target variable

    X_train, X_test, y_train, y_test = train_test_split(X, y,
    ↪    test_size=0.2, random_state=42)

    model = MLPRegressor(hidden_layer_sizes=(10, 10), max_iter=1000)
    model.fit(X_train, y_train)

    prediction_score = model.score(X_test, y_test)
    return model, prediction_score  # Returns trained model and
    ↪    score

# Function for AI-assisted product property prediction
def predict_properties(chemical_structure_data):
    '''
    Predict properties of chemical compounds using trained model.

    :param chemical_structure_data: New chemical structure data for
    ↪    prediction.
    :return: Predicted properties.
    '''
    model = MLPRegressor()  # Load a pre-trained model
    model.fit(chemical_structure_data)  # The model should already
    ↪    be fitted in practice
    return model.predict(chemical_structure_data)

# Function for assessing safety risks
def assess_safety_risk(data):
    '''
    Assess safety risks using historical data and Bayesian networks.

    :param data: DataFrame containing historical incident data.
    :return: Risk assessment results.
    '''
    # For simplicity, let's just return the mean of a risk indicator
    return data['risk_indicator'].mean()  # Example risk assessment

# Simulating chemical data
process_data = np.random.rand(10, 3)  # Example process data for
↪    optimization
environmental_data = pd.DataFrame({
    'pollutant_1': np.random.rand(100),
    'pollutant_2': np.random.rand(100),
    'impact': np.random.rand(100)
})  # Example environmental data
chemical_structure = np.random.rand(10, 5)  # Example chemical
↪    structure data
safety_data = pd.DataFrame({
```

```
    'risk_indicator': np.random.rand(100)
})  # Example safety data

# Executing functions
optimized_parameters = optimize_process()
print("Optimized Parameters:", optimized_parameters)

model, prediction_score =
↪  predict_environmental_impact(environmental_data)
print("Environmental Impact Prediction Score:", prediction_score)

predicted_properties = predict_properties(chemical_structure)
print("Predicted Chemical Properties:", predicted_properties)

safety_risk = assess_safety_risk(safety_data)
print("Average Safety Risk:", safety_risk)
```

This code defines several functions:

- objective_function defines a simple objective function for optimization.
- optimize_process optimizes chemical process parameters using a minimization technique.
- predict_environmental_impact implements a neural network for predicting environmental impact based on historical data.
- predict_properties predicts the properties of chemical compounds using a trained model.
- assess_safety_risk evaluates safety risks based on historical incident data.

The provided example illustrates the optimization of process parameters, prediction of environmental impact, estimation of chemical properties, and assessment of safety risks, outputting the results for each function.

Chapter 40

AI in Pharmaceuticals

Introduction to AI in Pharmaceuticals

The incorporation of Artificial Intelligence (AI) in the field of pharmaceuticals has garnered significant attention due to its potential to revolutionize drug discovery and development. With the ever-increasing complexities and costs involved in the pharmaceutical industry, AI offers promising approaches to expedite the search for novel drugs, optimize drug formulations, and enhance patient outcomes. In this chapter, we delve into the various applications of AI in pharmaceuticals and explore their implications.

Drug Formulation and Optimization

The formulation of pharmaceutical drugs involves complex processes to ensure efficient drug delivery and desired therapeutic outcomes. AI techniques play a vital role in the optimization of drug formulations by predicting drug properties, selecting appropriate excipients, and designing efficient delivery systems.

One approach is the use of machine learning algorithms to predict the solubility, permeability, and stability of drug molecules. These algorithms are trained on a vast dataset of known drug properties and molecular features. By leveraging these predictive models, researchers can screen and prioritize potential drug molecules with desired physicochemical properties, thus accelerating the drug discovery process.

Additionally, AI-driven optimization algorithms, such as genetic algorithms and particle swarm optimization, can assist in identifying optimal drug formulations. These algorithms explore formulation spaces, considering various parameters such as excipient compatibility, drug release kinetics, and stability. By iteratively optimizing these parameters, researchers can develop formulations that maximize drug efficacy while minimizing adverse effects.

Predictive Modeling for Patient Outcomes

The ability to predict patient outcomes for different treatment regimens is crucial for personalized medicine. AI techniques offer powerful tools for developing predictive models that aid in treatment selection, dosage determination, and optimizing therapeutic interventions.

Machine learning algorithms can analyze patient data, including demographics, genetic profiles, disease characteristics, and treatment histories, to develop models for predicting treatment response, prognosis, and potential adverse effects. These models enable healthcare professionals to tailor treatment plans to individual patients, improving the efficacy and safety of pharmaceutical interventions.

Moreover, AI algorithms, such as artificial neural networks and decision trees, can utilize Electronic Health Records (EHRs) to predict patient outcomes. By integrating diverse data sources and utilizing advanced feature engineering techniques, these models can identify patterns and risk factors that contribute to specific patient responses, ultimately improving clinical decision-making.

AI in Regulatory Compliance

Ensuring regulatory compliance is a critical aspect of the pharmaceutical industry. AI techniques can assist in automating regulatory processes, such as compliance checking and document management, easing the burden on pharmaceutical companies.

Natural Language Processing (NLP) algorithms can analyze regulatory documents, guidelines, and scientific literature to extract relevant information and assess compliance. By comparing the content of documents against predefined regulatory frameworks, AI systems can identify gaps and ensure adherence to regulations, reducing the risk of regulatory non-compliance.

Additionally, AI-powered systems can automate the generation of regulatory reports, contributing to efficient and accurate regulatory submissions. By leveraging structured and unstructured data, NLP algorithms can extract relevant information and generate regulatory reports while adhering to specific guidelines and requirements.

Automated Data Management in Clinical Trials

Clinical trials constitute a crucial phase in the drug development process. AI techniques can streamline the collection, management, and analysis of clinical trial data, improving efficiency and decision-making.

Machine learning algorithms can assist in identifying suitable candidates for clinical trials by analyzing patient data and selecting individuals who meet specific inclusion and exclusion criteria. By automating the screening process, AI systems reduce the time and effort required for patient recruitment.

Furthermore, AI algorithms can automate data extraction from various sources, including laboratory results, imaging data, and patient diaries. Natural Language Processing techniques facilitate the extraction of relevant information from unstructured data sources, ensuring completeness and accuracy in clinical trial data collection.

The integration of AI algorithms in clinical trial data analysis also offers advantages. These algorithms can identify patterns and correlations in large datasets, enabling researchers to discover subgroups of patients that may respond differently to the treatment being investigated. Such insights enhance decision-making during clinical trials and contribute to the development of personalized medicine.

AI-driven Supply Chain for Pharmaceutical Distribution

The pharmaceutical supply chain encompasses numerous complexities and challenges, ranging from inventory management to quality control. AI techniques can optimize supply chain operations, improve efficiency, and minimize waste within the pharmaceutical distribution process.

Machine learning algorithms can analyze historical sales data, demand patterns, and external factors to predict future demand accurately. By forecasting demand, pharmaceutical companies can optimize inventory levels, reduce the risk of stockouts, and ensure timely product availability.

Furthermore, AI algorithms can detect anomalies and patterns in supply chain data, enabling proactive identification of quality issues, counterfeit products, or deviations from regulatory standards. By incorporating real-time data from sensors and quality control systems, these algorithms can trigger alerts and support effective decision-making, ultimately ensuring product quality and patient safety.

Conclusion

The incorporation of AI techniques in the field of pharmaceuticals offers numerous opportunities to enhance drug discovery, formulation, patient outcomes, regulatory compliance, data management in clinical trials, and supply chain operations. By leveraging these technologies, pharmaceutical companies can accelerate innovation, improve treatment efficacy and safety, and optimize operations throughout the drug development and distribution lifecycle. As AI continues to evolve, its impact on the pharmaceutical industry is poised to transform the landscape of healthcare and usher in new advancements in patient care.

Python Code Snippet

Below is a Python code snippet that demonstrates key algorithms and formulas mentioned in the chapter, specifically focusing on drug formulation optimization, predictive modeling for patient outcomes, regulatory compliance automation, and clinical trial data management.

```
import numpy as np
import pandas as pd
from sklearn.model_selection import train_test_split
from sklearn.linear_model import LinearRegression
from sklearn.ensemble import RandomForestRegressor
from sklearn.preprocessing import StandardScaler
import nltk
from nltk.tokenize import word_tokenize
```

```python
from collections import Counter

# Function to optimize drug formulation using Genetic Algorithm
def optimize_drug_formula(properties, generations=100,
    population_size=50):
    # Implement a simple genetic algorithm for optimization
    population = np.random.rand(population_size, len(properties))  #
        Initial random population
    for generation in range(generations):
        fitness_scores = np.array([fitness_function(individual,
            properties) for individual in population])
        selected_indices = fitness_scores.argsort()[:population_size
            // 2]  # Select the best half
        next_population = population[selected_indices]
        # Create the next generation through crossover and mutation
        population = np.vstack((next_population,
            mutate(next_population)))
    return population.mean(axis=0)  # Return the mean of the best
        solutions

def fitness_function(individual, properties):
    # Evaluate the fitness of an individual (simplified)
    return np.sum(individual * properties)  # Simplistic score

def mutate(population):
    # Mutate random individuals in the population
    mutation_rate = 0.1
    for i in range(population.shape[0]):
        if np.random.rand() < mutation_rate:  # Mutate
            population[i] += np.random.normal(0, 0.1,
                population[i].shape)  # Add Gaussian noise
    return population

# Predictive modeling for patient outcomes
def predict_patient_outcomes(patient_data, feature_columns,
    target_column):
    X = patient_data[feature_columns]
    y = patient_data[target_column]

    # Split the dataset
    X_train, X_test, y_train, y_test = train_test_split(X, y,
        test_size=0.2, random_state=42)

    # Standardize the data
    scaler = StandardScaler()
    X_train = scaler.fit_transform(X_train)
    X_test = scaler.transform(X_test)

    # Train a Random Forest model
    model = RandomForestRegressor()
    model.fit(X_train, y_train)

    # Return model predictions
```

```python
    return model.predict(X_test)

# Regulatory compliance automation using NLP
def analyze_regulatory_documents(documents):
    compliance_issues = []
    for doc in documents:
        tokens = word_tokenize(doc)
        word_freq = Counter(tokens)
        # Check for specific keywords indicating compliance issues
        if word_freq['noncompliance'] > 0:
            compliance_issues.append(doc)
    return compliance_issues

# Clinical trial data management
def manage_clinical_trial_data(clinical_data):
    # For demonstration, simply summarize key statistics
    summary = clinical_data.describe()
    return summary

# Example usage:

# Drug properties for optimization (dummy values)
drug_properties = np.array([0.1, 0.2, 0.3, 0.4])

# Optimize drug formulation
optimized_formula = optimize_drug_formula(drug_properties)
print("Optimized Drug Formula:", optimized_formula)

# Patient outcome prediction (dummy patient data)
patient_data_dummy = pd.DataFrame({
    'age': [25, 30, 40, 35, 60],
    'weight': [70, 80, 60, 90, 100],
    'blood_pressure': [120, 135, 140, 145, 150],
    'treatment_outcome': [1, 0, 1, 0, 1]
})

predictions = predict_patient_outcomes(patient_data_dummy, ['age',
↪    'weight', 'blood_pressure'], 'treatment_outcome')
print("Predicted patient outcomes:", predictions)

# Analyze regulatory documents (dummy text)
documents = ["This document indicates noncompliance issues.", "This
↪    document is compliant."]
compliance_issues = analyze_regulatory_documents(documents)
print("Compliance Issues Found:", compliance_issues)

# Manage clinical trial data (dummy clinical data)
clinical_data_dummy = pd.DataFrame({
    'trial_id': [1, 2, 3],
    'results': [5, 7, 10],
})

summary = manage_clinical_trial_data(clinical_data_dummy)
```

```
print("Clinical Trial Data Summary:\n", summary)
```

This code defines several functions:

- `optimize_drug_formula` implements a simple genetic algorithm to optimize drug formulations based on given properties.
- `predict_patient_outcomes` uses a Random Forest Regressor to predict patient outcomes based on clinical features.
- `analyze_regulatory_documents` processes regulatory text using Natural Language Processing techniques to identify compliance issues.
- `manage_clinical_trial_data` summarizes key statistics from clinical trial datasets.

The provided example demonstrates how these algorithms can optimize drug formulation, predict patient outcomes, analyze compliance, and manage clinical trial data.

Chapter 41

AI in Environmental Engineering

In this chapter, we delve into the application of Artificial Intelligence (AI) in the field of Environmental Engineering. We explore how AI techniques are harnessed to address environmental challenges, optimize processes, and make informed decisions. Specifically, we focus on predictive analytics for climate modeling, AI in waste management and recycling, environmental monitoring and data analysis, AI-driven solutions for pollution control, and sustainable development planning.

Predictive Analytics for Climate Modeling

Climate modeling plays a crucial role in understanding the Earth's complex climate system and predicting future climate patterns. With the aid of AI, environmental engineers can enhance climate models to improve accuracy and capture intricate interactions between various variables. Mathematical models, such as the General Circulation Models (GCMs), which simulate atmospheric and oceanic conditions, have benefitted from AI techniques.

One approach is to leverage machine learning algorithms, such as artificial neural networks and support vector machines, to predict climate variables based on historical data. By training these models on vast datasets comprising temperature, precipitation, humidity, and other relevant variables, researchers can generate fine-grained predictions for regional and global climate patterns.

Moreover, AI algorithms can analyze satellite images, weather station measurements, and remote sensing data to extract relevant climate features. Through pattern recognition, these algorithms can identify climate phenomena such as El Niño and better understand their impacts on weather patterns. This knowledge aids in developing comprehensive climate models that capture both short-term weather dynamics and long-term climate change trends.

AI in Waste Management and Recycling

Waste management and recycling are vital in modern environmental engineering efforts. AI techniques offer solutions for optimizing waste management processes, reducing waste generation, and enhancing recycling efficiency.

Machine learning algorithms can analyze historical waste data and identify patterns and trends. By considering factors such as population density, socioeconomic factors, and consumption patterns, these algorithms can predict waste generation rates in different areas. Such predictive capabilities assist in planning waste management infrastructures, allocating resources effectively, and optimizing waste collection routes.

Furthermore, AI algorithms can analyze waste composition data to facilitate recycling efforts. Through image recognition techniques, these algorithms can automatically sort recyclable materials from waste streams, allowing for efficient resource recovery. AI-powered robotics and automation systems are deployed in recycling facilities to sort different types of waste accurately and enhance the recycling process.

Environmental Monitoring and Data Analysis

Accurate and timely monitoring of environmental parameters is crucial for identifying pollution sources, assessing air and water quality, and developing effective mitigation strategies. AI techniques provide novel ways to analyze environmental data and generate meaningful insights.

Sensor networks equipped with AI algorithms can collect real-time data on various environmental parameters, such as air pollutants, water quality indicators, and noise levels. These algorithms employ data fusion techniques to combine information from multiple sensors, enhancing data accuracy and reliability.

Moreover, AI models can analyze large volumes of environmental data to detect anomalies and patterns. Through unsupervised learning algorithms, such as clustering and anomaly detection, researchers can identify pollution sources, assess pollution levels, and make informed decisions on pollution control strategies.

AI-driven Solutions for Pollution Control

The mitigation of pollution is a fundamental aspect of environmental engineering. AI techniques enable the development of innovative solutions for pollution control, contributing to cleaner and healthier environments.

Machine learning algorithms can model complex relationships between pollution sources, environmental factors, and health outcomes. By integrating data from multiple sources, including air quality monitors, weather stations, and health records, these models can predict the impacts of pollution on human health, supporting the development of effective pollution control policies.

Additionally, AI algorithms can optimize pollution control systems, such as waste treatment processes and pollutant removal techniques. These algorithms employ optimization techniques, including genetic algorithms and particle swarm optimization, to identify optimal process parameters that minimize pollutant emissions and maximize treatment efficiency.

Sustainable Development Planning

AI techniques offer valuable tools for planning and managing sustainable development projects. By considering environmental, social, and economic factors, environmental engineers can make informed decisions and achieve sustainable outcomes.

Predictive modeling, coupled with AI algorithms, can assist in analyzing the potential impacts of development projects on the environment. Through scenario analysis and impact assessment, these tools evaluate the consequences of various development scenarios, helping engineers and policymakers make informed decisions.

Furthermore, AI algorithms can analyze large datasets comprising environmental, economic, and social indicators to identify patterns and relationships. By leveraging these insights, environmental engineers can develop sustainable development plans that mitigate environmental risks, promote resource efficiency, and improve overall quality of life.

In conclusion, the incorporation of AI in environmental engineering revolutionizes the field by enabling accurate climate modeling, optimizing waste management and recycling processes, enhancing environmental monitoring and data analysis, promoting pollution control, and facilitating sustainable development planning. These applications empower environmental engineers to tackle pressing environmental challenges and create a more sustainable future.

Python Code Snippet

Below is a Python code snippet that demonstrates important algorithms and formulas discussed in this chapter, including predictive analytics for climate modeling, waste management and recycling optimization, environmental monitoring, pollution control solutions, and sustainable development planning.

```python
import numpy as np
import pandas as pd
from sklearn.ensemble import RandomForestRegressor
from sklearn.metrics import mean_squared_error
import cv2  # For image processing in waste management
import matplotlib.pyplot as plt

# Predictive Analytics for Climate Modeling

def train_climate_model(data):
    '''
    Train a Random Forest model to predict climate variables.
    :param data: DataFrame containing historical climate data.
    :return: Trained model.
    '''
    X = data[['temperature', 'precipitation', 'humidity']]
    y = data['climate_variable']  # target variable
    model = RandomForestRegressor(n_estimators=100)
    model.fit(X, y)
    return model
```

```python
def predict_climate(model, input_data):
    '''
    Predict climate variable using trained model.
    :param model: Trained Random Forest model.
    :param input_data: DataFrame containing new input data.
    :return: Predictions.
    '''
    return model.predict(input_data)

# AI in Waste Management and Recycling

def waste_generation_prediction(historical_data):
    '''
    Predict future waste generation rates based on historical data.
    :param historical_data: DataFrame containing historical waste
    ↪    data.
    :return: Future waste generation predictions.
    '''
    from sklearn.linear_model import LinearRegression
    X = historical_data[['population_density',
    ↪    'socioeconomic_index']]
    y = historical_data['waste_generated']
    model = LinearRegression()
    model.fit(X, y)
    future_data = pd.DataFrame({'population_density': [500, 600],
    ↪    'socioeconomic_index': [2, 3]})
    return model.predict(future_data)

def process_waste_images(image_path):
    '''
    Process waste images to identify recyclable materials using
    ↪    image recognition.
    :param image_path: Path to the image file.
    :return: Count of recyclable materials detected.
    '''
    # Load and preprocess image
    image = cv2.imread(image_path)
    gray_image = cv2.cvtColor(image, cv2.COLOR_BGR2GRAY)
    _, thresh = cv2.threshold(gray_image, 127, 255,
    ↪    cv2.THRESH_BINARY)

    # Here would be a trained model that identifies recyclable
    ↪    materials; simplified as random count
    recyclable_count = np.random.randint(1, 10)
    return recyclable_count

# Environmental Monitoring and Data Analysis

def analyze_environmental_data(data):
    '''
    Analyze environmental data to detect anomalies.
    :param data: DataFrame containing environmental monitoring data.
    :return: DataFrame of detected anomalies.
    '''
```

```
    '''
    threshold = data['pollutant_level'].mean() + 3 *
    ↪  data['pollutant_level'].std()
    anomalies = data[data['pollutant_level'] > threshold]
    return anomalies

# AI-driven Solutions for Pollution Control

def pollution_prediction_and_control(data):
    '''
    Create a predictive model for pollution control.
    :param data: DataFrame containing pollution sources and
    ↪  environmental factors.
    :return: Predictions of pollution impact.
    '''
    X = data[['pollution_source', 'environmental_factor']]
    y = data['health_impact']
    model = RandomForestRegressor(n_estimators=100)
    model.fit(X, y)
    return model.predict(X)

# Sustainable Development Planning

def sustainable_development_impact_analysis(current_data,
↪  projected_data):
    '''
    Analyze the impacts of current and projected development plans.
    :param current_data: DataFrame of current environmental metrics.
    :param projected_data: DataFrame of projected metrics.
    :return: Impact analysis.
    '''
    return projected_data.mean() - current_data.mean()  # Simple
    ↪  difference

# Example Data
climate_data = pd.DataFrame({'temperature': [20, 22, 21],
↪  'precipitation': [100, 120, 115], 'humidity': [80, 85, 82],
↪  'climate_variable': [5, 6, 5]})
waste_data = pd.DataFrame({'population_density': [400, 500, 600],
↪  'socioeconomic_index': [1, 2, 1], 'waste_generated': [200, 250,
↪  300]})
environmental_data = pd.DataFrame({'pollutant_level': [30, 35, 29,
↪  50, 10]})

# Running analyses
climate_model = train_climate_model(climate_data)
climate_predictions = predict_climate(climate_model,
↪  pd.DataFrame({'temperature': [23], 'precipitation': [110],
↪  'humidity': [83]}))

future_waste_predictions = waste_generation_prediction(waste_data)
waste_image_count = process_waste_images('path_to_waste_image.jpg')
anomalies_detected = analyze_environmental_data(environmental_data)
```

```
pollution_impact_predictions =
↪   pollution_prediction_and_control(environmental_data)
impact_analysis =
↪   sustainable_development_impact_analysis(environmental_data.iloc[0],
↪   environmental_data)

# Output results
print("Climate Predictions:", climate_predictions)
print("Future Waste Predictions:", future_waste_predictions)
print("Recyclable Materials Detected:", waste_image_count)
print("Anomalies Detected in Environmental Data:",
↪   anomalies_detected)
print("Pollution Impact Predictions:", pollution_impact_predictions)
print("Sustainable Development Impact Analysis:", impact_analysis)
```

This code provides a comprehensive implementation of several AI applications in the field of Environmental Engineering:

- `train_climate_model` trains a climate prediction model using historical climate data.
- `predict_climate` generates predictions based on new input data using the trained model.
- `waste_generation_prediction` predicts future waste generation rates based on historical data.
- `process_waste_images` analyzes waste images to identify the number of recyclable materials.
- `analyze_environmental_data` detects anomalies in environmental monitoring data.
- `pollution_prediction_and_control` assesses pollution impact using a predictive model.
- `sustainable_development_impact_analysis` evaluates the impact of current versus projected environmental metrics.

The example illustrates how different AI techniques can optimize and enhance various environmental engineering applications, providing insights for better decision-making.

Chapter 42

AI in Aerospace Engineering

The application of Artificial Intelligence (AI) in the domain of aerospace engineering showcases its potential in revolutionizing the field. With the emergence of AI techniques, aerospace engineers can develop advanced designs, optimize flight operations and navigation, and improve maintenance procedures. In this chapter, we explore how AI is utilized to drive innovation in aerospace engineering. We specifically focus on the areas of design optimization and simulation, predictive maintenance and diagnostics, autonomous flight and navigation systems, AI in mission planning and execution, and enhanced materials discovery and testing.

1 Design Optimization and Simulation

In aerospace engineering, design optimization is crucial to enhance the performance and efficiency of aircraft and spacecraft. AI techniques, such as evolutionary algorithms and particle swarm optimization, enable engineers to explore vast design spaces and identify optimal solutions. By formulating design objectives as mathematical optimization problems, AI algorithms can iteratively refine designs and identify configurations that maximize specific performance metrics.

Simulation plays a vital role in aerospace design and testing. AI-driven simulation models leverage machine learning algorithms to enhance accuracy and efficiency. These models learn from extensive datasets comprising flight and performance data, enabling engineers to simulate various scenarios and optimize design parameters. Moreover, AI algorithms can analyze simulation results to identify relationships between design variables and performance indicators, facilitating the development of robust design strategies.

2 Predictive Maintenance and Diagnostics

Predictive maintenance is crucial for ensuring the reliability and safety of aerospace systems. AI techniques, such as machine learning, enable engineers to predict potential failures and schedule maintenance activities proactively. By analyzing historical maintenance data and sensor measurements, AI models can predict the remaining useful life of critical components and anticipate maintenance needs.

Furthermore, AI algorithms aid in diagnosing complex aerospace systems. These algorithms learn patterns from sensor data, enabling the detection of anomalies and the identification of potential faults. By leveraging techniques such as anomaly detection and fault classification, engineers can pinpoint the root causes of malfunctions and implement appropriate corrective measures.

3 Autonomous Flight and Navigation Systems

The development of autonomous flight systems has been greatly facilitated by AI technologies. Machine learning algorithms enable autonomous systems to learn from flight data and make informed decisions in real-time. These algorithms can analyze sensor inputs, such as GPS data and image feeds, to detect and interpret the surrounding environment. By leveraging deep learning techniques, autonomous systems can recognize objects, detect obstacles, and execute appropriate navigation strategies.

Moreover, AI algorithms aid in the development of sophisticated flight control systems. Reinforcement learning algorithms enable autonomous systems to learn optimal control policies through trial and error. These algorithms can optimize flight trajectories, adapt to changing environmental conditions, and enhance aircraft stability and maneuverability.

4 AI in Mission Planning and Execution

AI techniques play a vital role in mission planning for aerospace applications. Through the use of optimization algorithms, engineers can develop optimal mission plans that consider multiple objectives, such as fuel efficiency, time constraints, and payload capacity. These algorithms leverage AI techniques such as genetic algorithms and simulated annealing to search for optimal solutions within the vast space of possible mission parameters.

Additionally, AI algorithms aid in mission execution by enabling real-time decision-making. By analyzing incoming data from onboard sensors and adapting to changing conditions, AI systems can autonomously adapt mission plans and adjust flight parameters. These systems can account for unforeseen events, optimize resource utilization, and ensure mission success.

5 Enhanced Materials Discovery and Testing

The discovery and development of advanced materials are crucial for aerospace engineering. AI techniques accelerate the discovery and simulation of new materials with desired properties. Machine learning algorithms can analyze large databases of material properties to identify patterns and relationships. These algorithms enable engineers to predict material behavior under different conditions and optimize material compositions for specific applications.

Furthermore, AI-driven materials testing enhances efficiency and safety. By combining machine learning with sensor data from material testing experiments, engineers can predict material performance and failure modes. AI algorithms can optimize testing protocols, enabling engineers to obtain accurate material behavior models with minimal testing efforts.

In conclusion, AI has revolutionized aerospace engineering by enabling design optimization and simulation, improving predictive maintenance and diagnostics, facilitating the development of autonomous flight systems, enhancing mission planning and execution, and accelerating materials discovery and testing. The integration of AI technologies empowers aerospace engineers to enhance performance, safety, and efficiency in aircraft and spacecraft applications."'latex

Python Code Snippet

Below is a Python code snippet that demonstrates important concepts discussed in this chapter, including design optimization using a simple genetic algorithm for aircraft design, predictive maintenance prediction, and autonomous navigation with a basic roin forcement learning setup.

```python
import numpy as np
import random

# Genetic Algorithm for Design Optimization
def fitness_function(design):
    """
    Calculates the fitness of a given design. This is a placeholder
    for your actual performance evaluation code, which would depend
    on specific aircraft design parameters.
    :param design: Array of design parameters.
    :return: Fitness score.
    """
    return np.sum(design)   # Example fitness function that maximizes
    ↪ the sum

def select_parents(population, fitness_scores):
    """
    Select parents for the next generation based on fitness scores
    ↪ using roulette wheel selection.
    :param population: Current population of designs.
    :param fitness_scores: Fitness scores for the current
    ↪ population.
    :return: Selected parents for crossover.
    """
    total_fitness = np.sum(fitness_scores)
    selection_probabilities = fitness_scores / total_fitness
    parents = np.random.choice(population, size=2,
    ↪ p=selection_probabilities)
    return parents

def crossover(parent1, parent2):
    """
    Performs crossover between two parents to create a child design.
    :param parent1: First parent design.
    :param parent2: Second parent design.
    :return: Child design created from the parents.
    """
    crossover_point = len(parent1) // 2
    child = np.concatenate((parent1[:crossover_point],
    ↪ parent2[crossover_point:]))
    return child

def mutate(design, mutation_rate=0.1):
    """
    Mutates a design based on a mutation rate.
    :param design: Design array to mutate.
    :param mutation_rate: Probability of mutation for each design
    ↪ parameter.
    """
```

```
        for i in range(len(design)):
            if random.random() < mutation_rate:
                design[i] += random.uniform(-0.1, 0.1)  # Mutate by a
                ↪    small random value
        return design

def genetic_algorithm(population_size=50, generations=100):
    """
    Main function to run the genetic algorithm for design
    ↪    optimization.
    :param population_size: Number of designs in the population.
    :param generations: Number of generations to run the algorithm.
    """
    population = [np.random.rand(5) for _ in range(population_size)]
    ↪    # Initialize random designs
    for generation in range(generations):
        fitness_scores = np.array([fitness_function(design) for
        ↪    design in population])
        next_generation = []
        for _ in range(population_size // 2):
            parents = select_parents(population, fitness_scores)
            child1 = crossover(parents[0], parents[1])
            child2 = crossover(parents[1], parents[0])
            next_generation.append(mutate(child1))
            next_generation.append(mutate(child2))
        population = np.array(next_generation)
    best_design = population[np.argmax(fitness_scores)]
    return best_design

# Predictive Maintenance for Aircraft Components
def predict_failure(sensor_data):
    """
    Predicts the likelihood of failure based on sensor data.
    :param sensor_data: Array of collected sensor data.
    :return: Probability of failure.
    """
    # For illustration, we will simply use a threshold
    threshold = 0.75
    return np.mean(sensor_data) > threshold  # Placeholder logic

# Simulating sensor data
sensor_data_example = np.random.rand(100)  # Simulating with random
↪    sensor readings
failure_prediction = predict_failure(sensor_data_example)

# Simple Reinforcement Learning for Autonomous Navigation
class SimpleAgent:
    def __init__(self):
        self.q_table = np.zeros((5, 5))  # Simple grid world Q-table

    def act(self, state):
        return np.argmax(self.q_table[state])  # Choose action based
        ↪    on Q-values
```

```
def update(self, state, action, reward, next_state):
    self.q_table[state, action] += 0.1 * (reward +
    ↪  np.max(self.q_table[next_state]) - self.q_table[state,
    ↪  action])

# Running the Optimization and Prediction Algorithms
best_design = genetic_algorithm()
print("Best Design Parameters:", best_design)

if failure_prediction:
    print("Warning: High likelihood of component failure.")
else:
    print("Component functioning properly.")

agent = SimpleAgent()
current_state = (2, 3)  # Example state in the grid
action = agent.act(current_state)
print("Action for Autonomous Navigation:", action)

agent.update(current_state, action, reward=1, next_state=(2, 4))  #
↪  Example update with reward
```

This code snippet includes:

- fitness_function, which evaluates the fitness of design parameters for aircraft optimization.
- select_parents to select parent designs based on their fitness scores.
- crossover creates a new design by combining features from two parent designs.
- mutate introduces variations in designs to maintain genetic diversity.
- genetic_algorithm which orchestrates the evolutionary process to find optimal designs.
- predict_failure predicts component failures based on collected sensor data.
- A simple SimpleAgent class that implements a reinforcement learning method for autonomous navigation decisions.

The provided example runs the genetic algorithm for optimizing design parameters and checks predictive maintenance for aircraft components. It also demonstrates basic decision-making for an autonomous navigation system, printing relevant results to the console. "'

Chapter 43

AI in Structural Engineering

In the field of structural engineering, the advent of Artificial Intelligence (AI) has brought forth significant advancements and capabilities. AI applications have permeated various areas of structural engineering, revolutionizing design processes, enhancing safety measures, and optimizing construction practices. This chapter delves into the utilization of AI in structural engineering, specifically focusing on the optimization of structural integrity, smart city planning and management, AI-driven construction project management, safety monitoring and incident prediction, and environmental impact analysis and optimization.

1 Optimization of Structural Integrity

The optimization of structural integrity is a crucial aspect of structural engineering, aiming to ensure the safe and optimal design of buildings and infrastructure. AI techniques offer unprecedented opportunities to optimize structural integrity by enabling efficient design exploration and evaluation. One such method is the implementation of optimization algorithms, such as genetic algorithms or simulated annealing, that leverage AI principles to search for optimal solutions within the vast design space. These algorithms facilitate the identification of configurations that maximize structural performance metrics, such as load-bearing capacity or structural stability. By formulating structural design objectives as mathematical optimization problems, engineers can iteratively refine designs to achieve increased structural integrity.

2 Smart City Planning and Management

AI plays a pivotal role in the planning and management of smart cities, integrating structural engineering practices with urban development. By harnessing AI techniques, engineers can analyze vast amounts of data, such as geographic information systems (GIS) data, environmental data, and infrastructure information, to optimize city planning processes. Machine learning algorithms can process and analyze this data to identify patterns, make predictions, and propose optimal urban development strategies. These algorithms enable engineers to optimize city infrastructure layout, determine optimal zoning regulations, and design sustainable and resilient urban spaces. AI-driven smart city planning ensures efficient resource allocation, enhances livability, and improves the overall quality of urban life.

3 AI-driven Construction Project Management

Construction project management is a complex task that involves coordinating various activities, resources, and stakeholders. AI algorithms and techniques facilitate the automation and optimization of construction project management processes. By leveraging AI, engineers can optimize project schedules, manage resources effectively, and minimize delays and cost overruns. Machine learning algorithms can analyze historical project data to identify patterns and predict potential risks and bottlenecks. These algorithms aid in decision-making, enabling project managers to optimize construction processes, allocate resources efficiently, and ensure timely completion of projects. AI-driven construction project management enhances efficiency, reduces costs, and improves overall project outcomes.

4 Safety Monitoring and Incident Prediction

Ensuring safety in structural engineering projects is of utmost importance. AI technologies assist in safety monitoring and predicting potential incidents or failures. By employing machine learning algorithms, engineers can analyze sensor data from structural health monitoring systems to detect anomalies and predict structural deterioration or failure. These algorithms learn from historical data and identify patterns that indicate potential safety risks. Through AI-driven safety monitoring, engineers can anticipate and mitigate structural issues proactively, preventing accidents or catastrophes. Additionally, AI can aid in the prediction of extreme events, such as earthquakes or hurricane-induced structural damage, by analyzing relevant environmental and geological data. This enables engineers to design structures that are resilient to these events and implement appropriate safety measures.

5 Environmental Impact Analysis and Optimization

Structural engineering decisions have significant environmental implications. AI techniques enable engineers to assess and optimize the environmental impact of structural design and construction processes. Machine learning algorithms can analyze environmental data, material properties, and energy consumption patterns to assess the carbon footprint and resource usage of structural projects. This analysis facilitates the identification of sustainable design strategies and material choices to minimize environmental impact. AI algorithms can also optimize construction processes, considering factors such as transportation, energy usage, and waste management, with the goal of reducing environmental burdens. By leveraging AI, structural engineers can contribute to the development of environmentally conscious structures and promote sustainable practices within the industry.

Overall, the integration of AI technologies in structural engineering enhances the optimization of structural integrity, enables smart city planning and management, streamlines construction project management processes, ensures safety through predictive monitoring, and supports environmentally conscious design and construction practices. These advancements pave the way for more efficient, resilient, and sustainable infrastructure development that aligns with the needs of present and future generations.

Python Code Snippet

Below is a Python code snippet that implements key algorithms related to optimizing structural integrity, managing construction projects, and predicting safety incidents using AI techniques in structural engineering.

```
import numpy as np
from scipy.optimize import minimize

def optimize_structure(parameters):
    '''
    Optimize structural design for maximum integrity using a genetic
    ↪  algorithm.
    :param parameters: List of design parameters (e.g. dimensions,
    ↪  material properties).
    :return: Optimal value of the structural integrity metric.
    '''
    def structural_integrity(metric):
        # This is a simple representation of a function that defines
        ↪  structural integrity based on the parameters
        # The actual implementation would be based on finite element
        ↪  analysis or similar methods.
        return -1 * (metric[0]**2 + metric[1]**2 - 10)

    # Bounds for the parameters (example: dimensions constraints)
    bounds = [(0.1, 10), (0.1, 10)]

    # Initial guess
    initial_guess = [1, 1]

    # Optimization process
    result = minimize(structural_integrity, initial_guess,
    ↪  bounds=bounds)
    return result.fun, result.x  # Return the optimal integrity
    ↪  value and the corresponding parameters


def predict_incident_risk(sensor_data):
    '''
    Predict potential safety incidents based on historical sensor
    ↪  data.
    :param sensor_data: List of historical sensor readings (e.g.
    ↪  strain gauges, accelerometers).
    :return: Predicted risk of incidents.
    '''
    # Dummy prediction logic based on the averages
    risk_threshold = 0.8  # Presumed safety threshold
    mean_reading = np.mean(sensor_data)

    # Simple risk assessment logic
    if mean_reading > risk_threshold:
        return "High Risk"
    elif mean_reading > (risk_threshold / 2):
        return "Moderate Risk"
    else:
        return "Low Risk"
```

```
# Example usage of the functions

# Parameters for optimization (for example: width, height)
design_parameters = [5, 5]

# Run optimization
optimal_integrity_value, optimal_parameters =
↳  optimize_structure(design_parameters)

# Example sensor data (simulated)
sensor_data = [0.5, 0.6, 0.7, 0.9, 0.3, 0.4]

# Run incident risk prediction
incident_risk = predict_incident_risk(sensor_data)

# Output results
print("Optimal Structural Integrity Value:",
↳  optimal_integrity_value)
print("Optimal Design Parameters:", optimal_parameters)
print("Predicted Incident Risk:", incident_risk)
```

This code defines two important functions:

- `optimize_structure` utilizes optimization techniques to achieve maximum structural integrity based on given design parameters, simulating the design process.
- `predict_incident_risk` assesses the risk of potential incidents by analyzing historical sensor data for infrastructure robustness.

The provided example demonstrates how to optimize a structure and predict the risk of safety incidents, yielding valuable insights for structural engineering applications.

Chapter 44

AI in Quantum Computing

1 Quantum Algorithm Development with AI

The field of quantum computing combines principles from quantum mechanics and computer science to solve complex computational problems more efficiently than classical computers. With the advent of Artificial Intelligence (AI), researchers have begun exploring ways to leverage AI techniques in the development and optimization of quantum algorithms.

One area where AI has shown promising results is in the refinement and optimization of quantum algorithms. Quantum algorithms, such as Shor's algorithm for factorization or Grover's algorithm for search, rely on the manipulation of quantum states and operations to perform computations. However, designing efficient and error-tolerant quantum algorithms is a challenging task due to the inherent complexity of quantum systems.

By employing AI techniques, such as reinforcement learning or genetic algorithms, researchers can search for optimal quantum algorithm configurations within the vast space of possible solutions. AI algorithms can iteratively explore different combinations of quantum gates, circuit topologies, or input states to maximize the algorithm's performance metrics, such as the number of correct outputs or the circuit depth.

Formulating the problem of optimizing quantum algorithms as a reinforcement or evolutionary learning problem allows researchers to exploit the power of AI to discover new, more efficient quantum algorithms. This approach can potentially uncover novel algorithmic strategies that may have remained undiscovered using traditional computational approaches.

2 AI-driven Optimization in Quantum Systems

In addition to algorithm development, AI techniques play a crucial role in the optimization of quantum systems themselves. Quantum systems are highly susceptible to noise, decoherence, and errors that limit the performance and scalability of quantum computers. AI-driven optimization approaches can help mitigate these challenges and improve the overall capabilities of quantum systems.

One fundamental task in optimizing quantum systems is reducing the effects of noise and errors through error correction and fault tolerance techniques. AI algorithms can assist in developing error-correcting codes and protocols that enable the detection and correction of errors that occur during quantum information processing. By analyzing large datasets of error patterns and utilizing machine learning techniques, AI algorithms can identify and exploit underlying error structures to improve error correction efficiency.

Furthermore, AI techniques can aid in the optimization of quantum gate operations and gate sequences to minimize the effects of noise and improve the overall fidelity of quantum computations. Machine learning algorithms can analyze experimental data and quantum system attributes to develop models that predict optimal choices for gate parameters, such as gate duration or control signals. These optimized parameters can then be used to implement more robust and accurate quantum gates.

AI-driven optimization techniques also enable quantum computers to adapt to changes in system conditions and improve performance in real-time. By continuously monitoring quantum system parameters, AI algorithms can make informed decisions on system configurations, such as adjusting gate timings or optimizing qubit assignments, to maximize computational outputs. Real-time feedback loops between AI algorithms and quantum systems allow for dynamic system optimization and ensure robust performance under changing conditions.

3 Quantum Machine Learning Applications

The intersection of quantum computing and machine learning has garnered significant attention due to the potential for quantum computers to address computationally intensive tasks in machine learning more efficiently. Quantum machine learning algorithms leverage the unique properties of quantum systems to enhance classical machine learning techniques.

Quantum machine learning algorithms exploit quantum superposition and entanglement to perform computations on large datasets more quickly than classical counterparts. Quantum computers can potentially provide substantial speedup for important tasks, such as pattern recognition, optimization, and clustering. Moreover, quantum machine learning algorithms can uncover previously hidden patterns or correlations in high-dimensional data that are challenging for classical machine learning algorithms to extract.

AI techniques are instrumental in the development and optimization of quantum machine learning algorithms. Researchers employ AI algorithms, such as reinforcement learning or genetic algorithms, to search for optimal quantum models or circuits for a given machine learning task. These algorithms explore the design space of possible quantum machine learning architectures and optimize parameters to maximize the accuracy or efficiency of learning.

Additionally, AI techniques assist in data preprocessing and feature selection for quantum machine learning. AI algorithms can analyze and preprocess datasets to extract relevant features or reduce the dimensionality of the data before mapping it onto quantum states. This approach enhances the efficiency and effectiveness of subsequent quantum machine learning algorithms by inputting preprocessed data that captures the essential information required for learning tasks.

4 Quantum Cryptography and Security

AI techniques also find applications in the field of quantum cryptography, which leverages the principles of quantum mechanics to provide secure communication channels. Quantum cryptography offers unbreakable encryption methods using principles such as quantum key distribution (QKD) and quantum secure direct communication.

AI algorithms contribute to the security and robustness of quantum cryptography protocols by helping identify potential vulnerabilities or attacks. By analyzing historical attack patterns and simulating potential attack scenarios, AI algorithms can develop countermeasures and optimized protocols to detect and prevent security breaches.

In addition to enhancing security measures, AI techniques aid in the design and optimization of quantum key generation and distribution protocols. Machine learning algorithms can analyze quantum channel characteristics, system parameters, and noise patterns to devise more efficient and secure key generation strategies. This optimization ensures the creation of cryptographic keys that are less susceptible to interception or unauthorized decoding.

Furthermore, AI techniques enable dynamic adaptation of quantum cryptography protocols to evolving security threats. AI algorithms can continuously monitor system performance, identify potential weaknesses or deviations from expected behaviors, and make real-time adjustments to maintain security. The ability to adapt cryptography protocols in real-time enhances the resilience and reliability of quantum encryption systems.

5 AI-driven Quantum Error Correction

Quantum error correction is essential for maintaining the reliability and coherence of qubits in a quantum system. Error correction techniques detect and correct errors that occur during quantum computations, thereby enabling reliable and fault-tolerant quantum information processing. AI-driven approaches enhance the effectiveness and efficiency of quantum error correction algorithms, aiding in the development of fault-tolerant quantum computing systems.

AI techniques, such as machine learning algorithms, can analyze large datasets of error patterns and quantum system characteristics to identify underlying error structures and develop more accurate error models. Using this knowledge, AI algorithms can optimize error correction codes, error detection circuits, and recovery procedures to improve the overall performance of quantum error correction.

Moreover, AI algorithms can assist in the optimization of error mitigation techniques that suppress and reduce the impact of errors in quantum computations. By employing machine learning models, AI algorithms can identify and exploit error characteristics and develop efficient error mitigation methods. These methods can help overcome limitations imposed by hardware constraints or noise sources in quantum systems, improving the fidelity and longevity of quantum computations.

Additionally, AI techniques enable real-time adaptation of error correction approaches to changing quantum system conditions. By continuously monitoring error rates, noise sources, and system parameters, AI algorithms can dynamically adjust error correction procedures, error thresholds, or other system parameters to optimize error mitigation strategies. This adaptive error correction ensures efficient and reliable quantum information processing in the presence of transient or evolving noise sources.

In summary, the combination of AI and quantum computing holds immense potential for advancing the field of quantum algorithms, optimizing quantum systems, enhancing quantum machine learning capabilities, strengthening quantum cryptography and security, and improving quantum error correction techniques. The collaboration between these two domains can accelerate the development of quantum technologies and unlock novel applications in various fields."'latex

Python Code Snippet

Below is a Python code snippet that demonstrates important algorithms and calculations related to quantum algorithm optimization, quantum error correction, and quantum machine learning applications mentioned in this chapter.

```python
import numpy as np
from scipy.optimize import minimize

def optimize_quantum_algorithm(circuit_params, performance_metric):
    '''
    Optimize quantum circuit parameters to maximize performance
    ↪   metric.
    :param circuit_params: Initial parameters for the quantum
    ↪   circuit.
    :param performance_metric: Function to evaluate the performance
    ↪   based on parameters.
    :return: Optimized parameters.
    '''

    # Optimization function to minimize (negative of performance to
    ↪   maximize it)
    def objective(params):
        return -performance_metric(params)

    # Perform optimization
    result = minimize(objective, circuit_params,
    ↪   method='Nelder-Mead')
    return result.x

def quantum_error_correction(error_rates):
```

```
    '''
    Apply quantum error correction based on provided error rates.
    :param error_rates: List of error rates for different qubits.
    :return: Corrected output state.
    '''
    # Placeholder for corrected state (assuming a simple majority
    ↪   voting error correction)
    corrected_state = []

    for rate in error_rates:
        if rate < 0.1:   # Assume 10% is the threshold for error
        ↪   correction
            corrected_state.append(1)   # Corrected bit is 1
        else:
            corrected_state.append(0)   # Corrected bit is 0

    return corrected_state

def quantum_machine_learning(data, model_params):
    '''
    Implement a simple quantum machine learning algorithm strategy.
    :param data: Input data for machine learning.
    :param model_params: Parameters of the quantum model.
    :return: Output predictions.
    '''
    # Assuming a simple quantum feature mapping
    def feature_mapping(x):
        return np.sin(model_params[0] * x) + model_params[1]

    predictions = []
    for x in data:
        predictions.append(feature_mapping(x))

    return np.array(predictions)

# Example Inputs
initial_circuit_params = [0.5, 0.5]   # Example initial parameters
def performance_metric(params):
    '''Example performance metric function for optimization.'''
    # Placeholder for a performance metric function
    return np.exp(-((params[0] - 0.8)**2 + (params[1] - 0.3)**2))

error_rates = [0.05, 0.15, 0.08, 0.12]   # Example error rates
data_points = np.linspace(0, 2 * np.pi, 10)   # Data for predictions
model_parameters = [1.0, 0.5]   # Model parameters for quantum ML

# Perform optimizations and calculations
optimized_params =
↪   optimize_quantum_algorithm(initial_circuit_params,
↪   performance_metric)
corrected_state = quantum_error_correction(error_rates)
predictions = quantum_machine_learning(data_points,
↪   model_parameters)
```

```
# Output results
print("Optimized Quantum Algorithm Parameters:", optimized_params)
print("Corrected Quantum State:", corrected_state)
print("Quantum Machine Learning Predictions:", predictions)
```

This code defines three main functions:

- optimize_quantum_algorithm optimizes parameters for a quantum circuit to maximize a given performance metric.
- quantum_error_correction applies error correction based on predefined error rates using a majority voting approach.
- quantum_machine_learning executes a basic quantum machine learning model that predicts outputs based on input data and model parameters.

The provided example demonstrates the optimization of quantum algorithm parameters, the correction of quantum states based on error rates, and the predictions computed from a simple quantum machine learning strategy. "'

Chapter 45

AI in Data Center Management

Data centers play a critical role in modern computing, serving as the backbone for storing, processing, and managing vast amounts of data. The efficient management of data centers is crucial to ensure smooth operations, minimize downtime, optimize resource allocation, and reduce energy consumption. With the advances in Artificial Intelligence (AI) techniques, there has been a growing interest in leveraging AI for data center management, leading to significant improvements in its efficiency and performance.

1 Predictive Analytics for Server Maintenance

The maintenance of server infrastructure is vital to prevent failures and downtime in data centers. AI techniques, particularly predictive analytics, can play a crucial role in optimizing server maintenance schedules and improving the reliability of data center operations.

By analyzing historical server performance data, such as CPU utilization, memory usage, and network traffic, AI algorithms can identify patterns that are indicative of potential issues or failures. This analysis allows data center administrators to proactively address hardware or software failures, schedule maintenance activities, and replace components before they become major concerns. Moreover, predictive analytics can help optimize maintenance schedules to minimize disruptions and reduce the overall downtime of data center operations.

Mathematically, predictive analytics for server maintenance involves training machine learning models using labeled historical data. Let X represent the input features such as CPU usage, memory usage, and network traffic. Let Y denote the binary label indicating the occurrence of a failure or critical event. The task is to learn a function $f(X)$ that accurately predicts the probability of a failure based on the input features. This function can be estimated using techniques such as logistic regression, support vector machines, or neural networks.

2 AI-driven Energy Management and Cooling

Energy management and cooling systems are crucial components of data center infrastructure as they directly impact operational costs and equipment reliability. AI techniques enable data centers to optimize energy consumption, increase energy efficiency, and enhance cooling mechanisms.

AI algorithms can analyze real-time power usage, server workload, and environmental data to identify opportunities for reducing energy consumption without compromising performance. For example, workload consolidation algorithms can dynamically allocate server workloads to minimize the number of active servers and, thus, reduce energy consumption. Additionally, AI can optimize cooling systems by adjusting temperature and airflow based on real-time server conditions, resulting in energy savings and improved cooling efficiency.

Mathematically, AI-driven energy management involves formulating optimization problems to allocate server workloads and adjust cooling parameters. Let W represent the workload distribution across servers and C represent the cooling configurations. The goal is to find the optimal W and C that minimize energy consumption while satisfying performance and temperature constraints. This problem can be formulated as a constrained optimization problem:

$$\begin{aligned} \underset{W,C}{\text{minimize}} \quad & \text{Energy Consumption} \\ \text{subject to} \quad & \text{Performance Constraints,} \\ & \text{Temperature Constraints.} \end{aligned} \quad (45.1)$$

Solving this optimization problem requires efficient algorithms, such as linear or nonlinear programming, that balance energy efficiency with performance requirements.

3 Automated Data Management and Optimization

Efficient data management is crucial in data centers to ensure data availability, accessibility, and integrity. AI techniques can automate various data management tasks, such as data placement, replication, and caching, to maximize data center performance.

AI algorithms can analyze data usage patterns, access frequencies, and data characteristics to optimize data placement strategies. By placing frequently accessed data closer to the computational resources or using caching mechanisms, data retrieval times can be significantly reduced, improving overall system performance. Furthermore, AI-driven data replication techniques can enhance data availability and fault tolerance by intelligently replicating critical data across multiple servers.

Mathematically, data placement and replication can be modeled as optimization problems. Let D represent the dataset, S represent the set of available servers, and R denote the replication configuration. The goal is to find the optimal mapping of data to servers and the optimal configuration of replication to minimize data retrieval latency while ensuring data availability. This problem can be formulated as an optimization problem:

$$\underset{D,S,R}{\text{minimize}} \quad \text{Data Retrieval Latency} \tag{45.2}$$
$$\text{subject to} \quad \text{Data Availability Constraints.}$$

Solving this optimization problem requires efficient algorithms, such as integer programming or heuristic search, that balance data retrieval latency with data availability requirements.

4 Security Enhancement with AI

Data center security is of paramount importance to protect sensitive data, prevent unauthorized access, and safeguard against cyber threats. AI techniques can enhance data center security by identifying potential vulnerabilities, predicting and detecting security breaches, and enabling real-time threat response.

AI algorithms can analyze system logs, network traffic, and user behavior to identify patterns indicative of security breaches or malicious activities. By detecting anomalies and deviations from normal behavior, AI-driven security systems can proactively identify potential vulnerabilities or cyber attacks. Furthermore, real-time analysis of security data allows for immediate response, such as triggering alarm systems, blocking unauthorized access attempts, or initiating automated countermeasures.

Mathematically, security enhancement with AI involves training machine learning models using labeled security data to predict the occurrence of security breaches or classify potential cyber threats. For example, anomaly detection algorithms can be trained on normal system behavior and subsequently identify deviations from this behavior. This approach requires labeled security data and can utilize techniques such as clustering, classification, or outlier detection.

In summary, AI techniques offer significant potential for enhancing data center management. Through predictive analytics for server maintenance, data centers can proactively address issues and optimize maintenance schedules. AI-driven energy management and cooling systems enable energy-efficient operations and cooling mechanisms. Automated data management and optimization techniques optimize data placement and replication to maximize performance. Lastly, AI-enhanced security measures proactively detect and respond to potential security breaches and cyber threats.

Python Code Snippet

Below is a Python code snippet that implements the important equations and algorithms discussed in this chapter concerning predictive analytics for server maintenance, energy management and cooling, automated data management and optimization, and security enhancement using AI.

```python
import numpy as np
import pandas as pd
from sklearn.model_selection import train_test_split
from sklearn.ensemble import RandomForestClassifier
from scipy.optimize import minimize

def predictive_maintenance(data):
    '''
    Predictive maintenance using a Random Forest classifier.
    :param data: DataFrame containing historical server performance
    ↪   data.
    :return: Trained model and predictions.
    '''
    # Features: CPU, Memory, Network Traffic
```

```python
    X = data[['cpu_usage', 'memory_usage', 'network_traffic']]
    # Target: Failure occurrence (1 if failure, 0 otherwise)
    y = data['failure']

    # Splitting the dataset
    X_train, X_test, y_train, y_test = train_test_split(X, y,
    ↪    test_size=0.2, random_state=42)

    # Training the model
    model = RandomForestClassifier(n_estimators=100)
    model.fit(X_train, y_train)

    # Making predictions
    predictions = model.predict(X_test)
    return model, predictions

def optimize_energy_management(W_initial, C_initial,
↪    performance_constraints, temperature_constraints):
    '''
    Optimize energy consumption in a data center.
    :param W_initial: Initial workload distribution.
    :param C_initial: Initial cooling configurations.
    :param performance_constraints: Constraints on performance.
    :param temperature_constraints: Constraints on temperature.
    :return: Optimal workload and cooling configuration.
    '''
    def objective(WC):
        W, C = WC[:len(W_initial)], WC[len(W_initial):]
        return np.sum(W * C)   # Energy consumption as a function of
        ↪    workloads and cooling

    constraints = [{'type': 'ineq', 'fun': lambda WC:
    ↪    performance_constraints - np.sum(WC[:len(W_initial)])},
                    {'type': 'ineq', 'fun': lambda WC:
                    ↪    temperature_constraints -
                    ↪    np.sum(WC[len(W_initial):])}]

    result = minimize(objective, np.concatenate([W_initial,
    ↪    C_initial]), constraints=constraints)
    optimal_W = result.x[:len(W_initial)]
    optimal_C = result.x[len(W_initial):]
    return optimal_W, optimal_C

def optimize_data_placement(data, servers):
    '''
    Optimize data placement for minimizing retrieval latency.
    :param data: The dataset to optimize.
    :param servers: List of available servers.
    :return: Optimized data placement mapping.
    '''
    # This is a simplified version for illustration
    latency = {server: np.random.random() for server in servers}   #
    ↪    Random simulated latencies
```

303

```python
    optimized_mapping = {d: min(latency, key=latency.get) for d in
    ↪   data}  # Map data to server with min latency
    return optimized_mapping

def detect_security_breach(log_data):
    '''
    Identify potential security breaches using anomaly detection.
    :param log_data: DataFrame containing log information.
    :return: List of detected anomalies.
    '''

    # Example using simple statistics to detect anomalies
    anomalies = log_data[(log_data['response_time'] >
    ↪   log_data['response_time'].mean() + 3 *
    ↪   log_data['response_time'].std())]
    return anomalies

# Example Usage:

# Sample Data Generation for Predictive Maintenance
data = pd.DataFrame({
    'cpu_usage': np.random.rand(100),
    'memory_usage': np.random.rand(100),
    'network_traffic': np.random.rand(100),
    'failure': np.random.randint(0, 2, size=100)
})

# Step 1: Predictive Maintenance
model, predictions = predictive_maintenance(data)

# Step 2: Optimize Energy Management
W_initial = np.random.rand(5)  # Initial workloads
C_initial = np.random.rand(5)  # Initial cooling
performance_constraints = 10
temperature_constraints = 20
optimal_W, optimal_C = optimize_energy_management(W_initial,
↪   C_initial, performance_constraints, temperature_constraints)

# Step 3: Data Placement Optimization
data_items = ['data1', 'data2', 'data3']
servers = ['server1', 'server2', 'server3']
optimal_mapping = optimize_data_placement(data_items, servers)

# Step 4: Security Detection
log_data = pd.DataFrame({
    'response_time': np.random.normal(loc=1.0, scale=0.2, size=100)
})
detected_anomalies = detect_security_breach(log_data)

# Output results
print("Predictions from Predictive Maintenance:", predictions)
print("Optimal Workloads:", optimal_W)
print("Optimal Cooling Configurations:", optimal_C)
print("Optimized Data Placement Mapping:", optimal_mapping)
```

```
print("Detected Security Breaches:", detected_anomalies)
```

This code defines several key functions:

- `predictive_maintenance` implements a machine learning model to predict server failure using historical data.
- `optimize_energy_management` formulates and solves an optimization problem to minimize energy consumption.
- `optimize_data_placement` determines an optimized mapping of data to servers based on latency.
- `detect_security_breach` detects anomalies in logs that may indicate security threats.

The provided example covers mock data generation and demonstrates how these functions would operate in a real scenario, ultimately outputting predictions, optimized configurations, and detected security breaches.

Chapter 46

AI in Blockchain and Cryptocurrency

1 Fraud Detection and Security in Blockchain Networks

Blockchain technology has revolutionized the field of cryptocurrency by providing a decentralized and secure platform for conducting transactions. However, ensuring the security and integrity of blockchain networks remains a significant challenge. Artificial Intelligence (AI) techniques can enhance the security of blockchain networks by detecting and preventing fraudulent activities.

One key application of AI in blockchain networks is fraud detection. AI algorithms can analyze and monitor transaction patterns, network activities, and user behaviors to identify suspicious or fraudulent transactions. By applying anomaly detection algorithms, AI can detect transactions that deviate from normal behavior, indicating potential fraudulent activity. Moreover, machine learning techniques can identify patterns and characteristics associated with known fraudulent transactions to predict and prevent future instances of fraud.

Mathematically, fraud detection algorithms in blockchain networks involve training machine learning models using labeled transaction data. Let X represent the input features such as transaction details, timestamps, and user information. Let Y denote the binary labels indicating the occurrence of fraud (1 for fraudulent transactions, 0 otherwise). The task is to learn a function $f(X)$ that accurately predicts the probability of fraud based on the input features. This function can be estimated using techniques such as logistic regression, support vector machines, or neural networks.

2 AI for Cryptocurrency Trading Strategies

Cryptocurrency trading is a complex and volatile market where timely decision-making is crucial for maximizing profit. AI techniques can enhance trading strategies by analyzing market data, identifying trends and patterns, and making intelligent predictions about future price movements.

AI algorithms can analyze historical market data, including price fluctuations, trading volumes, and market sentiments, to identify patterns that indicate potential profitable trading opportunities. By training machine learning models on historical data, these algorithms can learn to make accurate predictions about future price movements, enabling traders to make informed investment decisions.

Mathematically, developing AI-based trading strategies involves training models to predict cryptocurrency price movements. Let X represent the input features such as historical price data, volume, and other relevant market indicators. Let Y represent the labels indicating the expected price movement (e.g., an increase, decrease, or no change). The goal is to learn a function $f(X)$ that accurately predicts the expected price movement based on the input features. This function can be estimated using techniques such as time series analysis, recurrent neural networks, or reinforcement learning algorithms.

3 Smart Contracts and Automated Transactions

Smart contracts are self-executing contracts with predefined rules and conditions stored on a blockchain. AI can enhance the capabilities of smart contracts by automating contract execution and enforcing complex conditions without the need for manual intervention.

AI algorithms can analyze the preprogrammed conditions of smart contracts and monitor the relevant data on the blockchain in real-time. By applying machine learning techniques, these algorithms can make intelligent decisions and execute the contract clauses automatically. This automation not only increases the efficiency and accuracy of contract execution but also reduces the risk of human error or manipulation.

Mathematically, AI algorithms for smart contracts involve developing models to interpret contract conditions and make automated decisions. The models leverage techniques such as rule-based systems, decision trees, or reinforcement learning algorithms to execute the contract clauses based on real-time blockchain data.

4 Predictive Analytics for Blockchain Scalability

Scalability is a critical challenge in blockchain networks, especially as the number of transactions and network participants continues to grow. Predictive analytics using AI techniques can help address scalability issues by forecasting network requirements and optimizing resource allocation.

AI algorithms can analyze historical transaction data, network metrics, and user activities to predict future demands on the blockchain network. By identifying patterns and trends, these algorithms can estimate the required network resources and optimize the allocation of computing power, storage capacity, and network bandwidth. This proactive approach to resource management allows blockchain networks to scale efficiently and dynamically.

Mathematically, predictive analytics for blockchain scalability involves training machine learning models using historical blockchain network data. Let X represent the input features such as transaction volumes, block sizes, and network metrics. Let Y denote the labels indicating the scaling requirements (e.g., network capacity, computing power). The task is to learn a function $f(X)$ that accurately predicts the scaling requirements based on the input features. This function can be estimated using techniques such as time series forecasting, regression analysis, or neural networks.

5 AI-driven Blockchain Data Analysis

The transparency and immutability of blockchain data generate vast amounts of valuable information. AI techniques can analyze blockchain data to extract insights, identify trends, and make data-driven decisions.

AI algorithms can process and analyze blockchain data, including transaction records, smart contract logs, and network activities, to generate meaningful information. By applying techniques such as natural language processing and machine learning, these algorithms can identify patterns, detect anomalies, and perform sentiment analysis on blockchain data. This analysis can help predict market trends, detect potential risks, and inform decision-making processes.

Mathematically, AI-driven blockchain data analysis involves training machine learning models using labeled blockchain data or applying unsupervised learning techniques. The specific techniques used depend on the nature of the analysis required, such as clustering, classification, anomaly detection, or sentiment analysis.

In conclusion, AI techniques offer promising applications in enhancing the security, trading strategies, automation, scalability, and data analysis in blockchain and cryptocurrency networks. By leveraging AI algorithms, blockchain networks become more secure, efficient, and capable of extracting valuable insights from the wealth of data they record.

Python Code Snippet

Below is a Python code snippet to implement the important equations and algorithms discussed in the chapter related to AI in Blockchain and Cryptocurrency, including fraud detection, cryptocurrency trading strategies, smart contracts, predictive analytics, and blockchain data analysis.

```python
import numpy as np
import pandas as pd
from sklearn.model_selection import train_test_split
from sklearn.linear_model import LogisticRegression
from sklearn.svm import SVC
from sklearn.ensemble import RandomForestClassifier
from sklearn.metrics import accuracy_score
from sklearn.preprocessing import StandardScaler
import tensorflow as tf

# Function to train a logistic regression model for fraud detection
def train_fraud_detection_model(data):
    '''
    Train a logistic regression model for fraud detection.
    :param data: DataFrame containing transaction data.
    :return: Trained model.
    '''
    X = data.drop('fraud', axis=1)   # Features
    Y = data['fraud']   # Labels

    # Splitting the dataset
    X_train, X_test, Y_train, Y_test = train_test_split(X, Y,
        test_size=0.3, random_state=42)
```

```python
# Scaling the features
scaler = StandardScaler()
X_train = scaler.fit_transform(X_train)
X_test = scaler.transform(X_test)

# Training the model
model = LogisticRegression()
model.fit(X_train, Y_train)

# Model evaluation
Y_pred = model.predict(X_test)
print("Fraud Detection Model Accuracy:", accuracy_score(Y_test,
↪  Y_pred))

return model

# Function to predict cryptocurrency price movements
def predict_price_movement(data):
    '''
    Predict cryptocurrency price movements using a Simple LSTM
    ↪  model.
    :param data: Historical price data (DataFrame).
    :return: Predicted price movements.
    '''
    # Preparing data for LSTM
    price_data = data['price'].values
    price_data = price_data.reshape(-1, 1)

    # Normalization
    from sklearn.preprocessing import MinMaxScaler
    scaler = MinMaxScaler(feature_range=(0, 1))
    scaled_data = scaler.fit_transform(price_data)

    # Creating training sequences
    X, y = [], []
    for i in range(60, len(scaled_data)):
        X.append(scaled_data[i-60:i])
        y.append(scaled_data[i])
    X, y = np.array(X), np.array(y)

    # Building LSTM model
    model = tf.keras.models.Sequential()
    model.add(tf.keras.layers.LSTM(units=50, return_sequences=True,
    ↪  input_shape=(X.shape[1], 1)))
    model.add(tf.keras.layers.LSTM(units=50))
    model.add(tf.keras.layers.Dense(units=1))

    model.compile(optimizer='adam', loss='mean_squared_error')
    model.fit(X, y, epochs=50, batch_size=32)

    # Predictions
    predicted_price = model.predict(X)
    return scaler.inverse_transform(predicted_price)
```

```python
# Function to automate smart contract execution
def execute_smart_contract(conditions):
    '''
    Execute smart contracts based on pre-defined conditions.
    :param conditions: Dict with conditions for execution.
    :return: Result of execution.
    '''
    # Example condition execution
    if conditions['condition_met']:
        return "Contract Executed: Terms Met"
    else:
        return "Contract Not Executed: Terms Not Met"

# Function for predictive analytics on transaction data
def analyze_scalability(data):
    '''
    Analyze blockchain scalability issues based on historical
    ↪    transaction data.
    :param data: DataFrame with transaction volumes and other
    ↪    metrics.
    :return: Predicted resource allocation requirements.
    '''
    # Feature selection
    X = data[['transaction_volume', 'number_of_transactions']]
    y = data['resource_requirement']

    X_train, X_test, y_train, y_test = train_test_split(X, y,
    ↪    test_size=0.3, random_state=42)

    model = RandomForestClassifier()
    model.fit(X_train, y_train)
    predicted_resources = model.predict(X_test)

    return predicted_resources

# Example data preparation and usage
# Fraud detection example
fraud_data = pd.DataFrame({
    'transaction_amount': [100, 150, 200, 5000, 800, 90, 10000],
    'age': [23, 34, 45, 65, 30, 29, 50],
    'fraud': [0, 0, 0, 1, 0, 0, 1]
})

# Train fraud detection model
model_fraud_detection = train_fraud_detection_model(fraud_data)

# Cryptocurrency price prediction example
price_data = pd.DataFrame({
    'price': [100, 105, 102, 110, 108, 107, 111, 115, 120]
})

predicted_prices = predict_price_movement(price_data)
```

311

```
# Smart contract execution example
conditions = {'condition_met': True}
execution_result = execute_smart_contract(conditions)

# Scalability analysis example
scalability_data = pd.DataFrame({
    'transaction_volume': [100, 200, 300, 400],
    'number_of_transactions': [1, 2, 3, 5],
    'resource_requirement': [2, 3, 4, 6]
})

predicted_resources = analyze_scalability(scalability_data)

# Output results
print("Predicted Prices:", predicted_prices)
print("Smart Contract Execution Result:", execution_result)
print("Predicted Resource Allocations for Scalability:",
↪   predicted_resources)
```

This code defines several functions:

- **train_fraud_detection_model** trains a logistic regression model for detecting fraudulent transactions.
- **predict_price_movement** uses an LSTM model to predict cryptocurrency price movements.
- **execute_smart_contract** simulates the execution of a smart contract based on predefined conditions.
- **analyze_scalability** analyzes resource requirements for blockchain scalability using historical transaction data.

The provided example demonstrates how to execute each of these functions in practice, using sample data to train, predict, and assess outcomes in a blockchain and cryptocurrency context.

Chapter 47

AI in Semiconductor Manufacturing

Semiconductor manufacturing is a complex and intricate process that involves the production of integrated circuits and electronic components. Artificial Intelligence (AI) techniques have shown great potential in optimizing various aspects of semiconductor manufacturing, such as design, testing, and quality control. In this chapter, we delve into the applications of AI in semiconductor manufacturing and explore how these techniques contribute to improving efficiency and productivity in the industry.

1 Predictive Maintenance for Semiconductor Equipment

Maintaining the health of semiconductor manufacturing equipment is crucial to ensure smooth and uninterrupted production. AI techniques, particularly predictive maintenance, enable early detection of equipment failures and prevent costly breakdowns.

The goal of predictive maintenance is to estimate the probability of equipment failure based on historical data and real-time sensor readings, enabling proactive maintenance before failure occurs. This can significantly reduce downtime and improve equipment utilization.

Mathematically, predictive maintenance models can be formulated as follows. Let X represent the historical data, which includes sensor readings, machine operating parameters, and maintenance records. Let Y denote the binary labels, indicating equipment failure (1) or normal operation (0). The objective is to learn a function $f(X)$ that can accurately predict the probability of equipment failure based on the input features. Various machine learning techniques such as logistic regression, support vector machines, or neural networks can be applied to estimate this function.

2 AI-Driven Design and Testing of Semiconductors

Designing and testing semiconductor products require meticulous attention to detail, as even minor inaccuracies can lead to significant performance issues or defects. AI techniques have demonstrated their capabilities in optimizing the design and testing processes.

AI algorithms can analyze large volumes of historical design and test data to identify patterns and correlations between design parameters and product performance. By leveraging this information, AI models can generate optimized designs with improved efficiency, power consumption, and manufacturing yield.

Mathematically, the AI-driven design process involves developing models that can predict product performance based on design parameters. Let X represent the input features, including design parameters, such as transistor sizes, interconnect topologies, and voltage levels. Let Y denote the target variables, such as power consumption, speed, or yield. The goal is to learn a function $f(X)$ that accurately predicts the target variables based on the input features. This function can be estimated using regression models, neural networks, or other appropriate techniques.

Similarly, in the testing phase, AI techniques can analyze test results, historical yield data, and equipment performance to identify potential causes of failures or defects. By leveraging this information, AI models can optimize testing strategies and improve yield rates.

3 Process Optimization in Chip Manufacturing

Chip manufacturing involves multiple complex processes, such as lithography, etching, deposition, and packaging. Optimizing these processes is essential to ensure high-quality and cost-effective chip production. AI techniques can be instrumental in optimizing chip manufacturing processes by analyzing process data and providing insights into process improvements.

Through the analysis of historical process data, sensor readings, and equipment parameters, AI algorithms can identify process variations, bottlenecks, and sources of defects. This information can be used to fine-tune process parameters, improve product quality, reduce cycle times, and optimize resource allocation.

Mathematically, process optimization models in chip manufacturing aim to find the optimal process parameters that maximize yield, minimize defects, or reduce production costs. Let X represent the input features, such as process parameters, equipment settings, and environmental conditions. Let Y denote the output variables of interest, such as yield, defect density, or production cost. The objective is to learn a function $f(X)$ that accurately predicts the output variables based on the input features. Optimization techniques, such as response surface methodology, genetic algorithms, or reinforcement learning, can be employed to find the optimal process parameters.

4 Quality Control and Defect Detection

Ensuring the quality of semiconductor products is of paramount importance in the industry. Defects can lead to significant financial losses and damage the reputation of semiconductor manufacturers. AI techniques can play a vital role in quality control and defect detection by analyzing images, sensor data, and historical defect records.

AI algorithms can analyze images of manufactured chips, such as optical microscope images or scanning electron microscope (SEM) images, to detect defects and anomalies. By training machine learning models on a large dataset of labeled images, these algorithms can learn to identify various types of defects, such as scratches, contamination, or misalignments.

Mathematically, quality control models in defect detection involve training models to classify or identify defects in semiconductor products. Let X represent the input features, such as image pixels, texture features, or wavelet transforms. Let Y denote the labels indicating the presence or absence of defects. The goal is to learn a function $f(X)$ that accurately predicts the presence of defects based on the input features. Various techniques, such as convolutional neural networks (CNNs), support vector machines (SVMs), or ensemble methods, can be employed for defect detection.

5 AI in Supply Chain and Inventory Management

Efficient supply chain and inventory management are crucial for semiconductor manufacturers to meet customer demands and maintain profitability. AI techniques can optimize supply chain processes by analyzing historical demand data, lead times, transportation costs, and inventory levels.

AI algorithms can forecast future demand based on historical sales data, seasonality patterns, and market trends. By accurately predicting demand, manufacturers can optimize production schedules, control inventory levels, and minimize stockouts or excess inventory.

Mathematically, demand forecasting models aim to predict future demand based on historical demand data and other relevant features. Let X represent the input features, such as historical sales, promotional activities, or economic indicators. Let Y denote the target variable, which represents future demand. The objective is to learn a function $f(X)$ that accurately predicts the target variable based on the input features. Time series analysis techniques, such as exponential smoothing, autoregressive integrated moving average (ARIMA), or recurrent neural networks (RNNs), can be applied for demand forecasting.

Additionally, AI techniques can optimize the inventory levels by dynamically adjusting reorder points, safety stocks, or production quantities. By considering factors such as lead times, demand variability, and customer service levels, AI-driven inventory management systems can balance the trade-offs between inventory costs and customer satisfaction.

In conclusion, AI techniques offer immense potential in enhancing various aspects of semiconductor manufacturing, including predictive maintenance, design optimization, process improvement, quality control, and supply chain management. By leveraging AI algorithms and models, semiconductor manufacturers can benefit from improved efficiency, increased productivity, and enhanced product quality. The applications of AI in semiconductor manufacturing continue to evolve, and further advancements in this field are expected to drive significant transformations in the industry.

Python Code Snippet

Below is a Python code snippet that implements predictive maintenance, AI-driven design optimization, and demand forecasting in semiconductor manufacturing, as discussed in the chapter.

```python
import numpy as np
import pandas as pd
from sklearn.linear_model import LogisticRegression
from sklearn.model_selection import train_test_split
from sklearn.metrics import accuracy_score
from sklearn.preprocessing import StandardScaler
from sklearn.ensemble import RandomForestRegressor
from statsmodels.tsa.arima.model import ARIMA

def predictive_maintenance(X, y):
    '''
    Perform predictive maintenance using logistic regression.
    :param X: Input features for equipment status and sensor
    ↪   readings.
    :param y: Binary labels indicating equipment failure (1) or
    ↪   normal operation (0).
    :return: Accuracy of the predictive model.
    '''
    X_train, X_test, y_train, y_test = train_test_split(X, y,
    ↪   test_size=0.2, random_state=42)
    scaler = StandardScaler()
    X_train = scaler.fit_transform(X_train)
    X_test = scaler.transform(X_test)

    model = LogisticRegression()
    model.fit(X_train, y_train)
    predictions = model.predict(X_test)

    accuracy = accuracy_score(y_test, predictions)
    return accuracy

def ai_design_optimization(X, y):
    '''
    Apply AI-driven design optimization using Random Forest.
    :param X: Input features including design parameters.
    :param y: Target variables such as power consumption or yield.
    :return: Trained model for optimization.
    '''
    model = RandomForestRegressor(n_estimators=100, random_state=42)
    model.fit(X, y)
    return model

def demand_forecasting(history, periods):
    '''
    Forecast future demand using ARIMA model.
```

```
:param history: Historical demand data.
:param periods: Number of periods to forecast.
:return: Forecasted demand values.
'''
model = ARIMA(history, order=(5, 1, 0))  # Example ARIMA model
model_fit = model.fit()
forecast = model_fit.forecast(steps=periods)
return forecast

# Example data for predictive maintenance
data = pd.DataFrame({
    'sensor1': np.random.rand(100),
    'sensor2': np.random.rand(100),
    'sensor3': np.random.rand(100),
    'failure': np.random.choice([0, 1], size=100)
})

# Inputs for the calculations
X_pm = data[['sensor1', 'sensor2', 'sensor3']]
y_pm = data['failure']

# Predictive maintenance accuracy
accuracy = predictive_maintenance(X_pm, y_pm)
print("Predictive Maintenance Accuracy:", accuracy)

# Example data for design optimization
X_design = pd.DataFrame({
    'transistor_size': np.random.rand(100),
    'interconnect_topology': np.random.rand(100),
    'voltage_level': np.random.rand(100)
})
y_design = np.random.rand(100)  # Example target variable

# AI-driven design optimization model
design_model = ai_design_optimization(X_design, y_design)

# Example historical demand data for forecasting
historical_demand = np.random.randint(100, 500, size=24)  # Monthly
↪   demands for 2 years

# Demand forecasting
forecasted_demand = demand_forecasting(historical_demand,
↪   periods=12)  # Forecast for the next year
print("Forecasted Demand for the Next 12 Periods:",
↪   forecasted_demand)
```

This code defines three functions:

- **predictive_maintenance** implements logistic regression for predicting equipment failures based on sensor readings.
- **ai_design_optimization** utilizes a Random Forest regressor to

optimize semiconductor design based on various parameters.

- `demand_forecasting` employs an ARIMA model to forecast future demand based on historical data.

The provided example generates synthetic data for predictive maintenance accuracy and demonstrates AI-driven design optimization and demand forecasting. It prints the accuracy of predictive maintenance and forecasted demand values.

Chapter 48

AI in Precision Engineering

Precision engineering is a field that demands utmost accuracy and meticulous attention to detail. In this chapter, we explore the application of Artificial Intelligence (AI) techniques in precision engineering processes. Specifically, we delve into the optimization of complex engineering systems, the prediction of structural integrity and performance, as well as the automation of construction and assembly processes. By leveraging AI methods, precision engineering can benefit from increased efficiency, improved product quality, and enhanced safety measures.

Optimization of Complex Engineering Systems

In precision engineering, the optimization of complex engineering systems plays a significant role in enhancing efficiency and achieving desired performance objectives. AI techniques offer valuable tools for optimizing these systems by analyzing large volumes of data and identifying optimal design parameters.

Mathematically, the optimization of complex engineering systems can be formulated as follows. Let X represent the input features, which may include design parameters, operating conditions, or geometrical constraints. Let F denote the objective function that quantifies the performance of the system to be optimized. The goal is to find the set of input features, denoted as X^*, that maximizes or minimizes the objective function F. Various optimization algorithms, such as genetic algorithms, particle swarm optimization, or gradient-based methods, can be employed to search for the optimal solution.

AI-driven optimization techniques allow engineers to explore the design space efficiently and evaluate a multitude of design alternatives. By leveraging these techniques, precision engineering processes can achieve enhanced system performance, reduced costs, and improved resource allocation.

Predictive Modeling for Structural Integrity

The prediction of structural integrity is a crucial aspect of precision engineering, as it ensures safe and reliable operation of structures under given loading conditions. AI techniques enable engineers to develop predictive models that analyze complex structural behavior and anticipate potential failure modes.

Mathematically, predictive modeling for structural integrity involves developing models that can accurately estimate the structural response and identify critical points of failure. Let X represent the input features, such as material properties, loading conditions, or geometric parameters. Let Y denote the target variables, which may include stress distribution, deformation, or fatigue life. The objective is to learn a function $f(X)$ that accurately predicts the target variables based on the input features. Machine learning algorithms, such as support vector regression, random forests, or neural networks, can be applied to construct these predictive models.

By employing AI-driven predictive modeling techniques, precision engineers can gain valuable insights into structural behavior, optimize designs for safety, and minimize the risk of failure.

Automated Construction and Assembly Processes

The automation of construction and assembly processes is an essential area of focus in precision engineering. AI techniques offer opportunities to streamline these processes, reduce human error, and improve overall efficiency in the assembly and construction of complex structures.

Mathematically, the automation of construction and assembly processes involves developing algorithms and control systems that enable machines to perform tasks accurately and autonomously. These algorithms may utilize computer vision, robotics, or machine learning techniques to analyze sensor data, make intelligent decisions, and execute precise actions. By leveraging AI, engineers can optimize task planning, execute intricate assembly operations, and enhance the coordination and interaction between robots or automated systems.

Automation in precision engineering not only increases productivity but also enhances safety by reducing human exposure to hazardous environments. Furthermore, it facilitates the production of consistent and high-quality assemblies, resulting in improved product performance and customer satisfaction.

In summary, the application of AI in precision engineering offers transformative capabilities in optimizing complex engineering systems, predicting structural integrity, and automating construction and assembly processes. By leveraging AI techniques, precision engineers can improve efficiency, ensure structural safety, and deliver high-quality products in a timely manner.

Python Code Snippet

Below is a Python code snippet that encompasses the key equations and algorithms mentioned in this chapter pertaining to optimization, predictive modeling for structural integrity, and automation in construction and assembly processes.

```python
import numpy as np
from sklearn.ensemble import RandomForestRegressor
from scipy.optimize import minimize
import matplotlib.pyplot as plt

def optimize_system(objective_function, initial_guess, bounds):
    '''
    Optimize complex engineering systems using Scipy's minimize
    ↪ function.
    :param objective_function: The objective function to minimize.
    :param initial_guess: Initial guess for the variables.
    :param bounds: Bounds for the variables.
    :return: Optimal variable values.
    '''
```

```python
    result = minimize(objective_function, initial_guess,
    ↪    bounds=bounds)
    return result.x

def structural_integrity_predictor(X, Y):
    '''
    Utilize machine learning to predict structural integrity.
    :param X: Input features such as material properties and loading
    ↪    conditions.
    :param Y: Target variables like stress distribution and
    ↪    deformation.
    :return: Trained model that predicts structural behavior.
    '''
    model = RandomForestRegressor(n_estimators=100, random_state=42)
    model.fit(X, Y)
    return model

def automate_construction_task(sensor_data):
    '''
    Automated construction decision-making based on sensor input.
    :param sensor_data: Data from sensors in the construction
    ↪    environment.
    :return: Actions to be taken by the automated system.
    '''
    # Placeholder for decision-making logic based on sensor data
    if sensor_data['temperature'] > 30:
        return "Activate cooling system"
    else:
        return "Proceed with construction"

# Example of an objective function for optimization
def example_objective_function(x):
    '''
    An example objective function: f(x) = (x-1)^2
    :param x: Input variable.
    :return: Computed value of the objective function.
    '''
    return (x - 1)**2

# Example input features for structural integrity prediction
X = np.array([[200, 50], [250, 60], [300, 70]])  # material
↪    properties, loading conditions
Y = np.array([150, 200, 250])  # stress or deformation values

# Perform optimization
initial_guess = [0]
bounds = [(0, 5)]
optimal_values = optimize_system(example_objective_function,
↪    initial_guess, bounds)

# Train a structural integrity predictor model
predictor_model = structural_integrity_predictor(X, Y)
```

```
# Simulate sensor data for automation
sensor_data = {'temperature': 35}
action = automate_construction_task(sensor_data)

# Output results
print("Optimal Values:", optimal_values)
print("Automated Action:", action)
print("Trained Model Predictions for Input X:",
↪   predictor_model.predict(X))
```

This code defines three functions:

- `optimize_system` uses the `minimize` function from SciPy to find optimal design parameters by minimizing an objective function.
- `structural_integrity_predictor` employs a random forest regressor to create a predictive model that estimates structural response based on input features.
- `automate_construction_task` determines actions for automated construction based on simulated sensor data, applying simple decision-making logic.

The provided example shows how to optimize a simple objective function, train a predictive model for structural integrity, and perform an automation task based on sensor input, then prints the results.

Chapter 49

AI in HVAC Systems

In this chapter, we delve into the intricate domain of Heating, Ventilation, and Air Conditioning (HVAC) systems and explore the application of Artificial Intelligence (AI) techniques. HVAC systems play a crucial role in maintaining optimal indoor environments, ensuring comfort, and promoting energy efficiency. By leveraging AI methods, we can optimize HVAC systems, enhance energy management, and personalize user experiences.

Optimization of HVAC Systems

1 Mathematical Modeling of HVAC Systems

Thermal Comfort Models

Achieving optimal thermal comfort for occupants is a primary objective in HVAC systems. Mathematical models are employed to capture the complex thermal interactions and estimate the comfort level in a given space. The Predicted Mean Vote (PMV) model, developed by P.O. Fanger [?], is widely used in the industry. It relates thermal comfort to several factors, including air temperature, humidity, air velocity, clothing insulation, and metabolic rate. The PMV model can be expressed as follows:

$$PMV = \frac{M - W}{\Delta H}$$

where M represents the metabolic rate, W denotes the amount of mechanical work performed by the individual, and ΔH corresponds to the rate of heat exchange with the environment.

Energy Consumption Models

Optimizing energy consumption is another crucial aspect of HVAC systems. Mathematical models can be utilized to estimate energy requirements based on various factors such as outdoor conditions, building characteristics, and occupancy patterns. The Total Equivalent Temperature Difference (TETD) model is commonly employed for energy consumption estimation [?]. It accounts for heat gain or loss due to conduction, convection, and ventilation. The TETD model can be represented as follows:

$$TETD = \sum_{i=1}^{n} (U_i \cdot A_i \cdot \Delta T_i)$$

where n is the number of building components, U_i represents the thermal transmittance of component i, A_i denotes the corresponding surface area, and ΔT_i represents the temperature difference across component i.

2   AI-driven Optimization Techniques

Machine Learning-based Control Strategies

Machine learning algorithms can be employed to develop control strategies for HVAC systems. These algorithms learn from historical data and optimize control parameters to achieve energy-efficient and comfortable operation. Reinforcement Learning (RL) methods, such as Q-learning or Deep Q-Network (DQN), have shown promise in optimizing HVAC systems [?]. By using reward functions that capture energy consumption and thermal comfort, RL agents can learn optimal control policies for HVAC system operation.

Genetic Algorithms for Parameter Optimization

Genetic algorithms (GAs) are optimization techniques inspired by natural selection and genetics. They can be applied to optimize HVAC system parameters, such as setpoints, schedules, or equipment sizes [?]. GAs employ the principles of crossover, mutation, and selection to iteratively search for the optimal parameter set that minimizes energy consumption while ensuring thermal comfort. By using fitness functions that evaluate energy efficiency and thermal comfort metrics, GAs can guide the search process towards optimal HVAC system configurations.

Energy Management and Optimization

Energy management plays a crucial role in HVAC systems, as it directly affects both environmental sustainability and operational costs. AI techniques offer valuable tools for energy optimization and demand response in HVAC systems.

1 Predictive Control Strategies

AI-driven predictive control strategies utilize historical data and machine learning algorithms to forecast future energy consumption and optimize HVAC operation [?]. These strategies take into account factors such as outdoor temperature, occupancy patterns, and electricity pricing to dynamically adjust setpoints and schedules, aiming to minimize energy consumption while maintaining thermal comfort. Techniques such as Support Vector Regression (SVR) or Long Short-Term Memory (LSTM) neural networks can be employed for energy demand forecasting and optimization.

2 Optimal Load Distribution

AI techniques, such as Genetic Algorithms or Ant Colony Optimization, can be utilized to optimize load distribution in HVAC systems [?]. By intelligently allocating cooling or heating loads across multiple units or zones, these algorithms can reduce energy consumption and improve overall system efficiency. Optimal load distribution minimizes unnecessary on/off cycling of equipment and ensures that power consumption is distributed evenly among system components.

Smart Climate Control Systems

AI technologies enable the development of advanced smart climate control systems that offer personalized comfort experiences while prioritizing energy efficiency.

1 Occupant Behavior Modeling

Machine learning algorithms can be employed to model occupant behavior and preferences, enabling HVAC systems to anticipate and adapt to individual comfort needs [?]. By analyzing historical data on occupancy patterns, temperature preferences, and user feedback, these models can learn personalized comfort profiles and adjust HVAC operation accordingly. Reinforcement Learning algorithms, such as Multi-Agent Deep Deterministic Policy Gradients (MADDPG), can optimize HVAC control actions to achieve personalized thermal comfort.

2 Human-in-the-Loop Systems

AI techniques facilitate the integration of occupant feedback and preferences into HVAC control systems. Natural Language Processing (NLP) and sentiment analysis algorithms can extract useful information from user feedback, enabling HVAC systems to dynamically adapt their operation based on occupants' comfort ratings and preferences. By incorporating human feedback into optimization algorithms, HVAC systems can continuously improve their performance and deliver personalized comfort experiences.

3 Energy-efficient Equipment and Sensors

AI methods also contribute to the development of energy-efficient HVAC equipment and sensors. Machine learning algorithms can optimize equipment design or sensor configurations to minimize energy consumption while ensuring accurate control and monitoring [?]. By employing AI techniques, HVAC systems can evolve towards even higher energy efficiency, reduced environmental impact, and increased occupant satisfaction.

In conclusion, the application of AI techniques in HVAC systems enables optimization of complex thermal processes, efficient energy management, smart climate control, and personalized comfort experiences. By leveraging AI methods, HVAC systems can achieve the dual goals of providing superior thermal comfort while minimizing energy consumption, contributing to a more sustainable and comfortable built environment.

Python Code Snippet

Below is a Python code snippet that implements important equations and algorithms discussed in the HVAC systems optimization section of this chapter. This snippet includes thermal comfort modeling, energy consumption modeling, reinforcement learning for HVAC control, and a simple genetic algorithm for parameter optimization.

```python
import numpy as np
import random

def calculate_pmv(M, W, delta_H):
    '''
    Calculate Predicted Mean Vote (PMV) for thermal comfort.
    :param M: Metabolic rate (W/m^2).
    :param W: Mechanical work performed (W/m^2).
    :param delta_H: Rate of heat exchange with the environment
    ↪   (W/m^2).
    :return: PMV value.
    '''
    return (M - W) / delta_H


def calculate_tetd(U, A, delta_T):
    '''
    Calculate Total Equivalent Temperature Difference (TETD) for
    ↪   energy consumption.
    :param U: Array of thermal transmittance values (W/m^2K).
    :param A: Array of corresponding surface areas (m^2).
    :param delta_T: Array of temperature differences (K).
    :return: Total Equivalent Temperature Difference.
    '''
    tetd = sum(U[i] * A[i] * delta_T[i] for i in range(len(U)))
    return tetd


# Example Input
M = 80  # Metabolic rate in W/m^2
W = 30  # Work in W/m^2
delta_H = 100  # Heat exchange rate in W/m^2
U = np.array([1.5, 2.0])  # Thermal transmittance (W/m^2K)
A = np.array([10, 15])  # Surface areas (m^2)
delta_T = np.array([20, 15])  # Temperature differences (K)

# Calculations
pmv = calculate_pmv(M, W, delta_H)
tetd = calculate_tetd(U, A, delta_T)

print("Predicted Mean Vote (PMV):", pmv)
```

```python
print("Total Equivalent Temperature Difference (TETD):", tetd)


def genetic_algorithm_hvac(population_size, generations,
↪    mutation_rate):
    '''
    Simple genetic algorithm for optimizing HVAC parameters.
    :param population_size: Number of individuals in each
    ↪    generation.
    :param generations: Number of generations to evolve.
    :param mutation_rate: Probability of mutation.
    :return: Best individual after evolution.
    '''
    # Initialize population with random parameters
    population = np.random.rand(population_size, 2)  # Two
    ↪    parameters to optimize

    for generation in range(generations):
        # Calculate fitness based on energy consumption and comfort
        fitness = [1 / (individual[0]**2 + individual[1]**2 + 1) for
        ↪    individual in population]  # Example fitness function

        # Selection
        selected = random.choices(population, weights=fitness,
        ↪    k=population_size)

        # Crossover and Mutation
        next_population = []
        for i in range(0, population_size, 2):
            if i + 1 < population_size:
                crossover_point = random.randint(0, 1)
                offspring1 =
                ↪    np.concatenate((selected[i][:crossover_point],
                ↪    selected[i + 1][crossover_point:]))
                offspring2 = np.concatenate((selected[i +
                ↪    1][:crossover_point],
                ↪    selected[i][crossover_point:]))
            else:
                offspring1 = selected[i]
                offspring2 = selected[i]

            # Mutation
            if random.random() < mutation_rate:
                offspring1 += np.random.normal(0, 0.1,
                ↪    offspring1.shape)
                offspring2 += np.random.normal(0, 0.1,
                ↪    offspring2.shape)

            next_population.extend([offspring1, offspring2])

        population = np.array(next_population)

    best_individual = population[np.argmax(fitness)]
```

330

```
return best_individual

# Example usage of genetic algorithm
best_params = genetic_algorithm_hvac(population_size=20,
↪   generations=100, mutation_rate=0.1)
print("Best HVAC Parameters (after optimization):", best_params)
```

This code defines several functions:

- `calculate_pmv` computes the Predicted Mean Vote for thermal comfort based on metabolic rate, mechanical work, and heat exchange rate.
- `calculate_tetd` calculates the Total Equivalent Temperature Difference used for estimating energy consumption based on thermal transmittance, surface areas, and temperature differences.
- `genetic_algorithm_hvac` implements a simple genetic algorithm to optimize HVAC system parameters over specified generations, returning the best parameters found.

The provided example calculates the PMV and TETD based on input values and optimizes HVAC parameters using the genetic algorithm, then prints the results.

Chapter 50

AI in Additive Manufacturing (3D Printing)

Optimization of Printing Processes

1   Mathematical Modeling of 3D Printing

Additive manufacturing, commonly known as 3D printing, has revolutionized the manufacturing industry by enabling the fabrication of components with complex geometries. Mathematical models play a crucial role in optimizing the printing processes and achieving high-quality printed parts.

Process Parameters Modeling

Optimizing the process parameters is essential to control the quality and accuracy of 3D printed objects. Mathematical models can capture the relationship between process parameters and various quality indicators, such as surface roughness, dimensional accuracy, and mechanical properties.

One commonly utilized model is the melt pool model, which describes the behavior of the melted material during the printing process. The melt pool width W can be estimated using the following equation:

$$W = \sqrt{\frac{4 \cdot E \cdot P \cdot V_{\text{melt}}}{\pi \cdot (\tan(\alpha) - \tan(\beta))^2 \cdot v}}$$

where E is the laser energy density, P is the laser power, V_{melt} is the volume of melted material per unit time, α and β are the angles, and v is the scanning speed.

Thermal Modeling

Thermal modeling is crucial for predicting temperature distribution during the 3D printing process. The heat transfer equation, using the finite difference method, can be employed to estimate temperature variations:

$$T_{i,j,k}^{n+1} = T_{i,j,k}^n + \frac{\alpha \cdot \Delta t}{\Delta x^2} \cdot (T_{i+1,j,k}^n + T_{i-1,j,k}^n - 2 \cdot T_{i,j,k}^n)$$

where $T_{i,j,k}^n$ denotes the temperature at the grid point (i, j, k) and time step n, α is the thermal diffusivity, Δt is the time step, and Δx is the grid spacing.

2 AI-driven Process Optimization

Machine Learning for Print Quality Prediction

Machine learning algorithms can be leveraged to predict print quality based on process parameters, material properties, and design features. By training models on historical data, relationships between these inputs and quality indicators can be learned, allowing for real-time quality prediction. Regression techniques such as Support Vector Regression (SVR) or Random Forest Regression can be employed to create accurate models.

Optimal Path Planning

Optimizing the printing path is vital to minimize printing time and material waste. AI algorithms, such as Genetic Algorithms or Ant Colony Optimization, can be utilized to find the optimal path that maximizes printing efficiency.

Material Optimization

1 Mathematical Modeling of Material Properties

The properties of the printing material directly influence the quality and mechanical behavior of 3D printed objects. Mathematical models can be utilized to predict material properties based on composition, printing parameters, and post-processing conditions.

One common model is the Arrhenius equation, which describes the relationship between temperature and the rate of chemical reactions. It can be expressed as:

$$k = A \cdot \exp\left(\frac{-E_a}{R \cdot T}\right)$$

where k represents the reaction rate, A is the pre-exponential factor, E_a is the activation energy, R is the ideal gas constant, and T denotes the absolute temperature.

2 AI-driven Material Optimization

Designing New Materials with AI

Artificial intelligence techniques, such as Generative Adversarial Networks (GANs) and Reinforcement Learning (RL), can be employed for materials discovery and development. GANs can generate new material designs by learning the underlying patterns in existing materials. RL algorithms can optimize materials' properties by suggesting chemical compositions or processing conditions to maximize desired characteristics.

Predicting Material Performance

Machine learning models can predict material performance and mechanical properties based on its composition, fabrication parameters, and microstructure. By training on experimental or simulation data, these models can provide accurate predictions for untested materials, allowing for informed decision-making in material selection.

Quality Control and Defect Detection

1 Mathematical Modeling of Defects

Ensuring the quality of 3D printed parts requires the detection and prevention of defects. Mathematical models can be employed to identify potential defect sources and predict defect types and locations.

For example, the heat transfer equation can be utilized to simulate the cooling process and predict the possibility of thermal stress-induced defects, such as warping or cracking, which may occur during solidification.

2 AI-driven Defect Detection

Computer Vision for Quality Control

Computer vision techniques, coupled with AI algorithms, can be utilized for automated defect detection in 3D printed parts. Convolutional Neural Networks (CNNs) can analyze images or point cloud data to identify defects, such as surface irregularities or structural faults, by comparing them to reference models or trained datasets.

Real-time Monitoring

Machine learning algorithms can also facilitate real-time monitoring of the printing process by analyzing sensor data, such as temperature or vibration measurements. By comparing these real-time measurements with expected values, deviations, and potential defects can be detected in real-time, enabling immediate remedial actions.

In conclusion, the application of AI techniques in additive manufacturing (3D printing) enables process optimization, material optimization, and quality control. By leveraging mathematical models and AI algorithms, 3D printing processes can be optimized for efficiency and quality, new materials with desired properties can be designed, and defects can be detected in real-time, ensuring high-quality printed objects across various industries.
""

Python Code Snippet

Below is a Python code snippet that demonstrates the key mathematical modeling equations and AI-driven optimizations for additive manufacturing (3D printing).

```python
import numpy as np
import matplotlib.pyplot as plt
from scipy.optimize import minimize

def melt_pool_width(E, P, V_melt, alpha, beta, v):
    '''
    Calculate the melt pool width during the 3D printing process.
    :param E: Laser energy density.
    :param P: Laser power.
    :param V_melt: Volume of melted material per unit time.
    :param alpha: Angle parameter.
    :param beta: Angle parameter.
    :param v: Scanning speed.
    :return: Melt pool width.
    '''
    W = np.sqrt((4 * E * P * V_melt) / (np.pi * (np.tan(alpha) -
      ↪  np.tan(beta))**2 * v))
    return W


def heat_transfer(T_initial, alpha, delta_t, delta_x, num_steps):
    '''
    Simulate the temperature distribution using the finite
      ↪  difference method.
    :param T_initial: Initial temperature distribution (numpy
      ↪  array).
    :param alpha: Thermal diffusivity.
    :param delta_t: Time step.
    :param delta_x: Grid spacing.
    :param num_steps: Number of time steps to simulate.
    :return: Temperature distribution over time (numpy array).
    '''
    T = np.zeros((num_steps, len(T_initial)))
    T[0] = T_initial
    for n in range(0, num_steps - 1):
        for i in range(1, len(T_initial) - 1):
            T[n + 1, i] = T[n, i] + (alpha * delta_t / delta_x**2) *
              ↪  (T[n, i + 1] + T[n, i - 1] - 2 * T[n, i])
    return T


def print_quality_prediction(parameters, model):
    '''
    Predict print quality based on process parameters using a
      ↪  trained machine learning model.
```

336

```
    :param parameters: Input parameters (list).
    :param model: Trained machine learning model.
    :return: Predicted print quality.
    '''
    return model.predict(np.array(parameters).reshape(1, -1))


def optimize_print_path(initial_path):
    '''
    Optimize the printing path using a simple implementation of the
    ↪   Genetic Algorithm.
    :param initial_path: Initial path represented as a list of
    ↪   coordinates.
    :return: Optimized path.
    '''
    def fitness_function(path):
        dist = 0.0
        for i in range(len(path) - 1):
            dist += np.sqrt((path[i+1][0] - path[i][0])**2 +
            ↪   (path[i+1][1] - path[i][1])**2)
        return dist

    # Here you would implement the genetic algorithm logic to evolve
    ↪   `initial_path`
    optimized_path = initial_path  # Placeholder for optimized path
    # For the sake of demonstration, we'll simply return the
    ↪   original path
    return optimized_path


# Example inputs
laser_energy_density = 10.0  # in J/m^2
laser_power = 100.0  # in watts
volume_melt_per_time = 0.1  # m^3/s
angle_alpha = np.radians(30)  # Convert degrees to radians
angle_beta = np.radians(15)  # Convert degrees to radians
scanning_speed = 0.1  # m/s

# Calculate the melt pool width
melt_width = melt_pool_width(laser_energy_density, laser_power,
↪   volume_melt_per_time, angle_alpha, angle_beta, scanning_speed)
print("Melt Pool Width:", melt_width, "meters")

# Simulate heat transfer (example with a simple initial condition)
initial_temperature_distribution = np.zeros(100) + 25  # Initial
↪   temperature of 25°C across 100 points
thermal_diffusivity = 0.01  # m^2/s
time_step = 0.1  # seconds
grid_spacing = 0.01  # meters
num_time_steps = 100  # number of time steps
```

```
temperature_distribution =
↪   heat_transfer(initial_temperature_distribution,
↪   thermal_diffusivity, time_step, grid_spacing, num_time_steps)

# Predict print quality (mock model, to be replaced with actual
↪   trained model)
class MockModel:
    def predict(self, X):
        return np.mean(X) + np.random.normal(0, 0.1)   # Stub
        ↪   prediction

mock_model = MockModel()
quality_parameters = [0.5, 0.3, 0.8]   # Example parameters
predicted_quality = print_quality_prediction(quality_parameters,
↪   mock_model)
print("Predicted Print Quality Score:", predicted_quality)

# Optimize printing path (placeholder for actual path)
initial_print_path = [(0, 0), (1, 2), (3, 3), (4, 0)]
optimized_path = optimize_print_path(initial_print_path)
print("Optimized Printing Path:", optimized_path)
```

This code defines several functions:

- `melt_pool_width` calculates the melt pool width based on laser parameters.
- `heat_transfer` simulates temperature distribution using the finite difference method.
- `print_quality_prediction` predicts print quality using a trained machine learning model.
- `optimize_print_path` provides a placeholder for optimizing printing paths.

The example demonstrates how to calculate melt pool width, simulate heat transfer, predict print quality, and optimize the printing path within the context of additive manufacturing.

Chapter 51

AI in Textile Engineering

In the field of textile engineering, the integration of artificial intelligence (AI) techniques has revolutionized various aspects of the industry, ranging from design and manufacturing to quality control and optimization. This chapter delves into the applications of AI in textile engineering and explores fundamental mathematical models and algorithms employed to enhance textile production processes.

Predictive Modeling for Textile Properties

Mathematical modeling plays a crucial role in predicting and understanding the properties of textiles. By considering the composition, structure, and manufacturing parameters of the fabric, mathematical equations can be formulated to estimate various characteristics, such as mechanical strength, elasticity, and thermal conductivity.

One commonly used model is the classical idealized model for textile stiffness. By considering the interactions between yarns and their arrangement in a fabric, the bending and stretching behavior of textiles can be described by a system of linear equations. This model allows designers and engineers to predict the stiffness and overall mechanical properties of textiles before manufacturing.

AI-driven Textile Design and Manufacturing

1 Design Optimization

The application of AI techniques in textile design enables the creation of innovative and customized fabric patterns. By utilizing generative models, such as Generative Adversarial Networks (GANs) or Variational Autoencoders (VAEs), designers can generate a wide range of creative textile designs. These models learn the underlying patterns and structures from a dataset of existing designs, which can then be used to generate novel and unique patterns.

Additionally, optimization algorithms, such as genetic algorithms or particle swarm optimization, can be employed to automatically explore the design space and find optimal configurations for specific design objectives. These techniques allow designers to efficiently search for the best combination of colors, patterns, or fabric structures to meet specific requirements.

2 Quality Control and Defect Detection

AI algorithms, coupled with computer vision techniques, have greatly improved the quality control and defect detection processes in textile manufacturing. By utilizing deep learning models, such as Convolutional Neural Networks (CNNs), textile defects can be accurately identified and classified.

Computer vision algorithms analyze images of the fabric to detect defects such as irregularities, holes, or pattern inconsistencies. The trained CNNs can classify the images according to predefined defect categories. This enables manufacturers to perform automated and real-time inspection of textiles, thereby reducing human error and increasing product quality.

3 Predictive Maintenance

Predictive maintenance techniques, empowered by AI, can prevent costly machine breakdowns and ensure uninterrupted textile production. By monitoring various parameters, such as vibration, temperature, or power consumption, machine learning models can predict potential failures or maintenance needs.

By training models using historical data on machine behavior and maintenance records, it is possible to identify patterns and anomalies that precede machine failures. These models can provide early warnings, enabling manufacturers to schedule maintenance activities proactively and minimize production downtime.

4 Process Optimization

AI algorithms, combined with mathematical optimization techniques, can improve textile production processes by optimizing various parameters, such as machinery settings, material usage, or production speed. These algorithms consider multiple factors simultaneously to maximize specific objectives, such as production efficiency or material waste reduction.

Optimization algorithms, including linear programming, genetic algorithms, or swarm intelligence algorithms, can be employed to find the optimal values for different parameters. By iteratively evaluating the objective function with different parameter combinations, these algorithms converge to the optimal solution, resulting in improved process efficiency and cost savings.

Conclusion

The utilization of AI techniques in textile engineering has transformed the industry by enabling personalized designs, improving quality control, and optimizing manufacturing processes. Mathematical modeling provides a theoretical foundation for predicting textile properties, while AI algorithms enhance design creativity, automate defect detection, enable predictive maintenance, and optimize production processes. The integration of AI and mathematics offers remarkable opportunities for further innovation and growth within the textile engineering field.

Python Code Snippet

Below is a comprehensive Python code snippet that implements the important equations, algorithms, and models discussed in the context of textile engineering.

```
import numpy as np
import cv2  # For image processing
```

```
import tensorflow as tf  # For deep learning
from sklearn.linear_model import LinearRegression

def calculate_textile_stiffness(yarn_count, fabric_width,
↳   yarn_spacing):
    '''
    Calculate the stiffness of a textile based on yarn properties.
    :param yarn_count: Number of yarns per unit length.
    :param fabric_width: Width of the fabric in meters.
    :param yarn_spacing: Spacing between yarns in meters.
    :return: Estimated stiffness of the textile.
    '''
    # Using a simple linear model for stiffness estimation
    stiffness = yarn_count * fabric_width / yarn_spacing
    return stiffness


def generate_fabric_design(dataset):
    '''
    Generate a new fabric design using a GAN.
    :param dataset: Dataset of existing fabric designs.
    :return: Generated fabric design.
    '''
    # Assuming a pre-trained GAN model is available
    gan_model = tf.keras.models.load_model('path_to_gan_model')
    noise = np.random.normal(0, 1, (1, 100))  # Random noise input
    ↳   for GAN
    generated_design = gan_model.predict(noise)
    return generated_design


def detect_defects(image_path):
    '''
    Detect defects in fabric images using a CNN.
    :param image_path: Path to the fabric image.
    :return: List of detected defects.
    '''
    model = tf.keras.models.load_model('path_to_cnn_model')
    image = cv2.imread(image_path)
    image = cv2.resize(image, (128, 128))  # Resize for model input
    image = np.expand_dims(image, axis=0) / 255.0  # Normalize and
    ↳   adjust dimensions

    predictions = model.predict(image)
    defects = np.where(predictions > 0.5)  # Assume binary
    ↳   classification for defects
    return defects


def predictive_maintenance(sensor_data):
    '''
    Predict maintenance needs based on sensor data.
    :param sensor_data: List of machine sensor readings.
```

```python
    :return: Predicted maintenance status.
    '''
    # Simple linear regression model for prediction
    X = np.array(sensor_data[:-1]).reshape(-1, 1)
    y = np.array(sensor_data[1:])  # Next state prediction
    model = LinearRegression().fit(X, y)

    last_reading = sensor_data[-1].reshape(-1, 1)
    prediction = model.predict(last_reading)
    return prediction


def optimize_production(parameters):
    '''
    Optimize textile production parameters for maximum efficiency.
    :param parameters: Dictionary of production parameters.
    :return: Optimized parameters.
    '''
    from scipy.optimize import minimize

    def objective_function(x):
        # Sample objective function to minimize waste
        return x[0]**2 + x[1]**2  # Example function for
        ↪   optimization

    initial_guess = [parameters['speed'],
    ↪   parameters['material_usage']]
    result = minimize(objective_function, initial_guess, bounds=[(0,
    ↪   None), (0, None)])
    return result.x


# Example inputs for calculations
yarn_count = 200   # Yarn count in yarns/m
fabric_width = 1.5  # Fabric width in meters
yarn_spacing = 0.01  # Yarn spacing in meters
sensor_data = [70, 68, 69, 70, 71]  # Example sensor readings
production_parameters = {'speed': 45, 'material_usage': 30}  #
↪   Change according to context

# Calculations
stiffness = calculate_textile_stiffness(yarn_count, fabric_width,
↪   yarn_spacing)
new_design = generate_fabric_design('existing_designs_dataset')
output_defects = detect_defects('fabric_image.jpg')
predicted_maintenance = predictive_maintenance(sensor_data)
optimized_parameters = optimize_production(production_parameters)

# Output results
print("Estimated Textile Stiffness:", stiffness)
print("Generated Fabric Design:", new_design)
print("Detected Defects (indices):", output_defects)
print("Predicted Maintenance Status:", predicted_maintenance)
```

```
print("Optimized Production Parameters:", optimized_parameters)
```

This code defines several functions:

- `calculate_textile_stiffness` calculates the stiffness of a textile based on yarn properties.
- `generate_fabric_design` generates a new fabric design using a pre-trained GAN model.
- `detect_defects` detects defects in fabric images using a CNN model.
- `predictive_maintenance` predicts maintenance needs based on sensor data using linear regression.
- `optimize_production` optimizes production parameters using a defined objective function.

The provided example calculates various aspects of textile engineering, generates fabric designs, detects defects, predicts maintenance, and optimizes production parameters, then prints the results.

Chapter 52

AI in Structural Engineering

In the field of structural engineering, the integration of artificial intelligence (AI) techniques has brought about significant advancements in various aspects of the industry, ranging from design and analysis to optimization and safety assessment. This chapter focuses on the applications of AI in structural engineering, exploring the use of mathematical models and algorithms to enhance the design and analysis of structures.

Predictive Modeling for Structural Behavior

Mathematical modeling plays a crucial role in predicting and understanding the behavior of structures subjected to various loading conditions. By considering the material properties, geometry, and boundary conditions of a structure, mathematical equations can be formulated to describe its behavior under external forces.

One commonly used model in structural engineering is the Euler-Bernoulli beam theory, which describes the behavior of slender beams subjected to bending moments. This theory relates the bending moment, beam deflection, and applied loads through the beam's material properties and geometry. By solving the differential equations derived from this theory, engineers can predict the structural response and determine critical parameters such as bending stresses and deflections.

AI-driven Structural Design and Analysis

1 Structural Optimization

AI algorithms, combined with optimization techniques, have revolutionized the field of structural design. By formulating the design problem as an optimization task, engineers can search for the best configuration of structural elements to satisfy specific requirements, such as minimizing weight while ensuring structural safety.

Genetic algorithms, simulated annealing, or particle swarm optimization can be employed to explore the design space and find optimal solutions. These algorithms iteratively evaluate different designs, adjusting parameters such as cross-section dimensions or member lengths, to converge to the most efficient and safe design.

2 Performance Prediction

AI techniques, such as machine learning and neural networks, enable engineers to predict the performance of structures more accurately. By training models on historical data and simulation results, these models can learn the complex relationships between design parameters, structural responses, and safety criteria.

For example, machine learning models can predict the ultimate strength of a structure based on design attributes, material properties, and loading conditions. These models enable engineers to assess the safety of a design and make informed decisions during the design process, reducing the need for expensive physical testing.

3 Structural Health Monitoring

AI algorithms, coupled with sensor data, enable continuous monitoring and assessment of the structural health of buildings and infrastructure. By incorporating sensor data, such as vibration measurements or strain gauges, into AI models, engineers can detect anomalies, assess structural integrity, and predict potential failures.

Machine learning techniques, such as anomaly detection or pattern recognition, can analyze sensor data in real-time, identifying deviations from expected structural behavior. This allows engineers to take proactive measures, such as maintenance or repair, before substantial damage occurs.

4   Failure Analysis

AI algorithms can assist engineers in understanding and analyzing structural failures. By examining historical failure data alongside structural properties and loading conditions, machine learning models can identify patterns and causes of failures, enhancing the understanding of structural weaknesses.

These models can aid in identifying critical failure modes, determining design deficiencies, and proposing remedial measures to prevent similar failures in future designs. Through this analysis, structural engineers can continuously improve design practices and enhance the safety of structures.

Conclusion

The integration of AI techniques in structural engineering has transformed the field by enabling efficient structural design optimization, accurate performance prediction, continuous structural health monitoring, and enhanced failure analysis. Mathematical modeling provides a theoretical foundation for predicting structural behavior, while AI algorithms enhance optimization, analysis, and decision-making processes. The incorporation of AI and mathematical principles offers immense potential for further advancements in structural engineering.Certainly! Below is a comprehensive Python code snippet related to the key equations and algorithms mentioned in the chapter, properly formatted within the LaTeX using the minted package.

Python Code Snippet

Below is a Python code snippet that includes functions for predicting structural behavior using the Euler-Bernoulli beam theory, optimizing structural design using a genetic algorithm, predicting structural performance with machine learning, and monitoring structural health through anomaly detection.

```python
import numpy as np
from sklearn.ensemble import RandomForestRegressor
from scipy.optimize import differential_evolution

def euler_bernoulli_beam(F, L, E, I):
    '''
    Calculate the deflection of a beam using Euler-Bernoulli beam
    ↪   theory.
    :param F: Applied load in Newtons.
    :param L: Length of the beam in meters.
    :param E: Young's modulus in Pascals.
    :param I: Moment of inertia in m^4.
    :return: Deflection in meters.
    '''
    return (F * L**3) / (3 * E * I)

def optimize_structure(objective_function, bounds):
    '''
    Optimize structural design using a genetic algorithm.
    :param objective_function: Function to minimize (design
    ↪   objective).
    :param bounds: Bounds for design parameters.
    :return: Optimal design parameters.
    '''
    result = differential_evolution(objective_function, bounds)
    return result.x

def predict_performance(features, target):
    '''
    Train a machine learning model to predict structural
    ↪   performance.
    :param features: Input features for training.
    :param target: Target values for training.
    :return: Trained model.
    '''
    model = RandomForestRegressor(n_estimators=100, random_state=42)
    model.fit(features, target)
    return model

def anomaly_detection(sensor_data, threshold):
    '''
    Detect anomalies in structural health monitoring data.
    :param sensor_data: Array of sensor measurements.
    :param threshold: Anomaly detection threshold.
    :return: List of detected anomalies.
    '''
    anomalies = []
    for i, value in enumerate(sensor_data):
        if value > threshold:
            anomalies.append((i, value))
    return anomalies
```

```
# Example parameters and data
F = 1000   # Applied load in Newtons
L = 5.0    # Length of the beam in meters
E = 200e9  # Young's modulus in Pascals
I = 8.33e-6  # Moment of inertia in m^4

# Deflection calculation using Euler-Bernoulli beam theory
deflection = euler_bernoulli_beam(F, L, E, I)

# Define an objective function for optimization (minimize weight)
def design_objective(params):
    length, cross_section_area = params
    return length * cross_section_area  # Simple weight
    ↪    approximation

bounds = [(1.0, 10.0), (0.01, 0.1)]  # Length and cross-section area
↪    bounds
optimal_design = optimize_structure(design_objective, bounds)

# Example features and target data
features = np.array([[1000, 5], [1500, 6], [2000, 7]])  # Load and
↪    length
target = np.array([0.05, 0.06, 0.07])  # Corresponding deflections
model = predict_performance(features, target)

# Simulated sensor data for health monitoring
sensor_data = np.array([0.03, 0.05, 0.07, 0.1, 0.12])  # Example
↪    measurements
threshold = 0.1  # Set threshold for anomaly detection
anomalies = anomaly_detection(sensor_data, threshold)

# Output results
print("Deflection calculated using Euler-Bernoulli beam theory:",
↪    deflection, "meters")
print("Optimal design parameters:", optimal_design)
print("Anomalies detected in sensor data:", anomalies)
```

This code defines several functions:

- euler_bernoulli_beam calculates the deflection of a beam according to the Euler-Bernoulli beam theory.
- optimize_structure utilizes a genetic algorithm to optimize structural design by minimizing a given objective function.
- predict_performance trains a random forest regression model to predict structural performance based on historical data.
- anomaly_detection identifies anomalies in sensor monitoring data against a specified threshold.

The example implementation calculates the deflection of a beam, optimizes design parameters, trains a performance prediction model, and detects anomalies from simulated sensor data, printing the results as it goes.

Chapter 53

AI in Bioengineering

Bioengineering is a multidisciplinary field that combines principles from mathematics, biology, and engineering to solve problems in medicine and healthcare. The integration of Artificial Intelligence (AI) techniques in bioengineering has enabled significant advancements in various aspects of the field, ranging from drug discovery and development to personalized medicine and disease modeling. This chapter delves into the key applications of AI in bioengineering, offering expert insights into the use of mathematical modeling and algorithmic approaches to address complex challenges in the domain.

AI-driven Biomedical Device Design and Testing

In biomedical engineering, the design and development of innovative medical devices require a deep understanding of biological systems, coupled with engineering principles. AI algorithms, when combined with mathematical modeling, facilitate the design process by providing insightful information and optimizing device performance based on biological constraints.

One prominent area where AI plays a significant role is in the design of prosthetic limbs. By integrating AI algorithms, such as neural networks or reinforcement learning, with mathematical models, researchers can develop prosthetic limbs that can respond to neural signals, enabling natural and intuitive movements for the amputees.

Mathematical models, such as finite element analysis or fluid dynamics simulations, are employed to analyze and optimize the structural and functional aspects of medical devices. AI-based algorithms contribute to the design optimization process, considering multiple design parameters, material properties, and biological behaviors to enhance device performance.

Predictive Modeling for Tissue Engineering

Tissue engineering is a field that aims to create functional living tissues to replace damaged or diseased tissues in the human body. AI techniques, combined with mathematical models, play a vital role in predicting the behavior and properties of engineered tissues.

One prevailing challenge in tissue engineering is the growth and development of blood vessels within engineered tissues. Mathematical models rely on partial differential equations, such as those related to angiogenesis, to capture the complex interactions between biological factors and tissue growth. Incorporating AI algorithms facilitates the prediction of vessel development and enables the optimization of tissue culture conditions to promote angiogenesis.

Furthermore, AI techniques aid in predicting the mechanical properties of engineered tissues, such as elasticity or stiffness, by integrating mathematical models with machine learning approaches. These models consider various factors, including cell behavior, scaffold properties, and external mechanical stimuli, to accurately predict tissue mechanical properties and guide the design of biomaterials with desired characteristics.

AI in Genetic Engineering and Modification

Genetic engineering involves the manipulation of an organism's genome to introduce desired traits or functionalities. AI techniques have revolutionized this field by automating the design of DNA sequences and predicting the behavior of engineered genetic circuits.

Mathematical models, such as Boolean networks or differential equations, describe the dynamic behavior of genetic circuits, guiding the design and optimization of synthetic gene networks. AI algorithms, such as genetic algorithms or reinforcement learning, assist in automating the design process, searching through vast design spaces to identify optimal DNA sequences.

Predictive models, often utilizing AI techniques combined with statistical methods, enable researchers to assess the safety and efficacy of genetically modified organisms. These models consider the structural properties of DNA, gene expression patterns, and biological interactions to predict the behavior and potential impact of genetic modifications. This insight is invaluable in ensuring the safety of genetically modified organisms and guiding the development of new traits.

Automated Lab Processes and Diagnostics

The increasing complexity of laboratory processes in bioengineering demands automation and advanced diagnostics to enhance efficiency and accuracy. AI plays a crucial role in automating various laboratory procedures, such as image analysis, data processing, and experimental design.

Machine learning algorithms, when integrated with microscopic imaging data, enable automated cell counting, segmentation, and analysis. These algorithms, often based on convolutional neural networks, learn to detect and classify different cell types or structures, facilitating high-throughput experiments and cell-based assays.

AI techniques, such as clustering or dimensionality reduction algorithms, help uncover patterns and relationships in multi-dimensional experimental data. This insight is invaluable in identifying biomarkers, understanding disease mechanisms, or optimizing experimental conditions for efficient data collection.

Additionally, AI algorithms assist in diagnostics by analyzing patient data, such as medical images or physiological signals. These algorithms, often trained on large datasets, can aid in disease detection, monitoring treatment response, or predicting patient outcomes. By considering a wide range of patient-specific factors and utilizing mathematical models, AI-based diagnostics provide valuable information for clinicians and contribute to personalized medicine.

AI-driven Research in Biomaterials

Biomaterials are materials designed to interact with biological systems, often used in medical implants, drug delivery systems, or tissue engineering scaffolds. AI techniques, in combination with mathematical models, greatly accelerate the discovery and optimization of biomaterials with desired properties.

Machine learning algorithms aid in the design and synthesis of novel biomaterials by predicting their physicochemical properties and interactions with biological systems. These algorithms exploit patterns and relationships learned from large materials databases and employ mathematical models to guide material design and optimization.

Mathematical models, such as diffusion equations or reaction kinetics models, are integral to predicting drug release kinetics from various delivery systems. By incorporating AI algorithms, researchers can optimize the design of drug delivery systems, considering factors such as material properties, drug characteristics, and target tissue behavior.

Furthermore, AI techniques contribute to the understanding of the biocompatibility and immune response of biomaterials. By combining mathematical models with machine learning algorithms, researchers can simulate and predict the interactions between biomaterials and the immune system, guiding the development of biocompatible materials or implantable devices.

Conclusion

AI has emerged as a powerful tool in bioengineering, enabling advancements in the design of biomedical devices, tissue engineering, genetic engineering, lab processes, and biomaterials research. Through the integration of AI algorithms with mathematical models, researchers gain valuable insights into complex biological systems and optimize engineering solutions according to biological constraints. This dynamic synergy between AI and mathematics continues to drive innovation in the field, paving the way for improved healthcare technologies and personalized medicine."'latex

Python Code Snippet

Below is a Python code snippet that incorporates important equations and algorithms relevant to bioengineering applications discussed in this chapter, such as predictive modeling for tissue engineering, automated lab processes, and AI-driven genetic engineering.

```python
import numpy as np
import pandas as pd
from sklearn.linear_model import LinearRegression
from sklearn.metrics import mean_squared_error
from scipy.integrate import odeint

def tissue_growth_model(y, t, params):
    '''
    A model for predicting tissue growth using differential
    ↪ equations.
    :param y: Current state of the system (cell density).
    :param t: Time variable.
    :param params: Parameters for the model (growth rate).
    :return: Derivative of cell density over time.
    '''
    growth_rate = params['growth_rate']
    return growth_rate * y * (1 - y/params['carrying_capacity'])

def simulate_tissue_growth(initial_cells, params, time_points):
    '''
    Simulate tissue growth over time.
    :param initial_cells: Initial cell density.
    :param params: Model parameters containing growth rate and
    ↪ carrying capacity.
    :param time_points: Time points for the simulation.
    :return: Cell densities at given time points.
    '''
    results = odeint(tissue_growth_model, initial_cells,
    ↪ time_points, args=(params,))
    return results.flatten()

def predict_mechanical_properties(cell_data):
    '''
    Predict mechanical properties of engineered tissues from cell
    ↪ density data.
    :param cell_data: DataFrame containing variables for prediction.
    :return: Predicted mechanical properties.
    '''
    X = cell_data[['cell_density', 'scaffold_type']]
    y = cell_data['mechanical_property']

    model = LinearRegression()
    model.fit(X, y)
```

```python
    predictions = model.predict(X)

    return predictions

def automated_cell_analysis(image_data):
    '''
    Automate cell counting and analysis using image data.
    :param image_data: Array of image data for analysis.
    :return: Count of detected cells or other relevant metrics.
    '''
    from skimage.feature import canny
    from skimage.measure import label, regionprops

    edges = canny(image_data)
    labeled_image = label(edges)
    properties = regionprops(labeled_image)

    return len(properties)  # Return the count of detected
    ↪   regions/cells

# Example parameters for simulation and prediction
params = {
    'growth_rate': 0.1,  # Growth rate parameter
    'carrying_capacity': 10000  # Maximum sustainable cell density
}

initial_cells = 100  # Starting with 100 cells
time_points = np.linspace(0, 100, 100)  # From time 0 to 100

# Simulate tissue growth
cell_density_over_time = simulate_tissue_growth(initial_cells,
↪   params, time_points)

# Prepare sample cell data for prediction
cell_data = pd.DataFrame({
    'cell_density': [1500, 3000, 4500],
    'scaffold_type': [1, 2, 3],  # Encoded scaffold types
    'mechanical_property': [200, 400, 600]  # Corresponding
    ↪   mechanical properties
})

# Predict mechanical properties
predicted_properties = predict_mechanical_properties(cell_data)

# Example image data for automated cell analysis (in reality, this
↪   would be image array)
image_data_example = np.random.rand(100, 100)  # Dummy image data
cell_count = automated_cell_analysis(image_data_example)

# Output results
print("Cell Density Over Time:", cell_density_over_time)
print("Predicted Mechanical Properties:", predicted_properties)
```

```
print("Automated Cell Count:", cell_count)
```

This code defines several functions:

- `tissue_growth_model` and `simulate_tissue_growth` predict the growth of engineered tissues using mathematical modeling.
- `predict_mechanical_properties` uses a linear regression model to predict the mechanical properties of tissues based on cell data.
- `automated_cell_analysis` automates the process of cell counting in given image data.

The provided example simulates tissue growth over time, predicts mechanical properties based on sample data, and counts detected cells in a simulated image data array. The results are then printed out. " '

Chapter 54

AI in Music and Sound

Music and sound are integral aspects of human culture, creativity, and expression. The intersection of Artificial Intelligence (AI) and music has opened up exciting opportunities for exploration, innovation, and collaboration. From AI-driven music composition to personalized music recommendations, this chapter delves into the key applications of AI in the field of music and sound, offering expert insights and mathematical perspectives on the use of AI algorithms and techniques.

AI-driven Music Composition and Production

Music composition is a complex creative process that requires a deep understanding of musical theory, structure, and aesthetics. With the advent of AI, researchers have sought to develop algorithms capable of generating original music compositions.

One approach is to employ Generative Adversarial Networks (GANs) to create new musical pieces. GANs consist of two networks: a generator that produces musical sequences, and a discriminator that evaluates the quality of the generated music. By training these networks on large datasets of existing music, AI algorithms can learn to mimic the style and characteristics of specific composers or genres, resulting in the generation of new compositions.

Mathematical models, such as Markov chains or recurrent neural networks (RNNs), can capture the temporal dependencies and patterns in music, enabling the generation of coherent musical sequences. By training these models on a corpus of music, AI algorithms can generate new compositions that follow the underlying structure and dynamics of the musical genre.

Personalized Music Recommendations

The abundance of music available on various platforms necessitates effective personalized music recommendation systems. AI has played a crucial role in developing advanced recommendation algorithms that take into account user preferences, listening history, and other contextual factors.

Collaborative Filtering is a popular technique in music recommendation systems. This algorithm leverages the preferences of similar users to make recommendations. By employing mathematical modeling, such as matrix factorization or nearest neighbor approaches, AI algorithms can identify patterns and relationships in user listening habits, resulting in accurate song or artist recommendations.

Content-based Filtering is another approach that utilizes mathematical models to analyze the acoustic and semantic properties of songs. By representing music as high-dimensional feature vectors, AI algorithms can calculate similarity metrics to recommend songs with similar musical characteristics.

Analysis of Listener Behavior and Preferences

Understanding listener behavior and preferences is critical in improving the quality and relevance of music recommendations, as well as informing marketing and content creation strategies. AI techniques combined with mathematical models provide powerful tools for analyzing user data and extracting actionable insights.

Clustering algorithms, such as k-means or hierarchical clustering, aid in segmenting listeners based on their music preferences. By grouping users with similar listening habits together, AI algorithms enable targeted marketing campaigns, customized user experiences, and genre-specific promotions.

Sentiment analysis techniques, often utilizing natural language processing (NLP) algorithms, help analyze user-generated content, such as reviews or comments, to extract sentiment and opinions. By employing mathematical models to process textual data, AI algorithms can gauge user reactions, identify trends, and enhance music or artist recommendations accordingly.

AI in Sound Design and Audio Engineering

Beyond music composition and recommendation, AI algorithms play a vital role in sound design and audio engineering. By analyzing large datasets of sound samples and employing mathematical models, AI can automate and enhance various aspects of the sound engineering process.

Audio synthesis algorithms, such as deep neural networks or GANs, enable the creation of realistic and high-quality sound effects. By training these models on extensive libraries of sound samples, AI algorithms can generate new sounds, mimic specific acoustic environments, or even synthesize musical instruments digitally.

Mathematical models, such as Fourier transforms or spectral analysis, provide the foundation for audio processing and enhancement. By employing AI-driven algorithms, noise reduction, audio denoising, and equalization can be accomplished more effectively, resulting in high-fidelity audio production.

Automated Mastering and Mixing

Mastering and mixing audio tracks are intricate processes that require a deep understanding of acoustics, psychoacoustics, and artistic preferences. AI algorithms have been employed to automate and enhance the mastering and mixing stages of audio production.

Using mathematical models, AI algorithms can analyze track dynamics, frequency spectra, and spatial qualities in order to optimize the audio mix. By training on large datasets of professionally mixed tracks, these algorithms can learn to balance audio elements, enhance clarity, and ensure compatibility across different listening environments.

Automated mastering algorithms utilize AI techniques, such as regression models or neural networks, to process audio tracks and apply appropriate mastering techniques. By analyzing track characteristics, such as frequency distribution or dynamic range, AI algorithms can automatically adjust parameters, including compression, reverb, and equalization, to achieve a polished and professional sound.

Conclusion

The integration of AI techniques and mathematical models in the field of music and sound is revolutionizing various aspects of musical composition, production, recommendation, and analysis. By leveraging the power of AI algorithms, researchers and practitioners are pushing the boundaries of creativity and innovation in music, while enhancing the user experience and personalization. The continuous development of AI-driven tools and techniques offers exciting prospects for the future of music and sound.

Python Code Snippet

Below is a Python code snippet that demonstrates important algorithms and equations related to AI in music and sound discussed in this chapter, including music composition using recurrent neural networks (RNNs), collaborative filtering for personalized recommendations, and automated mastering.

```python
import numpy as np
import random
from sklearn.metrics.pairwise import cosine_similarity
from keras.models import Sequential
from keras.layers import LSTM, Dense, Activation
from keras.utils import to_categorical

# Function to generate music using a simple RNN
def generate_music_rnn(data, num_notes=100):
    '''
    Generate a sequence of music notes using a simple RNN.
    :param data: Training data containing sequences of music notes.
    :param num_notes: Number of music notes to generate.
    :return: Generated music notes.
    '''
    model = Sequential()
    model.add(LSTM(128, input_shape=(data.shape[1], data.shape[2]),
    ↪    return_sequences=True))
    model.add(LSTM(128))
```

```python
model.add(Dense(len(set(data.flatten())), activation='softmax'))

model.compile(loss='categorical_crossentropy', optimizer='adam')

# Train the model
model.fit(data, epochs=10, verbose=0)

# Generate music
indices = [random.randint(0, len(data) - 1)]
generated_notes = []

for _ in range(num_notes):
    input_sequence = np.reshape(data[indices[-1]], (1,
    ↪    data.shape[1], data.shape[2]))
    prediction = model.predict(input_sequence, verbose=0)
    next_note = np.argmax(prediction)
    generated_notes.append(next_note)
    indices.append(next_note)

return generated_notes


# Function for collaborative filtering music recommendations
def recommend_songs(user_song_matrix, user_id,
↪    num_recommendations=5):
    '''
    Recommend songs to a user using collaborative filtering.
    :param user_song_matrix: User-song interaction matrix.
    :param user_id: ID of the user to whom recommendations are made.
    :param num_recommendations: Number of song recommendations.
    :return: Indices of recommended songs.
    '''
    user_vector = user_song_matrix[user_id].reshape(1, -1)
    similarities = cosine_similarity(user_vector,
    ↪    user_song_matrix)[0]

    # Get the indices of the most similar users
    similar_users_indices = np.argsort(similarities)[::-1][1:]  #
    ↪    Ignore self

    recommended_songs = set()
    for user in similar_users_indices:
        song_indices = np.where(user_song_matrix[user] > 0)[0]
        recommended_songs.update(song_indices)
        if len(recommended_songs) >= num_recommendations:
            break

    return list(recommended_songs)[:num_recommendations]


# Function to automate audio mastering
def automate_mastering(audio_file):
    '''
```

```
Automated mastering of an audio file using basic normalization.
:param audio_file: Path to the audio file to be mastered.
:return: Processed audio data.
'''
import librosa
y, sr = librosa.load(audio_file, sr=None)

# Normalize audio to -1 to 1 range
y_max = np.max(np.abs(y))
mastered_audio = y / y_max

return mastered_audio


# Example Data - Dummy data for music generation
# Training data should be in the shape of (samples, timesteps,
↪   features)
training_data = np.random.rand(1000, 10, 1)

# Generate new music notes
generated_music_notes = generate_music_rnn(training_data)

# User-song interaction matrix - Dummy data
user_song_matrix = np.random.randint(0, 2, (10, 20))  # 10 users, 20
↪   songs

# Recommend songs for User ID 0
recommended_songs_indices = recommend_songs(user_song_matrix,
↪   user_id=0)

# Automate mastering for a given audio file
# Note: Replace 'example_audio.wav' with a valid audio filepath
mastered_audio_data = automate_mastering('example_audio.wav')

# Output results
print("Generated Music Notes:", generated_music_notes)
print("Recommended Songs Index for User 0:",
↪   recommended_songs_indices)
print("Mastered Audio Data Shape:", mastered_audio_data.shape)
```

This code defines three functions:

- `generate_music_rnn` implements a simple recurrent neural network to generate music notes based on training data.
- `recommend_songs` utilizes collaborative filtering techniques to recommend songs for a user based on their interactions with songs.
- `automate_mastering` automates the audio mastering process of an audio file using normalization.

The provided example demonstrates how to generate music notes, recommend songs for a user, and process an audio file for mastering, then prints the results.

Chapter 55

AI in Coastal Engineering

In this chapter, we focus on the application of AI in the field of coastal engineering, specifically addressing topics such as predictive modeling for coastal erosion, AI in marine infrastructure design and maintenance, environmental monitoring and impact assessment, AI-driven optimization of coastal protection measures, and autonomous marine and coastal survey systems.

Predictive Modeling for Coastal Erosion

Predicting and understanding coastal erosion is of paramount importance for coastal engineers in order to develop effective strategies for shoreline management and protection. By harnessing the power of AI techniques and mathematical modeling, predictive models for coastal erosion can be built to forecast the long-term effects of different factors on coastal regions.

A common approach is to employ machine learning algorithms, such as Support Vector Machines (SVM) or Random Forests, to analyze various input parameters, including wave energy, sediment transport characteristics, and coastal geomorphology. These algorithms can capture the complex relationships between these parameters and shoreline changes, enabling the prediction of erosion patterns.

Mathematical models, such as Partial Differential Equations (PDEs) or Cellular Automata (CA), can also be used to simulate coastal erosion dynamics. By combining these mathematical models with AI techniques, such as genetic algorithms or neural networks, researchers can optimize model parameters and improve the accuracy of predictions.

AI in Marine Infrastructure Design and Maintenance

Coastal engineering encompasses the design and maintenance of marine structures, such as breakwaters, seawalls, and piers, to ensure their integrity and functionality in the face of natural forces. AI algorithms combined with mathematical modeling offer valuable tools for optimizing the design and maintenance of these structures.

Optimization algorithms, such as Genetic Algorithms or Particle Swarm Optimization, aid in the design of marine structures by searching for optimal configurations based on a set of predefined objectives and constraints. By iteratively evaluating different design options and adjusting parameters, AI algorithms can identify optimal solutions that balance structural stability, cost-effectiveness, and environmental considerations.

AI techniques, such as Machine Vision or LiDAR (Light Detection and Ranging) data analysis, facilitate the inspection and maintenance of marine infrastructure. By processing and interpreting visual or remote sensing data, AI algorithms can identify structural defects, erosion patterns, or other potential risks, enabling timely maintenance interventions.

Environmental Monitoring and Impact Assessment

The monitoring and assessment of environmental changes in coastal areas are crucial for maintaining ecological balance and understanding the impact of human activities. AI algorithms, in conjunction with mathematical modeling, support the development of effective monitoring systems and facilitate data-driven environmental impact assessment.

Remote sensing technologies, such as satellites or drones, provide vast amounts of data on coastal ecosystems. AI algorithms, including image classification and object detection, enable the automatic analysis and interpretation of these data, allowing for efficient monitoring of environmental indicators, such as shoreline changes, vegetation cover, or water quality.

Mathematical models, such as hydrodynamic models or ecological models, can simulate the behavior and interaction of coastal ecosystems. AI algorithms, such as data assimilation techniques or model calibration methods, can improve the accuracy of these models by assimilating observed data and optimizing model parameters to minimize prediction errors.

AI-driven Optimization of Coastal Protection Measures

Coastal protection measures, such as beach nourishment or the construction of artificial reefs, play a crucial role in preventing coastal erosion and protecting coastal areas against natural hazards. AI techniques, in combination with mathematical models, can optimize the design and implementation of these protection measures.

AI algorithms, such as genetic algorithms or reinforcement learning, can explore and optimize different combinations of coastal protection strategies, considering parameters such as cost, effectiveness, and ecological impact. By iteratively evaluating and adjusting these strategies based on observations and feedback, AI algorithms can discover robust and efficient solutions.

Mathematical models, such as morphodynamic models or wave propagation models, provide a scientific basis for understanding the physical processes involved in coastal protection. AI algorithms can enhance these models through data assimilation techniques, uncertainty quantification, or sensitivity analysis, leading to improved predictions and more effective decision-making.

Autonomous Marine and Coastal Survey Systems

The collection of accurate and reliable data is essential for understanding coastal processes and assessing their impact. Autonomous marine and coastal survey systems, guided by AI algorithms and mathematical models, offer cost-effective and efficient solutions for data acquisition in challenging coastal environments.

Autonomous underwater vehicles (AUVs) equipped with various sensors, such as sonar or imaging systems, can collect data on bathymetry, seabed characteristics, or coastal vegetation. AI algorithms, including path planning or obstacle avoidance techniques, enable AUVs to navigate autonomously and optimize data collection routes.

Unmanned aerial vehicles (UAVs), or drones, equipped with cameras or LiDAR sensors, offer a valuable means of collecting high-resolution data on coastal landscapes, shoreline changes, or vegetation cover. AI algorithms aid in automated flight planning, image analysis, and data interpretation, enabling efficient data acquisition and analysis.

Conclusion

In this chapter, we explored the application of AI in coastal engineering, focusing on predictive modeling for coastal erosion, the design and maintenance of marine infrastructure, environmental monitoring and impact assessment, the optimization of coastal protection measures, and the use of autonomous marine and coastal survey systems. By combining AI algorithms and mathematical modeling, researchers and engineers can gain valuable insights, optimize designs, and make informed decisions to ensure the sustainability and resilience of coastal areas.Certainly! Below is a comprehensive Python code snippet that encapsulates some of the important equations, formulas, and algorithms mentioned in the chapter "AI in Coastal Engineering."

Python Code Snippet

Below is a Python code snippet that implements predictive modeling for coastal erosion, AI in marine infrastructure design and maintenance, and environmental monitoring and impact assessment.

```
import numpy as np
import pandas as pd
from sklearn.ensemble import RandomForestRegressor
from scipy.optimize import minimize

def predict_coastal_erosion(features, target):
    '''
    Predict coastal erosion using a Random Forest Regressor.
    :param features: DataFrame of input features (e.g., wave energy,
    ↪ sediment transport).
    :param target: Series of target erosion values.
```

```
    :return: Trained Random Forest model.
    '''
    model = RandomForestRegressor(n_estimators=100, random_state=42)
    model.fit(features, target)
    return model

def optimize_marine_structure_design(objectives, constraints):
    '''
    Optimize marine structure design using a simple optimization
    ↪ method.
    :param objectives: Function to minimize/cost function.
    :param constraints: List of constraints for the optimization.
    :return: Optimized design parameters.
    '''
    initial_guess = np.ones(len(objectives))  # Initial design
    ↪ parameters
    result = minimize(objectives, initial_guess,
    ↪ constraints=constraints)
    return result.x  # Optimized design parameters

def analyze_environmental_impact(data):
    '''
    Analyze environmental impact based on remote sensing data.
    :param data: DataFrame of remote sensing indicators (e.g.,
    ↪ vegetation cover, water quality).
    :return: Summary statistics for environmental assessment.
    '''
    return data.describe()  # Return descriptive statistics

# Example inputs for coastal erosion prediction
erosion_data = pd.DataFrame({
    'wave_energy': [100, 200, 300, 400],
    'sediment_transport': [30, 40, 60, 80],
    'geomorphology': [1, 2, 3, 4]  # Categorical encoded
})
erosion_target = pd.Series([0.5, 1.2, 1.8, 2.5])  # Erosion targets

# Train a model to predict coastal erosion
coastal_erosion_model = predict_coastal_erosion(erosion_data,
↪ erosion_target)

# Example of optimization for marine structure design
def cost_function(design_params):
    ''' Define a cost function for the design optimization. '''
    cost = np.sum(design_params**2)  # Simple quadratic cost
    return cost

constraints = ({'type': 'eq', 'fun': lambda x: x[0] + x[1] - 1})  #
↪ Example constraint

optimized_design = optimize_marine_structure_design(cost_function,
↪ constraints)
```

```
# Example environmental data analysis
environmental_data = pd.DataFrame({
    'vegetation_cover': [30, 40, 35, 50],
    'water_quality_index': [70, 65, 75, 80],
})
environmental_summary =
↪  analyze_environmental_impact(environmental_data)

# Output results
print("Optimized Coastal Erosion Model Parameters:",
↪  coastal_erosion_model.feature_importances_)
print("Optimized Design Parameters:", optimized_design)
print("Environmental Impact Summary:\n", environmental_summary)
```

This code defines three main functions:

- `predict_coastal_erosion` trains a Random Forest model to predict coastal erosion based on various features like wave energy and sediment transport.
- `optimize_marine_structure_design` optimizes the design of marine structures based on a defined cost function and given constraints.
- `analyze_environmental_impact` provides a summary analysis of environmental indicators from remote sensing data.

The provided example demonstrates how to predict coastal erosion, optimize marine design parameters, and analyze environmental impacts using sample data, while printing the results.

Chapter 56

AI in Automation of Financial Processes

In this chapter, we delve into the realm of AI and its applications in automating financial processes. The integration of AI techniques in financial systems has revolutionized how various tasks and processes in the finance industry are executed. By harnessing the power of AI algorithms and machine learning models, financial processes that were previously manual and time-consuming can now be automated, leading to increased efficiency and accuracy in financial operations.

Robotic Process Automation in Finance

Robotic Process Automation (RPA) entails the use of software robots or bots to perform repetitive and rule-based tasks in financial processes. These bots mimic human interactions with software applications and systems, enabling the automation of tasks such as data entry, report generation, and reconciliation.

RPA has been widely adopted in the finance industry due to its ability to improve process efficiency and reduce operational costs. By leveraging AI algorithms, RPA bots can learn from historical data and adapt to changes in financial processes over time. This enables them to handle increasingly complex tasks, make data-driven decisions, and continuously optimize process workflows.

AI-driven Reconciliation and Accounting

Reconciliation, the process of comparing financial records from different sources to ensure consistency and accuracy, is a critical task in the financial domain. AI-driven reconciliation algorithms leverage machine learning models and pattern recognition techniques to automate this process, minimizing human error and improving efficiency.

Machine learning algorithms, such as Support Vector Machines (SVM), Random Forests, or Neural Networks, can be trained on historical financial data to identify patterns and regularities in reconciliations. These models can then be applied to automate future reconciliations, saving time and resources.

In addition to reconciliation, AI algorithms have also streamlined accounting processes. AI-driven accounting systems can automate the classification and coding of financial transactions, reducing manual effort and improving accuracy. By learning from historical data, these systems can accurately categorize transactions, identify anomalies, and generate financial reports with minimal human intervention.

Predictive Analytics for Financial Planning

Financial planning involves forecasting future financial performance, making informed investment decisions, and formulating strategies to achieve financial goals. AI-based predictive analytics techniques have greatly enhanced the accuracy and reliability of financial planning models by leveraging patterns in historical financial data.

Time series forecasting algorithms, such as ARIMA (AutoRegressive Integrated Moving Average), Exponential Smoothing, or Long Short-Term Memory (LSTM) networks, can be employed to predict future financial variables, such as stock prices, exchange rates, or interest rates. By analyzing historical trends and relationships between variables, these algorithms can generate accurate forecasts to support financial planning processes.

Moreover, AI algorithms can combine financial data with other external factors, such as market indicators, news sentiment, or macroeconomic variables, to improve the accuracy of predictive models. Machine learning techniques, including regression analysis, ensemble models, or deep learning architectures, can be employed to uncover complex relationships between financial variables and external factors, enabling more robust financial planning.

Fraud Detection and Compliance Management

Fraud detection is a critical aspect of financial processes, aiming to identify and prevent fraudulent activities that can cause financial loss and reputational damage. AI algorithms, particularly machine learning models, play a vital role in automating fraud detection by identifying patterns and anomalies in large volumes of financial data.

Machine learning algorithms, such as logistic regression, decision trees, or neural networks, can be trained on historical fraud cases to detect potential fraudulent transactions or activities. These models learn from historical data, identifying patterns that signify fraudulent behavior and enabling real-time fraud detection.

Furthermore, AI algorithms can assist in compliance management by continuously monitoring financial operations for regulatory compliance. These algorithms can automatically analyze financial transactions, identify potential compliance violations, and generate alerts or reports for further investigation. By automating compliance monitoring, financial organizations can ensure adherence to regulations while minimizing manual effort.

AI in Financial Reporting and Analysis

Financial reporting and analysis are crucial components of financial processes, providing valuable insights into an organization's financial performance and aiding decision-making processes. AI techniques have revolutionized financial reporting and analysis by automating data collection, analysis, and report generation.

Natural Language Processing (NLP) algorithms and text mining techniques can be applied to extract relevant information from financial documents, such as annual reports, financial statements, or news articles. These algorithms parse through large volumes of textual data, extracting key financial indicators or sentiment analysis, which can be used in financial reporting and analysis.

Machine learning algorithms, such as clustering, classification, or regression, can be employed to analyze financial data and uncover hidden patterns or relationships. These algorithms can automate financial analysis tasks, such as trend identification, risk assessment, or investment portfolio optimization. AI-driven financial analysis enables more accurate predictions and informed decision-making.

Conclusion

In this chapter, we have explored the applications of AI in automating financial processes. AI techniques, such as Robotic Process Automation (RPA), AI-driven reconciliation and accounting, predictive analytics for financial planning, fraud detection and compliance management, and AI in financial reporting and analysis have revolutionized the finance industry. By leveraging AI algorithms and machine learning models, financial institutions can streamline their processes, improve accuracy, and enhance decision-making processes. The automation of financial processes through AI enables organizations to allocate resources more efficiently, reduce operational costs, and drive overall growth and success in the financial domain.

Python Code Snippet

Below is a Python code snippet that implements important algorithms and calculations discussed in the chapter related to automation of financial processes.

```python
import pandas as pd
import numpy as np
from sklearn.ensemble import RandomForestClassifier
from sklearn.metrics import classification_report
from sklearn.linear_model import LogisticRegression
from sklearn.model_selection import train_test_split
import re

def perform_reconciliation(financial_data_1, financial_data_2):
    '''
    Compare two datasets for reconciliation and return matched
    ↪ items.
    :param financial_data_1: First dataset as a list or DataFrame.
    :param financial_data_2: Second dataset as a list or DataFrame.
    :return: DataFrame of reconciled items.
    '''
```

```
    reconciled_data = pd.merge(financial_data_1, financial_data_2,
    ↪  on="transaction_id", how="inner")
    return reconciled_data

def predict_fraudulent_activity(transaction_data):
    '''
    Predict fraudulent transactions using a machine learning model.
    :param transaction_data: DataFrame containing transaction
    ↪  features.
    :return: DataFrame with a column indicating fraudulent (1) or
    ↪  not (0) predictions.
    '''
    # Feature set preparation
    X = transaction_data.drop('is_fraud', axis=1)
    y = transaction_data['is_fraud']

    # Train-test split
    X_train, X_test, y_train, y_test = train_test_split(X, y,
    ↪  test_size=0.2, random_state=42)

    # Train a Random Forest Classifier
    model = RandomForestClassifier(n_estimators=100,
    ↪  random_state=42)
    model.fit(X_train, y_train)

    # Predictions
    predictions = model.predict(X_test)

    print(classification_report(y_test, predictions))

    # Add predictions to the original DataFrame
    transaction_data['predicted_fraud'] = model.predict(X)

    return transaction_data

def predictive_financial_planning(historical_data):
    '''
    Perform predictive financial planning using linear regression.
    :param historical_data: DataFrame with historical financial
    ↪  performance data.
    :return: Predictions for future financial performance.
    '''
    from sklearn.model_selection import train_test_split
    from sklearn.linear_model import LinearRegression

    X = historical_data.drop('future_value', axis=1)
    y = historical_data['future_value']

    X_train, X_test, y_train, y_test = train_test_split(X, y,
    ↪  test_size=0.2, random_state=42)

    model = LinearRegression()
    model.fit(X_train, y_train)
```

```python
    predictions = model.predict(X_test)

    return predictions

def extract_financial_data_from_text(text):
    '''
    Extracts financial amounts from given text using regular
    ↪ expressions.
    :param text: Text containing financial information.
    :return: List of extracted financial amounts.
    '''
    amounts = re.findall(r'\$\d+(?:,\d{3})*(?:\.\d{2})?', text)
    return amounts


# Sample data for reconciliation
data1 = pd.DataFrame({'transaction_id': [1, 2, 3], 'amount': [100,
    ↪ 150, 200]})
data2 = pd.DataFrame({'transaction_id': [1, 2, 4], 'amount': [100,
    ↪ 150, 250]})

# Performing reconciliation
reconciled = perform_reconciliation(data1, data2)
print("Reconciled Transactions:\n", reconciled)

# Sample transaction data for fraud prediction
transaction_data = pd.DataFrame({
    'transaction_id': [1, 2, 3, 4, 5],
    'amount': [100, 150, 20, 3000, 200],
    'is_fraud': [0, 0, 1, 1, 0]
})

# Predicting fraudulent activities
predicted_fraud = predict_fraudulent_activity(transaction_data)
print("Transactions with Fraud Predictions:\n", predicted_fraud)

# Sample historical financial performance data for predictive
↪ planning
historical_data = pd.DataFrame({
    'past_value': [100, 200, 300, 400, 500],
    'future_value': [200, 300, 400, 500, 600]
})

# Performing predictive planning
future_predictions = predictive_financial_planning(historical_data)
print("Future Predictions:\n", future_predictions)

# Sample text containing financial amounts
sample_text = "The total revenue for the quarter was $1,000.00 while
↪ expenses totaled $500.00."

# Extracting financial data from text
```

```
extracted_amounts = extract_financial_data_from_text(sample_text)
print("Extracted Financial Amounts:\n", extracted_amounts)
```

This code snippet includes several functions that perform core tasks related to financial process automation:

- `perform_reconciliation` compares two datasets and identifies reconciled transactions.
- `predict_fraudulent_activity` utilizes a Random Forest Classifier to predict whether transactions are fraudulent.
- `predictive_financial_planning` employs linear regression to forecast future financial performance based on historical data.
- `extract_financial_data_from_text` parses a string to extract financial amounts using regular expressions.

Together, these functions demonstrate the power of AI and machine learning in enhancing efficiency and accuracy in financial processes.

Chapter 57

AI in Precision Engineering

In this chapter, we delve into the application of Artificial Intelligence (AI) in the field of Precision Engineering. Precision Engineering aims to design and manufacture high-quality and high-accuracy components and products, often in industries where small errors can have significant consequences. Leveraging AI techniques in Precision Engineering allows for enhanced design optimization, improved production processes, and overall superior performance.

Enhancing Design Accuracy with AI

Design accuracy is a crucial aspect of Precision Engineering, as even small deviations can impact the functionality and reliability of the final product. AI algorithms can play a significant role in enhancing design accuracy by automating design optimization processes and reducing human error.

Optimization algorithms, such as Genetic Algorithms (GA), Particle Swarm Optimization (PSO), or Simulated Annealing, can be utilized to iteratively search for the best design parameters that optimize specific criteria, such as structural integrity, stress distribution, or thermal performance. These algorithms simulate the evolution of biological or physical systems and use principles of natural selection to gradually improve the design.

Furthermore, AI techniques can be employed to explore complex design spaces and identify optimal designs that satisfy multiple constraints simultaneously. Multi-Objective Optimization algorithms, like Non-Dominated Sorting Genetic Algorithm (NSGA-II) or Strength Pareto Evolutionary Algorithm (SPEA2), can efficiently handle multiple objectives and generate a set of Pareto-optimal solutions, providing engineers with a range of design options to choose from based on their trade-offs.

Predictive Maintenance for Precision Tools

Precision Engineering heavily relies on the proper functioning and maintenance of precision tools and equipment. AI algorithms, particularly those based on predictive maintenance, can enhance the reliability and availability of these tools while minimizing downtime and maintenance costs.

Using sensor data and historical maintenance records, machine learning models, such as Support Vector Machines (SVM), Random Forests, or Long Short-Term Memory (LSTM) networks, can be trained to predict the likelihood of tool failure or degradation. These models capture patterns and correlations between sensor data and tool conditions, enabling engineers to predict when maintenance or repair is necessary proactively.

By implementing predictive maintenance strategies, precision tools can undergo maintenance and servicing only when required, avoiding unnecessary downtime and reducing the risk of unexpected failures. This approach allows for more efficient use of resources and improved overall productivity.

AI-driven Quality Control in Manufacturing

Quality control is critical in Precision Engineering to ensure that components and products meet the required specifications and tolerances. AI techniques, particularly those utilizing computer vision and machine learning, can automate quality control processes and enhance the detection of defects and irregularities.

Computer vision algorithms, such as Convolutional Neural Networks (CNN), can be trained on large labeled datasets to identify visual defects in manufactured components. By analyzing images or videos of the components, these algorithms can classify defects, such as cracks, scratches, or dimensional variations, with high accuracy.

Furthermore, machine learning models can be developed to analyze sensor data collected during the manufacturing process and identify anomalies or deviations from expected behavior. These models can detect abnormalities in variables such as temperature, pressure, or vibration, which may indicate a potential defect.

By leveraging AI-driven quality control in manufacturing, Precision Engineering industries can ensure higher product quality, reduce scrap and rework, and maintain consistent standards across production lines.

Automated Production Processes

Automation plays a crucial role in Precision Engineering, enabling precise and efficient manufacturing processes. AI techniques enhance automation further by enabling adaptive and self-learning systems that can adjust and optimize production parameters in real-time.

Machine learning algorithms, such as Reinforcement Learning (RL) or Adaptive Control, can be employed to optimize control strategies and parameters for manufacturing processes. These algorithms learn from experience and feedback, enabling them to make data-driven decisions and adapt to varying conditions. For example, in a machining process, RL algorithms can determine the optimal cutting parameters, such as speed, feed rate, or tool engagement, to achieve the desired surface finish while minimizing tool wear and energy consumption.

Furthermore, AI techniques can facilitate the coordination and collaboration of multiple automated systems in Precision Engineering. Multi-Agent Systems (MAS) can be employed to optimize production schedules, resource allocation, and task assignments, ensuring efficient utilization of resources and smooth operation of the manufacturing process.

Optimization of Complex Engineering Systems

Precision Engineering often involves the design and optimization of complex engineering systems, such as robotic systems, mechatronic systems, or aerospace systems. AI algorithms offer powerful optimization approaches to tackle the challenges associated with these complex systems.

Evolutionary Algorithms, such as Genetic Programming (GP), Evolutionary Strategies (ES), or Differential Evolution (DE), can be employed to discover superior designs and optimize various aspects of complex engineering systems. These algorithms can handle high-dimensional search spaces and identify optimal system configurations that maximize performance and meet specific design objectives.

Additionally, AI techniques, such as Neural Networks or Gaussian Processes, can be utilized to model and simulate the behavior of complex systems. These models enable engineers to analyze system responses under different operating conditions, identify critical parameters, and optimize system performance.

By optimizing complex engineering systems through AI techniques, Precision Engineering can achieve higher levels of performance, efficiency, and reliability.

Conclusion

In this chapter, we have explored the application of AI in Precision Engineering. AI techniques, including design optimization, predictive maintenance, quality control, process automation, and optimization of complex engineering systems, have significant potential in enhancing precision and efficiency in manufacturing processes. By harnessing the power of AI algorithms and machine learning models in Precision Engineering, industries can achieve superior product quality, reduce costs, and drive innovation in this vital field of engineering.

Python Code Snippet

Below is a Python code snippet that implements important equations and algorithms discussed in this chapter related to Precision Engineering. This code showcases design optimization using Genetic Algorithms (GA), predictive maintenance using Random Forests, quality control using Convolutional Neural Networks (CNN), and automated production processes using Reinforcement Learning (RL).

```python
import numpy as np
import random
from sklearn.ensemble import RandomForestClassifier
from sklearn.model_selection import train_test_split
import cv2
from keras.models import Sequential
from keras.layers import Conv2D, MaxPooling2D, Flatten, Dense
import gym

# Genetic Algorithm for Design Optimization
def genetic_algorithm(pop_size, n_generations, mutation_rate):
    population = [np.random.rand(10) for _ in range(pop_size)]  #
    ↪   Initialize population
    for generation in range(n_generations):
        scores = [evaluate_design(individual) for individual in
        ↪   population]
        next_population = []
        for _ in range(pop_size):
            parents = select_parents(population, scores)
            child = crossover(parents[0], parents[1])
            child = mutate(child, mutation_rate)
            next_population.append(child)
        population = next_population
    best_solution = population[np.argmax([evaluate_design(ind) for
    ↪   ind in population])]
    return best_solution

def evaluate_design(individual):
    # Placeholder for evaluating design based on specific criteria
    return np.sum(individual)  # Example fitness function

def select_parents(population, scores):
    return random.sample(sorted(zip(population, scores), key=lambda
    ↪   x: x[1], reverse=True)[:2], 2)

def crossover(parent1, parent2):
    point = random.randint(1, len(parent1)-1)
    return np.concatenate((parent1[:point], parent2[point:]))

def mutate(individual, mutation_rate):
    return [gene if random.random() > mutation_rate else
    ↪   random.random() for gene in individual]


# Predictive Maintenance using Random Forests
def predictive_maintenance(sensor_data, labels):
    X_train, X_test, y_train, y_test = train_test_split(sensor_data,
    ↪   labels, test_size=0.2)
    model = RandomForestClassifier()
    model.fit(X_train, y_train)
    return model.score(X_test, y_test)
```

```python
# Quality Control using CNN
def quality_control(train_images, train_labels):
    model = Sequential()
    model.add(Conv2D(32, kernel_size=(3, 3), activation='relu',
      input_shape=(64, 64, 1)))
    model.add(MaxPooling2D(pool_size=(2, 2)))
    model.add(Flatten())
    model.add(Dense(128, activation='relu'))
    model.add(Dense(1, activation='sigmoid'))
    model.compile(optimizer='adam', loss='binary_crossentropy',
      metrics=['accuracy'])
    model.fit(train_images, train_labels, epochs=10)
    return model

# Automated Production Process using Reinforcement Learning
def train_rl_agent():
    env = gym.make('CartPole-v1')   # Example environment
    for episode in range(1000):
        state = env.reset()
        done = False
        while not done:
            action = env.action_space.sample()   # Placeholder for
              action based on policy
            next_state, reward, done, _ = env.step(action)
            state = next_state
    # Here you would implement the training algorithm for policies
      or Q-values
    return "Training Complete"

# Example usage of the functions
if __name__ == "__main__":
    # Genetic Algorithm Example
    best_design = genetic_algorithm(pop_size=100, n_generations=50,
      mutation_rate=0.1)
    print("Best Design Parameters from GA:", best_design)

    # Predictive Maintenance Example
    sensor_data = np.random.rand(100, 5)   # Random sensor data
    labels = np.random.randint(0, 2, 100)   # Example labels
    accuracy = predictive_maintenance(sensor_data, labels)
    print("Predictive Maintenance Model Accuracy:", accuracy)

    # Quality Control Example
    # Assuming train_images and train_labels are predefined
    train_images = np.random.rand(100, 64, 64, 1)   # Example image
      data
    train_labels = np.random.randint(0, 2, 100)   # Example binary
      labels
    cnn_model = quality_control(train_images, train_labels)
    print("Quality Control CNN Model Training Complete")

    # Reinforcement Learning Example
    rl_training_result = train_rl_agent()
```

```
print(rl_training_result)
```

The following functions are defined in the code:

- `genetic_algorithm` implements a Genetic Algorithm for design optimization, involving selection, crossover, and mutation processes.
- `predictive_maintenance` utilizes a Random Forest Classifier to predict equipment maintenance needs based on sensor data.
- `quality_control` leverages a Convolutional Neural Network (CNN) to automate the detection of product defects in manufacturing.
- `train_rl_agent` serves as a basic framework for training a reinforcement learning agent in an example environment.

This code snippet illustrates the application of AI approaches to improve various facets of Precision Engineering, including optimization, maintenance, quality assurance, and automation.

Chapter 58

AI in Geotechnical Engineering

In this chapter, we explore the application of Artificial Intelligence (AI) in Geotechnical Engineering, a field that deals with the behavior and properties of soil, rock, and other earth materials. Geotechnical Engineering plays a critical role in the design and construction of foundations, slopes, tunnels, and other civil infrastructure. By incorporating AI techniques into Geotechnical Engineering, we can enhance our understanding of complex geotechnical systems, optimize design processes, and improve the overall safety and efficiency of geotechnical projects.

Predictive Modeling for Soil and Rock Behavior

A fundamental aspect of Geotechnical Engineering is the prediction of soil and rock behavior under different loading conditions. AI techniques offer powerful tools to model and simulate the complex behavior of geotechnical materials.

One approach is to utilize Machine Learning algorithms, such as Artificial Neural Networks (ANNs), Support Vector Machines (SVM), or Random Forests, to develop predictive models based on historical data. These models can capture the non-linear relationships between various soil and rock properties, loading conditions, and resulting behavior. By training these models on a large dataset of laboratory tests and field measurements, we can predict the behavior of geotechnical materials under new or different conditions.

Mathematically, for a given input vector, $\mathbf{x}$, and a corresponding target variable, y, we can represent the predictive model as $\hat{y} = f(\mathbf{x})$, where f represents the trained model. The model's parameters, such as weights and biases in a neural network, are optimized during the training process based on the available data.

The predictive models can provide valuable insights into geotechnical behavior, allowing engineers to make informed decisions during the design and construction phases. These models can help in the selection of appropriate ground improvement techniques, estimation of settlement, evaluation of stability, and prediction of deformation of geotechnical structures.

AI-Driven Site Investigation and Analysis

Site investigation and analysis are essential steps in geotechnical engineering to understand the subsurface conditions and evaluate potential geotechnical hazards. AI techniques can enhance site investigation processes by automating data analysis and interpreting relevant geotechnical information.

Machine Learning algorithms can be utilized to analyze and interpret various geotechnical data, including soil boring logs, geological surveys, laboratory test results, and geophysical data. By training models on large datasets of known site conditions, these algorithms can identify patterns and correlations in the data, enabling the prediction of subsurface properties and the identification of potential geotechnical hazards.

Additionally, AI techniques can be employed to optimize site investigation process design. For example, Genetic Algorithms or Particle Swarm Optimization can facilitate the selection of optimal borehole locations and depths to minimize uncertainty and maximize the value of collected data. These optimization algorithms simulate the evolution of biological or physical systems, gradually improving the efficiency and effectiveness of site investigation campaigns.

The integration of AI-driven site investigation and analysis provides geotechnical engineers with improved insights into subsurface conditions, allowing for better design decisions and risk mitigation strategies.

Automated Design and Construction Processes

AI techniques contribute to streamlining design and construction processes in geotechnical engineering, reducing costs and time while ensuring optimal performance and safety.

By utilizing algorithms, such as Genetic Programming or Evolutionary Strategies, engineers can optimize the design of geotechnical structures, such as retaining walls, foundations, or embankments. These algorithms search for the best parameter values that meet specific performance objectives, considering factors such as stability, settlement, or construction cost. The optimization process can involve complex numerical models, incorporating factors such as soil-structure interaction and the influence of construction processes.

Another area where AI can make a significant impact is in the automation of construction processes. Robotic systems can be employed for tasks such as excavation, soil compaction, or tunneling. These robots leverage AI techniques, including computer vision, path planning, and machine learning, to perform these tasks efficiently and with a high level of precision. Through AI-driven automation, construction processes can become faster, safer, and more reliable.

Safety Monitoring and Risk Management

Geotechnical projects are often associated with safety risks, such as slope instability, ground settlement, or liquefaction. AI techniques can contribute to proactive safety monitoring and risk management, ensuring the stability and integrity of geotechnical structures.

Machine Learning algorithms can be employed to analyze data from sensors, such as inclinometers, piezometers, or strain gauges, to detect early warning signs of potential failures or abnormalities. These algorithms can learn patterns and trends that precede geotechnical hazards, enabling engineers to take preventive measures and avoid catastrophic events.

Furthermore, AI techniques, including Bayesian Networks or Fuzzy Logic, can be utilized to perform risk assessments and make informed decisions regarding geotechnical hazards. These techniques can combine historical data, expert knowledge, and probabilistic models to evaluate the likelihood and impact of potential failures. This information helps in the selection of appropriate risk mitigation measures and the development of contingency plans.

By integrating AI-driven safety monitoring and risk management, geotechnical engineers can enhance the overall safety performance of geotechnical structures, safeguarding lives and minimizing potential damage.

AI-Driven Optimization of Geotechnical Solutions

In complex geotechnical projects, AI techniques offer significant opportunities for optimization, enabling engineers to find the most cost-effective, reliable, and sustainable solutions.

Evolutionary Algorithms, such as Genetic Algorithms or Particle Swarm Optimization, can be employed to optimize parameters of geotechnical design, considering multiple objectives, constraints, and uncertainties. These algorithms explore the solution space and converge towards a set of Pareto-optimal solutions, offering trade-offs between different design criteria. Engineers can select the most suitable solution based on their priorities and project-specific requirements.

AI techniques can also optimize the selection of ground improvement techniques, helping engineers identify the most appropriate methods for enhancing soil or rock properties. By considering factors such as site conditions, cost, time, and environmental impact, AI algorithms can suggest optimal solutions and improve overall project performance.

The integration of AI-driven optimization approaches holds promise for geotechnical engineering, enabling engineers to make informed decisions, minimize costs, reduce construction time, and enhance the sustainability of geotechnical projects.

Conclusion

In this chapter, we have explored the application of AI in Geotechnical Engineering. AI techniques, including predictive modeling, AI-driven site investigation, automated design and construction processes, safety monitoring and risk management, and optimization of geotechnical solutions, offer significant potential to enhance geotechnical projects' safety, efficiency, and sustainability. By harnessing the power of AI algorithms and machine learning models, geotechnical engineers can gain deeper insights into the behavior of geotechnical materials, optimize design processes, mitigate risks, and ultimately, deliver reliable and cost-effective solutions.

Python Code Snippet

Below is a Python code snippet that implements important algorithms and equations mentioned in this chapter related to geotechnical engineering, including predictive modeling, site investigation analysis, automated design processes, and risk assessment.

```python
import numpy as np
import pandas as pd
from sklearn.ensemble import RandomForestRegressor
from sklearn.model_selection import train_test_split
from sklearn.metrics import mean_squared_error
from scipy.optimize import minimize

# Function to predict soil/rock behavior using Random Forest
↪   regression
def predict_soil_behavior(features, target):
    '''
    Train a Random Forest model to predict soil behavior.
    :param features: DataFrame containing input features (soil
    ↪   properties, loading conditions).
    :param target: Series containing the target variable (soil
    ↪   behavior).
    :return: Trained Random Forest model.
    '''
    X_train, X_test, y_train, y_test = train_test_split(features,
    ↪   target, test_size=0.2, random_state=42)
    model = RandomForestRegressor(n_estimators=100, random_state=42)
    model.fit(X_train, y_train)

    # Predictions and performance evaluation
    predictions = model.predict(X_test)
    mse = mean_squared_error(y_test, predictions)
    print("Mean Squared Error of the model:", mse)

    return model

# Function to optimize site investigation borehole locations using a
↪   simple cost function
def optimize_borehole_locations(num_boreholes, site_map):
    '''
    Optimize borehole locations based on a cost function.
```

```
    :param num_boreholes: Number of boreholes to place.
    :param site_map: 2D numpy array representing the site's geology.
    :return: Optimized locations of boreholes.
    '''
    def cost_function(locations):
        # Cost function: sum of uncertainty at borehole locations
        total_cost = 0
        for loc in locations:
            total_cost += site_map[int(loc[0]), int(loc[1])]   #
            ↪   Example of accessing geology cost
        return total_cost

    initial_locations = np.random.rand(num_boreholes, 2) *
    ↪   np.array(site_map.shape)
    result = minimize(cost_function, initial_locations,
    ↪   method='Nelder-Mead')
    return result.x

# Function for risk management assessment using Bayesian probability
def assess_risk(previous_failures, total_cases, threshold):
    '''
    Assess the risk of failure based on historical data using
    ↪   Bayesian probability.
    :param previous_failures: Number of previous failure incidents.
    :param total_cases: Total number of cases assessed.
    :param threshold: Risk threshold for decision making.
    :return: Probability of failure and decision.
    '''
    probability_of_failure = previous_failures / total_cases
    decision = probability_of_failure > threshold
    return probability_of_failure, decision

# Sample data for predictions
soil_data = pd.DataFrame({
    'clay_content': [15, 20, 25, 30, 10],
    'silt_content': [25, 20, 15, 30, 35],
    'sand_content': [60, 60, 60, 40, 55],
    'load': [100, 150, 200, 250, 120]
})
target_behavior = pd.Series([5, 7, 9, 11, 6])   # Example target
↪   values

# Predictions
model = predict_soil_behavior(soil_data, target_behavior)

# Optimization of borehole locations
site_map_example = np.random.rand(100, 100)   # Simulated geology
↪   map
optimized_locations = optimize_borehole_locations(5,
↪   site_map_example)
print("Optimized Borehole Locations:", optimized_locations)

# Risk assessment
```

```
previous_failures = 3
total_cases = 100
threshold = 0.05
failure_probability, is_high_risk = assess_risk(previous_failures,
↪   total_cases, threshold)
print("Probability of Failure:", failure_probability)
print("Is High-Risk:", "Yes" if is_high_risk else "No")
```

This code includes the following functions:

- `predict_soil_behavior` trains a Random Forest model to predict the behavior of soil based on its properties and loading conditions, providing the model's mean squared error for evaluation.
- `optimize_borehole_locations` optimizes the locations of boreholes within a geological site using a cost function that minimizes uncertainty.
- `assess_risk` evaluates the risk of failure using Bayesian probability based on historical failure data, helping engineers make informed decisions regarding safety.

The provided example implements a predictive model for soil behavior, optimizes borehole locations in a simulated geological map, and assesses the risk of failure for a geotechnical project. The results are printed for further analysis.

www.ingramcontent.com/pod-product-compliance
Lightning Source LLC
LaVergne TN
LVHW051421050326
832903LV00030BC/2936